THE GREATEST SPY STORIES EVER TOLD

THE GREATEST SPY STORIES
EVER TOLD

EDITED BY LAMAR UNDERWOOD

For Bill—
Our protector and friend.
Here's my latest.
With warmest best wishes
for good reading.

LP
LYONS
PRESS

Guilford, Connecticut

An imprint of The Rowman & Littlefield Publishing Group, Inc.
4501 Forbes Blvd., Ste. 200
Lanham, MD 20706
www.rowman.com

Distributed by NATIONAL BOOK NETWORK

British Library Cataloguing in Publication Information available

Library of Congress Cataloging-in-Publication Data available

ISBN 978-1-4930-3912-8 (paperback)
ISBN 978-1-4930-3913-5 (e-book)

♾™ The paper used in this publication meets the minimum requirements of American National Standard for Information Sciences—Permanence of Paper for Printed Library Materials, ANSI/ NISO Z39.48-1992.

CONTENTS

INTRODUCTION

Lamar Underwood

As a teenager staggering through the difficulties of pimples, voice breaks, and unrequited love, I knew what telescopes did and how they worked. Sort of. Only I never used that word: telescope.

A long, tubular glass device that could pull distant images into detailed closeup was called a spyglass.

Spyglass.

The name says it all: Prying into things in secret. The neighbor's backyard, or front porch. The playground down the street. The busy corner where roads crossed. Fields and forests where birds and wildlife could be seen and, of course, the moon and stars. With the immense pleasure that visions of all these interests, and others, were yours in secrecy. Your spyglass doing its thing.

The names "binocular" and "telescope" don't ignite the sense of drama that the word "spyglass" sparks into motion. Spies and spying, usually with hostile intentions, have been prominent in our culture through decades of war and peace, including business interests and personal affairs. Hardly a day goes by without buzz words of spying activities popping up in the media. Hacking, mole, code book, safe houses, disinformation, drone, double agent, cryptanalysis, security clearance—spies are busier than ever it seems. The tensions inherent in their mischief has not been lost on the creators of literature, film and TV.

The predicaments spies find themselves snared in have led to countless lines of movie-goers, from "The Third Man" to all the James Bond movies. Then there's the Hitchcock classic "Rear Window," where a magazine photographer uses his telescopic lens as a "spyglass" to peek at his neighbors across a courtyard. Avid readers like myself have not been left behind in the spy-inspired fiction sweepstakes. From dusty, mellow classics like James Fenimore Cooper's *The Spy*, to today's bestseller lists with names like Henry Silva, John Le Carré, and Frederic Forsyth, spy stories provide so much great reading that keeping up with the latest yarns takes time. That includes rereading some of the works of such spy-story giants as Eric Ambler and Len Deighton.

While the old "cloak-and-dagger" label still applies to many spies, not all their tricks and adventures create good reading. A great deal of spy activity makes dull stuff when related on the printed page. Talented storytellers, however, deliver prose that can grip us through every turn of a secret safe combination, footsteps in hallways, the opening and closing of file cabinet drawers. Spies doing their thing create drama of a quieter type than the machine-gun fire and explosions of so many books and films. The tension that tightens its grip on spies, moment by moment, is the fear of being caught. History shows that such fear is not misplaced. Spies have been dealt with harshly over the years, even when their mischief did little damage to the places they targeted.

The heartbeats and blood pressure of spies not only soar when confronted by the vigilance of the anti-espionage sleuths opposing them; they are constantly being betrayed. Cold, hard cash; a better life in a country of choice; escape from punishment. The rewards can be great for individuals who can turn over a name or two to authorities.

"Your papers!"

That cliché'd line, spoken with a heavy accent, heard in films set during World War II or the Cold War era, accompanied by the hand of a uniformed or civilian officer outstretched toward a character we have been cheering for, emotionally connected with, slams into us with a force more devasting than explosions or gunshots. Is our hero doomed? Caught and destined to soon be in irons? The scene always works, because the tension reaches the breaking point.

The spies in the pages ahead are sometimes truly evil in the damage they did to our country, while some are heroic in defending our country. Their stories are revealing and intriguing. Danger seems to lurk on every page, along with reader rewards.

CHAPTER ONE

The Spy and the Traitor

Ben Macintyre

"The best true spy story I have ever read."

Those words from distinguished author John Le Carré on the cover of Ben Macintyre's The Spy and the Traitor *provide the launching of this new spy stories book with liftoff power. Macintyre's book is subtitled: "The Greatest Espionage Story of the Cold War." If that description and John Le Carré's quote don't grab you, as they have this editor, I'm afraid you've come to the wrong pew.*

Since the publication of The Spy Who Came in from the Cold, *in 1963, John Le Carré has been my favorite spymaster. From George Smiley tales, like* Tinker, Tailor, Soldier, Spy *and* The Honorable Schoolboy, *through the years to more recent bestsellers like* The Night Manager, *Le Carré's prose has carried me into spying adventures. A writer of fiction, Le Carré worked in British Intelligence for years and knows what he's speaking about.*

This excerpt from The Spy and the Traitor *is a clear-cut chase story, a tense feel-the-heartbeats account of a Russian turncoat agent on the run from the KGB, Russia's biggest and most vicious Intelligence agency. This was 1985, and Oleg Gordievsky had been delivering Russian secrets to British Intelligence for years while working for the KGB.*

Ben Macintyre opens his book with this clear and powerful statement: "Oleg Gordievsky was born into the KGB, shaped by it, loved by it, twisted, damaged, and very nearly destroyed by it."

Gordievsky was well-educated, knew languages, and despite his background he came to see the savagery and terror of the Communist regime. He became an agent for MI6, the British Intelligence Service and delivered criti-cal information during the Margaret Thatcher and Ronald Reagan era. MI6 fiercely guarded Gordievsky's identity, even from the CIA. Good thing too, because at this same time the Russian spy Aldrich Ames was tearing the CIA apart.

As the KGB began moving in on Gordievsky, Margaret Thatcher launched Operation PIMLICO to get Gordievsky out of Russia, across Finland, and to England. Our excerpt begins with Gordievsky on the run for his life.

Friday, July 19

10 a.m., British embassy, Moscow

As the hour of departure approached, Roy Ascot's mounting excitement competed with a rising dread. He had spent much of the night praying. "I was pretty certain that, however we prepared ourselves, only prayer would see us through the operation." MI6 had never attempted to smuggle any-one across the Russian border before. If PIMLICO arrived at the rendez-vous alone, it would be hard enough, but if, as expected, he brought his wife and two children, the chance of success was infinitesimal. "I thought: this man will be shot. The plan could not work. We all knew how flimsy the whole thing was. We were fulfilling a promise, and we had to do it even though we were walking into something that wasn't going to work. I put the chances at twenty percent or lower."

A telegram arrived from Century House. The bosses in London "detected signs of wobbliness" on the part of the embassy management, and had composed a message "to stiffen the sinews." It read: "The Prime Minister has personally approved this operation and expressed her com-plete confidence in your ability to carry it out. We all here join in stand-ing 100% behind you and are confident you will succeed." Ascot showed it to Cartledge, to demonstrate the "continuing top-level clearance in London."

Then another potentially lethal snag emerged. In order to leave the Soviet Union by car, foreign diplomats needed formal permission and special license plates. The official garage doing the plating closed at mid-day on Fridays. Gee's Ford was replated without a hitch, but Ascot's

Saab was sent back with the message: "Sorry. We can't plate this because your wife hasn't got a driving license." Caroline's handbag containing her Soviet license had been stolen the month before, and to obtain a new one, she had sent in her British license to the consular authorities. This had not yet been returned and a new Soviet license issued. Diplomats were not permitted to drive alone; without a codriver with a valid Soviet license. Ascot could not get the official plates; without these plates they could not leave the Soviet Union. PIMLICO was about to founder on a tiny but immoveable rock of Russian bureaucracy. At 11 a.m., an hour before the traffic authorities shut for the weekend, Ascot was still racking his brains for a solution when a package arrived from the Soviet Foreign Ministry containing Caroline's British license and a new Soviet one. "We had an hour to get our car plated in time. I couldn't believe it, this incredible stroke of luck."

But, on second thought, Ascot wondered if the unexpected and timely return of the license really was serendipity, or part of the KGB setup: "We had cleared the last obstacle to travel, but it all looked very pat.

11 a.m., Leninsky Prospekt, Moscow

Gordievsky spent the morning cleaning the flat from top to bottom. In a very short time, the KGB would tear it apart, rip up the floorboards, demolish his library page by page, and dismantle every stick of furniture. But some odd pride made him determined that his home should look "shipshape" when they arrived to destroy it: he did the washing up, arranged the crockery, washed his clothes in the sink, and hung them out to dry. On the counter he left money for Leila, 220 rubles, enough to cover household expenses for a few days. It was a small gesture . . . but of what? His continuing care? Apology? Regret? The money would probably never reach her. The KGB would surely confiscate or steal it. Like the meticulous cleaning of the flat, he was sending a message that said more about him, perhaps, than he realized: Gordievsky wanted to be thought of as a good man; he wanted the KGB, which he had deceived so comprehensively, to respect him. He left no note of self-justification, no explanation for having betrayed the Soviet Union. If they caught him, the KGB would extract all that, and this time with nothing so gentle as a truth drug. He left a spotless flat, and a lot of clean laundry. Like Mr. Harrington, he would not flee without doing his washing.

Then Gordievsky prepared to throw off the KGB surveillance squad for a fourth and final time. The timing was crucial. If he left the flat and evaded his watchers too early, they might finally spot what was afoot and raise the alarm. But if he left it too late, he might not be able to complete his dry-cleaning, and would reach the railway station with the KGB still on his tail.

He did his packing, meager enough, in an ordinary plastic bag: a light jacket, his Danish leather cap, sedatives, and a small, Soviet-printed road atlas that covered the Finnish border region, doubtless inaccurate since the area was militarily sensitive. He forgot to pack the snuff. *[Editor's note: Intended to throw police dogs off the scent at vehicle checkpoints.]*

11 a.m., Vaalimaa Motel, Finland

The Finnish end of Operation PIMLICO was running according to schedule. The team assembled at a small motel, about ten miles from the border. Veronica Price and Simon Brown, traveling under false passports, had arrived in Helsinki the previous evening, and spent the night in an airport hotel.

Martin Shawford, the young MI6 officer in charge of coordinating matters in Finland, was already waiting when they drew up in the motel parking lot, followed a few minutes later by the two Danish PET officers, Eriksen and Larsen. Coincidentally, the cars had all been booked through the same rental company at the airport, and to Shawford's horror three identical cars were now parked in the lot: three bright-red, brand-new Volvos, with sequential license plates. "We looked like a convention. It could hardly have been more conspicuous." At least one car would have to be changed before the next day.

The rendezvous point on the Finnish side of the border had been selected when Veronica Price first formulated the plan. Five miles north-west of the border crossing, a forestry track turned off to the right and led into the woods. About a mile along it on the left was a small clearing, where the logging trucks turned, surrounded by trees and invisible from the main road: the spot was close enough to the frontier to ensure Oleg and his family would not remain cramped in the car trunks a moment longer than necessary, but far enough away to be well clear of the border security zone.

The combined MI6-PET team thoroughly reconnoitered the area around the rendezvous point. The Finnish pine forest stretched away unbroken on every side. There were no houses in sight. Here they would meet the getaway team, swiftly move escapees from the MI6 cars into the Finnish rental cars, and then split up into two groups. The Finnish team would reassemble at a second rendezvous point in the woods about ten miles farther on, where they could check the escapees' health, change their clothing, and speak freely without fear of being overheard through the bugged diplomatic cars. Meanwhile, the Moscow team would take the road toward Helsinki, and wait at the first petrol station. The escape team would begin the long journey north to the Finnish-Norwegian border: Leila and one child would travel in the Danes' car, Gordievsky and the other girl with Brown and Price. Shawford would rejoin the MI6 Moscow team at the petrol station; debrief Ascot and Gee, and make an important call from the public telephone kiosk in the forecourt.

The call would be automatically routed through to the Sovbloc controller, waiting with the P5 team in Century House. The petrol station telephone might be monitored by the KGB or Finnish intelligence, so the outcome of PIMLICO would have to be reported in veiled language. If Gordievsky and his family were out and safe, Shawford would say that his fishing holiday had been successful. If, however, the escape had failed, he would report that he had caught nothing. Having thoroughly checked the rendezvous area, the team drove back to Helsinki, swapped one of their fleet of bright-red Volvos for another model, and dispersed to separate hotels.

12 p.m., Kutuzovsky Prospekt, Moscow

In the diplomatic flats, Caroline Ascot and Rachel Gee did the packing. They could take no personal clothing, since all the space in the trunks was needed to accommodate PIMLICO and his family. Instead, they assembled a number of empty travel bags that looked realistically bulky, when stuffed with cushions, but could be folded flat when emptied. The escape kit, first assembled seven years earlier, was retrieved from the British embassy safe: water bottles and children's plastic "sippy cups" (which would be easier for the girls to drink from in the cramped trunks), two large empty bottles to urinate into, and four "space blankets" made of heat-reflective thin plastic sheeting, of the sort used to reduce heat loss in cases of hypothermia or exertion. Heat sensors and infrared cameras at the Soviet border were believed to be capable of picking up a concealed body, but no one in MI6 was sure how the technology worked, or whether it really existed. The escapees would have to strip to their underwear before pulling the blankets over themselves; it would be hot inside the trunks, and the lower their body temperatures, the less the likelihood of attracting the sniffer dogs and heat sensors.

Caroline put together a picnic—hamper, blankets, sandwiches, and potato crisps—which they could spread out at the turnout as a form of camouflage. The escapees might take time to emerge from hiding. They might be late reaching the rendezvous. There could be others in the turnout, who might become suspicious if four foreigners simply appeared on the scene with no obvious purpose. The two couples needed to have an innocent explanation for turning off the road, and an English picnic would provide perfect cover. Caroline also prepared a travel bag for Florence, with clothes, baby food, and spare nappies. Rachel Gee took her two small children and mother-in-law to the park. Every so often, she would stop and clutch her back as if in pain. Her performance was so convincing that Gee's mother asked him: "Are you sure she's not ill? She doesn't look a bit well to me, you know."

3 p.m., British embassy, Moscow

The assistant naval attaché, one of several military experts at the embassy, arrived back in Moscow, following a trip to Finland, having inadvertently thrown a very large wrench in the works: he reported that he had been challenged by the KGB border guards at Vyborg, both on leaving and again on reentering the Soviet Union. Against all the diplomatic rules, the guards had demanded to search his car, and the attaché had not objected. "The stupid man had let them put a dog through it," fumed Ascot. If the border authorities were flouting convention and using sniffer dogs to search British diplomatic vehicles, the escape plan was sunk. Four hot people crammed into the trunks of two cars give off a powerful scent. The attaché had unknowingly set a dangerous precedent, at the worst possible moment. Ascot hurriedly forged a formal diplomatic note of protest for the ambassador to the Ministry of Foreign Affairs complaining that the attaché's car had been searched and insisting that British diplomatic immunity had been violated. The note was not sent, but Ascot took a copy indicating that it had, along with a translation, into Russian, of the relevant clauses of the Vienna Convention. If the KGB tried to search the cars at the border, he would brandish the fake letter. But there was no guarantee that this would work: if the border guards wanted to see what was inside the car trunks, no amount of official protest would stop them.

There was one final bit of paperwork. Violet, the MI6 secretary, typed up a copy of the escape instructions on soluble paper. If the KGB arrested them, the aide-memoire "could be dissolved in water or, most uncomfortably, in one's mouth." In an extreme emergency, the MI6 team could eat Operation PIMLICO.

4 p.m., Leninsky Prospekt, Moscow

Gordievsky dressed in a thin green sweater, faded green corduroy trousers, and old brown shoes, selected from the back of the cupboard in the hope that they might have escaped contamination by radioactive dust or the other chemicals used to alert sniffer dogs. The outfit was probably sufficiently similar to his green tracksuit for the concierge (and watchers) to assume he was going for a run. He locked the front door of his flat. The KGB would be opening it again in a few hours. "I was closing it not only on my home and my possessions, but on my family and my life." He took no souvenir photographs with him or other emotional mementoes.

He made no farewell calls to his mother or sister, although he knew he would probably never see either of them again. He left no note of explanation or justification. He did nothing that might seem out of the ordinary, on the most extraordinary day of his life. The concierge did not look up as he passed through the lobby. He had exactly one and a half hours to make the journey across Moscow to Leningrad Station, and to lose his tail for the last time.

On his earlier dry-cleaning runs, he had made for the nearby shopping precinct. This time, he crossed over the avenue and into a wooded area on the other side that ran the length of the avenue. Once out of sight of the road, he broke into a jog, and steadily increased his speed, until he was almost sprinting. The fat KGB surveillance officer would never keep up. At the end of the park, he crossed over the road, doubled back, and then entered the shops from the opposite side. Plastic bags were rare enough to be distinctive, so he bought a cheap artificial leather valise, stuffed his few items into it, and left by the rear entrance.

Then he ran through the full surveillance-evasion menu, methodically and meticulously: jumping on a Metro train as the door closed, alighting after two stops, waiting for the next train to arrive and then making certain every passenger on the platform had boarded before letting the doors close and catching a train in the opposite direction; ducking down one street, doubling back and up another, into a shop by one entrance and then out of the back. Leningrad Station was awash with people, and police. By chance, 26,000 young leftists from 157 countries were pouring into Moscow for the Twelfth World Festival of Youth and Students, starting the following week, billed as a celebration of "antiimperialist solidarity, peace, and friendship." At a mass rally, Gorbachev would tell them: "Here, in the homeland of the great Lenin, you can directly feel how deeply our young people are devoted to the noble ideals of humanity, peace, and socialism."

Most festival-goers had come not for Lenin, but for the music: among the performers would be Dean Reed, the pro-Soviet American-born singer who had settled behind the Iron Curtain, the British pop duo Everything But the Girl, and Bob Dylan, who had been invited by the Soviet poet Andrei Voznesensky. Many of the youth delegates were arriving from Scandinavia, via Finland. Gordievsky was alarmed to see riot police patrolling the station, but then tried to reassure himself: with so many people crossing the northern border, the guards might be too preoccupied to pay much attention to diplomatic cars passing in the other direction. He bought bread and sausage at a stall. As far as he could tell, no one was following him.

The overnight train to Leningrad consisted largely of fourth-class sleeper carriages, with six bunks to each compartment, opening onto a corridor. Gordievsky found he was in the topmost bunk. He collected clean sheets and made up his bed. The female conductor, a student earning money during her vacation, did not seem to pay him particular attention. At 5:30 precisely the train pulled out. For a few hours, Gordievsky lay on the bunk, chewing his scanty supper and trying to remain calm, while beneath him his fellow passengers did the crossword together. He took two sedative pills, and in a few moments fell into a deep sleep, compounded by mental exhaustion, fear, and chemicals.

7 p.m., British embassy, Moscow

The ambassador's inaugural drinks party was a great success. Sir Bryan Cartledge, who had arrived the night before, gave a brief speech, of which the MI6 party could remember not a single word. Rachel stayed at home, moaning for the hidden microphones, and occasionally emitting "the odd sob."

After an hour of diplomatic chitchat beneath the chandeliers, the two intelligence officers made their excuses, explaining that they had to drive overnight to Leningrad to take Rachel to a doctor in Finland. Of those at the party, only the ambassador, the minister, David Ratford, and the MI6 secretary, Violet Chapman, knew the real purpose of their journey. At the end of the party, Violet retrieved the PIMLICO "medicine package" from the MI6 safe in the embassy, and handed it to Ascot: tranquilizer pills for the adults, and a pair of syringes for sedating two terrified little girls.

Back at Kutuzovsky Prospekt, while the men loaded up the cars, Rachel went into the bedroom where her children were sleeping and kissed them good night. She wondered when she would see them again. "If we get caught," she reflected, "we're going to be stuck for a very long time." Gee walked his stiff-backed and hobbling wife to the Ford Sierra, and settled her in the front seat.

At about 11:15 p.m., the two-car convoy pulled into the wide avenue and headed north, with Gee taking the lead in the Ford, while Ascot followed in his Saab. Both couples had brought a plentiful stock of music cassettes for the long journey to Helsinki. A single KGB surveillance car escorted them to Sokol, on the city's outskirts, and then peeled off. As they hit the wide highway, Ascot and Gee could detect no obvious surveillance cars following them. This was not necessarily reassuring. A tail car was not the KGB's only method of vehicle surveillance. Along every main road State Automobile Inspection Posts (GAI posts) were stationed at regular intervals, which would note when a car under observation passed by, radio ahead to alert the next post, and if necessary maintain contact with any surveillance cars that might be deployed out of sight. Inside the cars the atmosphere was otherworldly and tense. Since the vehicles were assumed to be bugged, recording or relaying sound to an unseen radio car, there could be no letup in the playacting. The performance was entering its second, mobile act. Rachel complained of her painful back. Ascot grumbled about having to drive hundreds of miles with a small baby, just as the new ambassador had arrived. No one mentioned the escape, or the man who was even now, they all hoped, in a train rumbling toward Leningrad.

"This has got to be a setup," Gee mused, as Rachel fell asleep. "We can't possibly get away with this."

Saturday, July 20 3:30 a.m., Moscow to Leningrad train

Gordievsky woke up on the bottom bunk, with a splitting headache and, for a long and unreal moment, no idea where he was. A young man was looking down on him from an upper bunk, with an odd expression: "You fell out," he said. The sedatives had plunged Gordievsky into such profound slumber that when the train braked suddenly he had rolled off the bunk and landed on the floor, cutting his temple as he fell. His jersey was covered in blood. He staggered into the corridor for some air. In the next compartment, a group of young women from Kazakhstan were talking animatedly. He opened his mouth to join in the conversation, but as he did so one of the women recoiled in horror: "If you speak one word to me, I'll scream." Only then did he realize what he must look like: disheveled, blood-spattered, and unsteady on his feet. He backed away, grabbed his bag, and retreated to the end of the corridor. There was still more than an hour to go before the train reached Leningrad. Would the other passengers report him for being drunk? He went to find the guard, handed her a five-ruble note, and said: "Thank you for your help," though she had done nothing but supply his bedsheets. She gave him a quizzical look, with what seemed to be a hint of reproach. But she pocketed the money anyway. The train rattled on through the lifting darkness.

4 a.m., Moscow to Leningrad highway

About halfway to Leningrad, in the Valdai Hills, the escape team drove into a spectacular dawn that moved Ascot to lyricism: "A thick mist had risen from the lakes and rivers, extending into long belts beside the hills and through the trees and villages. The land slowly coalesced into substantial forms out of these foaming banks of violet and rose. Three very bright planets shone out in perfect symmetry, one to the left, one to the right, and one straight ahead. We passed solitary figures already scything hay, picking herbs, or taking cows to pasture along the slopes and gullies of common land. It was a stunning sight, an idyllic moment. It was difficult to believe that any harm could come out of a day of such beginnings."

Florence slept happily in her car seat on the backseat.

A devout Catholic and a spiritual man, Ascot thought: "We are on a line and we are committed to it—there is only one line and that's the one we've got to go on."

In the second car, Arthur and Rachel Gee were experiencing their own transcendent moment, as the sun emerged over the horizon and light flooded the mist-cloaked Russian uplands. The Dire Straits album *Brothers in Arms* was playing on the cassette deck, with Mark Knopfler's virtuoso guitar seeming to fill the dawn.

"For the first time I thought: this is going to come out all right," Rachel recalled.

At that moment, a snub-nosed brown Soviet-made Fiat, known as a Zhiguli, the standard-issue KGB surveillance car, slotted in behind the convoy at a distance of about two hundred feet. "We were being followed."

5 a.m., Main railway station, Leningrad

Gordievsky was among the first passengers to alight when the train pulled in. He walked swiftly to the exit, not daring to look behind to see if the guard was already talking to station staff and pointing out the strange man who had fallen out of his berth and then over-tipped her. There were no taxis outside the station. But a number of private cars were milling around, their drivers touting for fares. Gordievsky climbed into one: "To the Finland Station," he said.

Gordievsky arrived at the Finland Station at 5:45. The almost deserted square in front was dominated by a vast statue of Lenin, commemorating the moment in 1917 when the great theorist of revolution arrived from Switzerland to take charge of the Bolsheviks. In Communist lore, the Finland Station is symbolic of revolutionary liberty and the birth of the Soviet Union; to Gordievsky it also represented the route to freedom, but in the opposite direction, in every sense, to Lenin.

The first train toward the border left at 7:05. It would take him as far as Zelenogorsk, thirty miles northwest of Leningrad and just over a third of the way to the Finnish border. From there he could catch a bus that would take him along the main road toward Vyborg. Gordievsky climbed aboard, and pretended to fall asleep. The train was excruciatingly slow.

7 a.m., KGB headquarters, Moscow Center

It is not clear exactly when the KGB noticed that Gordievsky had gone. But by dawn on July 20, the surveillance team from the First Chief Directorate (Chinese department) must have been seriously worried. He had last been seen on Friday afternoon, jogging into the woods on Leninsky Prospekt, carrying a plastic bag. On the previous three occasions that he had gone missing, Gordievsky reappeared within a few hours. This time, he had not returned to the flat. He was not with his sister, his father-in-law, or his friend Lyubimov, or at any other known address.

At this moment, the most sensible action would have been to raise the alarm. The KGB could then have launched an immediate manhunt, stripped Gordievsky's flat for clues to his whereabouts, pulled in for questioning every friend and relative, redoubled surveillance of British diplomatic personnel, and then shut down every avenue of escape, by air, sea, and land. There is no evidence, however, that the surveillance team did this on the morning of July 20. Instead, they seem to have done what timeservers do in every autocracy that punishes honest failure: they did nothing at all, and hoped the problem would go away.

7:30 a.m., Leningrad

The MI6 exfiltration team parked outside Leningrad's Astoriya hotel. The brown KGB surveillance car had followed them all the way to central Leningrad, before disappearing. "I assumed we had a new tail," wrote Ascot. They opened the trunks and "ostentatiously rummaged inside, to show the surveillance we had nothing to hide and our [trunks] were genuinely full of luggage." While Gee and the two women went inside to feed the baby and have breakfast ("disgusting hard-boiled eggs and wooden bread"), Ascot remained in his car, pretending to be asleep. "The KGB was sniffing around and I didn't want people to look inside." Two different men approached the car and peered through the window; on both occasions, Ascot pretended to wake up with a start, and glared at them.

The hundred-mile drive north to the turnout, he estimated, would take about two hours. So they would need to leave Leningrad at 11:45 to get there in plenty of time for the rendezvous at 2:30. The car that had shadowed them into Leningrad, and now the inquisitive types hanging around the car, suggested a worrying degree of KGB interest. "At that point I knew they were going to follow us to the border, and that took the enthusiasm out of me." The powerful Western cars might be able to outrun a single Soviet-made KGB car and get far enough ahead to swerve into the rendezvous turnout without being seen. But what if the KGB also put a surveillance car in front, as they sometimes did? If PIMLICO had been unable to shake off surveillance, they could be driving into an ambush. "I feared most of all that two sets of KGB surveillance would plan on meeting in a pincer movement at the rendezvous itself. My remaining optimism was evaporating fast."

With two hours to kill, Ascot suggested they use up the time by making an ironic pilgrimage to the Smolny Institute and Convent, one of Communism's most venerated sites. Originally the Smolny Institute for Noble Maidens, one of the first schools in Russia to educate women (aristocrats only), the great Palladian edifice was used by Lenin as his headquarters during the October Revolution, and became the seat of the Bolshevik government until it was moved to the Kremlin in Moscow. It was filled with what Ascot called "Leniniana."

In the gardens of the Smolny, the foursome sat on a bench, and ostensibly huddled over a guidebook. "It was a last council of war, rehearsing everything," said Ascot. If they successfully reached the rendezvous site, the contents of the car trunks would need to be rearranged to accommodate the passengers. Rachel would lay out the picnic while the men cleared the luggage from the trunks. Caroline, meanwhile, would walk to the entrance of the turnout with Florence in her arms, and look up and down the road. "If anything seemed amiss, she would remove her headscarf." But if the coast was clear Gee would open the hood of his car to signal to PIMLICO that it was safe to emerge. Any microphones would overhear the conversation, so the pickup should be conducted wordlessly. If he was the only escapee, he would be hidden in the trunk of Gee's car. The Ford suspension was higher than that of the Saab, and the extra weight of the body would be slightly less noticeable. "Arthur would lead the way out of the RV site," wrote Ascot. "And I would protect from behind, against any attempt to ram the boot."

Lenin's revolutionary headquarters seemed an appropriate place to be plotting. "It was two fingers to the KGB, really."

Before climbing back into their cars for the last leg, they wandered down to the banks of the Neva, and watched the river flowing past an abandoned wharf, "now strewn with rusting, wheelless buses and torn bales of cellophane floating into the river weed." Ascot suggested this might be a good opportunity for a brief communication with the Almighty. "All four of us had a moment of reflection. We felt very connected to something beyond—and we really needed to."

On the outskirts of Leningrad, they passed a large GAI police post with a watchtower. Moments later, a blue Zhiguli, with two male passengers and a tall radio aerial, tucked in behind them. "This was a depressing sight," wrote Ascot. "But worse was to follow."

8:25 a.m., Zelenogorsk

Gordievsky climbed down off the train and looked around. The town of Zelenogorsk, known until 1948 by its Finnish name, Terijoki, was waking up, and the station was busy. It seemed impossible that he could have been followed here, but back in Moscow the surveillance team must have raised the alarm by now. The border post at Vyborg, fifty miles to the northwest, might already be on alert. The escape plan called for him to catch a bus the rest of the way, and get off at the 836 marker post, 836 kilometers from Moscow and sixteen miles short of the border town. At the bus station he bought a ticket to Vyborg.

The ancient bus was half full, and as it wheezed out of Zelenogorsk, Gordievsky tried to make himself comfortable on the hard seat and closed his eyes. A young couple took the seat in front of him. They were talkative and friendly. They were also, in a way that is almost unique to Russia, stupendously drunk at nine o'clock in the morning. "Where are you going?" they hiccuped. "Where are you from?" Gordievsky gave a mumbled reply. As is the habit of drunks seeking conversation, they asked the same question, louder. He said he was visiting friends in a village near Vyborg, dredging up a name from his study of the mini-atlas. Even to his own ears, that sounded like a flat lie. But it seemed to satisfy the couple, who burbled on inconsequentially and then, after about twenty minutes, lurched to their feet and alighted, waving cheerily.

Dense woods lined either side of the road, conifers mixed with scrub birch and aspen, broken by the occasional clearing with picnic tables. It would be an easy place to get lost in, but also a good place to hide. Tourist buses streamed in the opposite direction, bringing Scandinavian youths to the music festival. Gordievsky noted a large number of military vehicles, including armored personnel carriers. The border area was heavily militarized, and some sort of training exercise was under way.

The road curved to the right, and suddenly the photographs Veronica Price had shown him so often seemed to come alive. He had not spotted the marker post, but felt certain this was the place. Jumping to his feet, he peered out of the window. The bus was almost empty now, and the driver was looking at him quizzically in his mirror. He brought the bus to a stop. Gordievsky hesitated. The bus started to move again. Gordievsky hurried up the aisle, one hand over his mouth. "Sorry, I'm feeling sick. Can you let me off?" Irritated, the driver stopped once again and opened the door. As the bus pulled away, Gordievsky bent over the roadside ditch, pretending to retch. He was making himself far too conspicuous. At least half a dozen people would now remember him clearly: the train guard, the man who had found him blacked out on the floor of the compartment, the drunk couple, and the bus driver, who would surely recall a sick passenger who seemed not to know where he was going.

The entrance to the turnout was three hundred yards ahead, marked by a distinctive rock. It turned off in a wide D-shaped loop a hundred yards in length, with a screen of trees on the roadside and thick undergrowth of bracken and scrub. A military track at the widest point of the D led deeper into the woods on the right. The dirt surface of the turnout was dusty, but the ground around it was boggy, with pools of semi-stagnant water. It was beginning to get warm, and the earth gave off a pungent, fetid aroma. He heard the whine of a mosquito, and felt the first bite. Then another. The forest seemed echoingly quiet. It was still only 10:30. The MI6 getaway cars would not arrive for another four hours, if they came at all.

Fear and adrenaline can have a strange effect on the mind; as well as the appetite. Gordievsky should have remained hidden in the undergrowth. He should have pulled his jacket over his head, and allowed the mosquitoes to do their worst. He should have waited. Instead he did something that was, with hindsight, very nearly insane.

He decided he would go into Vyborg, and have a drink.

12 p.m. Leningrad to Vyborg highway

The two MI6 cars were leaving the outskirts of Leningrad, with the blue KGB Zhiguli following, when a Soviet police car pulled out ahead of Ascot's Saab, and positioned itself at the head of the little convoy. A few moments later, a second police car passed in the opposite direction, then signaled and performed a U-turn, and slotted in behind the KGB car. A fourth car, a mustard-colored Zhiguli, joined the rear of the column. "We were bracketed," said Ascot. He exchanged an anxious look with Caroline but said nothing.

Some fifteen minutes later, the police car in front suddenly pulled ahead. At the same moment, the KGB car also accelerated, overtook the two British cars, and assumed the front position. A mile ahead, the first police car was waiting in a side road. Once the convoy had passed, it pulled out and took up the rear position. The convoy was bracketed again, but now with the KGB in front, and the two police cars behind. A classic Soviet power play had just taken place, coordinated by radio and performed as a bizarre motorized dance: "The KGB had said to the police: 'You can stay, but we're going to run this operation.'"

Whatever order they might choose to drive in, this was intense surveillance, with no effort made to disguise it. Ascot drove on gloomily. "At that point I thought we were in a pincer movement. I saw us turning into the place and meeting a reception committee, a whole lot of uniformed people coming out of the bushes."

The kilometer marker posts were counting down. "I had no plan formulated to deal with such a situation: I hadn't quite imagined that we might be moving toward the rendezvous with the KGB a few yards ahead and just behind us." With one car in front and three in the rear, it would be impossible to pull into the turnout. "If they are still with us at the rendezvous point," thought Ascot, "we are going to have to abort." PIMLICO and his family, if he had brought them, would be left high and dry. Assuming, that is, that he had ever left Moscow.

12:15 p.m., a cafe south of Vyborg

The first car on the road going in the direction of Vyborg had been a Lada, which obligingly stopped the moment Gordievsky stuck out his thumb. Hitchhiking, known as *Avtostop*, was common in Russia, and encouraged by the Soviet authorities. Even in a military zone, a lone hitchhiker was not necessarily suspicious. The young driver was smartly dressed in civilian clothes. Possibly military or KGB, Gordievsky reflected, but if so he was remarkably incurious, asked not a single question, and played loud Western pop music all the way to the edge of the town. When Gordievsky proffered three rubles for the short journey, the man accepted the money wordlessly and drove away without looking back. A few minutes later Gordievsky was sitting down to his fine lunch: two bottles of beer and a plate of fried chicken.

The first bottle of beer slipped down, and Gordievsky began to feel a delicious drowsiness as the adrenaline subsided. The chicken leg was one of the tastiest things he had ever eaten. The empty cafeteria on the outskirts of Vyborg seemed utterly nondescript, a glass and plastic bubble.

The waitress had barely glanced at him as she took his order. He began to feel, not safe exactly, but oddly calm and suddenly exhausted.

Vyborg had changed nationality repeatedly down the centuries, from Sweden to Finland to Russia, then the Soviet Union, back to Finland, and finally Soviet again. In 1917, Lenin had passed through the town at the head of his contingent of Bolsheviks. Before the Second World War its population of 80,000, though the majority were Finnish, also included Swedes, Germans, Russians, Gypsies, Tatars, and Jews. During the Winter War between Finland and the Soviet Union (1939–40), virtually the entire population was evacuated, and more than half the buildings were destroyed. After bitter fighting, it was occupied by the Red Army, and annexed by the Soviet Union in 1944, when the last Finns were expelled and replaced by Soviet citizens. It had the stark, inert atmosphere of every town that has been demolished, ethnically cleansed, and rebuilt swiftly and cheaply. It felt utterly unreal. But the cafe was warm.

Gordievsky came to with a jolt. Had he been asleep? Suddenly it was 1 p.m. Three men had entered the cafeteria, and were staring at him, Gordievsky thought, with suspicion. They were well dressed. Trying to appear unhurried, he picked up the second bottle of beer, put it in the bag, left money on the table, and walked out. Steeling himself, he walked casually south; after four hundred yards, he dared to look back. The men were still inside the cafe. But where had the time gone? The road was now deserted. With the arrival of lunchtime, the traffic had melted away. He began to run. The sweat was pouring off him after just a few hundred yards, but he picked up speed. Gordievsky was still an accomplished runner. Despite the trials of the last two months, he remained fit. He could feel his heart pumping, from fright and exertion, as he got into his stride. A hitchhiker might be unremarkable, but a man sprinting along an empty road would surely excite curiosity. At least he was running away from the border. He ran faster. Why had he not remained at the rendezvous? Could he possibly cover the sixteen miles back to the turnout in an hour and twenty minutes? Almost certainly not. But he ran anyway, as fast as he could. Gordievsky ran for his life.

1 p.m., two miles north of Vaalimaa village, Finland

On the Finnish side of the border, the MI6 reception team got into position early. They knew Ascot and Gee had set off from Moscow on time the previous evening, but had heard nothing since. Price and Brown parked their red Volvo off the track, on the edge of the clearing. Shawford and the Danes took up positions on either side of the road. If the two cars arrived with the KGB in hot pursuit, Eriksen and Larsen would use their vehicle to try to block or ram the pursuers. They seemed most cheerful at the possibility. It was hot and quiet, oddly peaceful after the frenetic activity of the previous four days.

"I felt an extraordinary period of stillness at the center of the turning world," Simon Brown recalled. He had brought along *Hotel du Lac*—the Booker Prize-winning novel by Anita Brookner. "I thought if I took a long book it would be tempting fate, so I took a short book." The Danes dozed. Veronica Price made a mental checklist of everything on the escape plan. Brown read as slowly as he could, and "tried not to think of the minutes ticking by." Dark forebodings kept intruding: "I wondered whether we had killed the kids by injecting drugs into them."

1:30 p.m., Leningrad to Vyborg highway

Russia's road-building authorities were proud of the highway running from Leningrad to the Finnish border, the main gateway between Scandinavia and the Soviet Union. It was a show road, wide and properly asphalted and cambered, with neat signs and road markings. The little convoy was making good progress, cruising at seventy-five miles per hour, with the KGB car in front, the MI6 cars corralled in the middle, and two police vehicles and a second KGB car following a little way behind. It was all far too easy for the KGB, so Ascot decided to make it more difficult.

"I had been under surveillance for years, and we had got to know the way the KGB Seventh Directorate thought. While they often knew that you knew they were around, what really offended and embarrassed them was when someone deliberately indicated that he had spotted them: psychologically, no surveillance team likes to be shown up by its target as obvious and incompetent. They hate you putting two fingers up, and saying in effect: 'We know you are there and we know what you're up to.'" On principle, Ascot always ignored surveillance, however overt. Now, for the first time, he broke his own rule.

The Viscount-spy reduced speed until he was traveling at just thirty-five miles per hour. The rest of the convoy did likewise. At Kilometer Post 800, Ascot slowed again, until they were crawling along at barely thirty miles per hour. The KGB car in front decelerated and waited for the British cars to catch up. Other cars began to stack up behind the convoy.

The KGB driver did not like it. The British were mocking him, deliberately impeding progress. "Finally, the nerve of the driver in front broke, and he shot off at top speed. He didn't like being shown up." A few miles farther on, the blue KGB Zhiguli was waiting in a side road leading to the village of Kaimovo. It tucked in behind the other surveillance cars. Ascot's Saab was once again in the lead.

Gradually, he increased speed. So did Gee, maintaining a distance of just fifty feet between his car and the Saab in front. The three following cars began to fall behind. The road ahead was straight and clear. Ascot accelerated again. They were now speeding at around eighty-five miles per hour. A gap of more than eight hundred yards had opened up between Gee and the Russian cars. Kilometer Post 826 shot past. The rendezvous point was just ten kilometers ahead.

Ascot swung around a bend and hit the brakes.

An army column was crossing the road, from left to right: tanks, howitzers, rocket launchers, armored personnel carriers. A bread van was already stopped ahead, waiting for the convoy to pass. Ascot drew to a halt behind the van. Gee pulled up behind him. The surveillance cars caught up, and bunched up behind. The Russian soldiers on top of the tanks spotted the foreign cars, and raised clenched fists and shouted, an ironic Cold War salutation.

"That's it," thought Ascot. "We are done."

2:00 p.m., Leningrad highway, ten miles southeast of Vyborg
Gordievsky heard the truck rumbling up behind him before he saw it, and stuck out his thumb. The driver beckoned the hitchhiker aboard. "What do you want to go there for? There's nothing there," he said when

Gordievsky, panting, explained that he would like to be dropped off at Kilometer Post 836.

Gordievsky shot him what he hoped was a conspiratorial look. "There are some dachas in the woods. I've got a nice lady waiting for me in one of them." The truck driver gave a snort of approval, and grinned in complicity.

"You lovely man," thought Gordievsky, when the driver dropped him, ten minutes later, at the rendezvous point, and drove away with a lascivious wink and three rubles in his pocket. "You lovely, Russian man."

At the turnout, he crawled into the undergrowth. The mosquitoes hungrily welcomed him back. A bus carrying women to the military base turned into the turnout and went down the track; Gordievsky flattened himself on the damp earth, wondering if he had been spotted. Silence fell, save for the whining mosquitoes, and his thumping heart. Dehydrated, he drank the second bottle of beer. 2:30 passed. Then 2:35.

At 2:40, another moment of madness gripped him, and he got to his feet and walked into the road, heading in the direction the MI6 getaway cars should be coming from. Perhaps he could save a few minutes by meeting them on the road itself. But after a few steps, sanity returned. If the cars had a KGB escort, they would all be caught in the open. He ran back to the turnout and dived into the concealing bracken once more.

"Wait," he told himself. "Control yourself."

2:40 p.m., Kilometer Post 826, Leningrad to Vyborg highway
The last vehicle of the military convoy finally trundled across the road. Ascot gunned the engine of the Saab, shot around the stationary bread van, and accelerated hard, with Gee just a few yards behind him. They were a hundred yards ahead before the KGB car had started its engine. The road ahead was clear. Ascot put his foot to the floor. Handel's *Messiah* was playing on the tape deck. Caroline turned it up to full volume. "The people that walked in darkness have seen a great light; and they that dwell in the land of the shadow of death, upon them hath the light shined." Ascot thought grimly: "If only . . ."

The MI6 officers had driven the route several times before, and both knew that the turnout was just a few miles ahead. In moments they were back up to eighty-five miles per hour, and the escort cars were already five hundred yards behind, the gap steadily increasing. Just before the 836 Marker Post, the road straightened and dipped for about half a mile, and then rose again before making a sharp bend to the right. The turnout was on the right, about two hundred yards farther on. Would it be full of Russian picnickers? Caroline Ascot still did not know whether her husband was going to attempt the pickup or drive on past the turnout. Nor did Gee. Nor, in fact, did Ascot.

At the brow of the dip, as Ascot turned into the curve, Gee glanced in his rearview mirror, to see the blue Zhiguli just coming into view on the straight, half a mile behind—a gap of half a minute, perhaps less.

The rock loomed into view, and almost before he knew he had done it, Ascot slammed on the brakes, shot into the turnout, and came to a screeching stop, with Gee just a few yards behind, their skidding tires kicking up a cloud of dust. They were screened from the road by the trees and the rock. The place was deserted. The time was 2:47. "Please God, don't let them see the dust," thought Rachel. As they clambered out of the cars, they heard the sound of three Zhiguli engines, screaming in protest, hurtle past on the main road, less than fifty feet away on the other side of the trees. "If just one of them looks in his rear mirror now," thought Ascot, "he will see us." The sound of the engines faded. The dust settled. Caroline tied on her headscarf, picked up Florence, and headed to the lookout point at the turnout entrance. Rachel, following the script, took out the hamper and laid out the picnic rug. Ascot set about transferring luggage from the trunks to the backseats, and Gee moved to the front of the Saab, preparing to open the hood as soon as Caroline gave the all-clear signal.

At that second, a tramp erupted from the undergrowth, unshaven and unkempt, covered in mud, ferns, and dust, dried blood in his hair, a cheap brown bag clutched in one hand, and a wild expression on his face, "He looked absolutely nothing like the photograph," thought Rachel. "Any fantasies we had of meeting a suave spy disappeared on the spot." Ascot thought the figure looked like "some forest troll or woodman in Grimms' *Fairy Tales*." Gordievsky recognized Gee as the man with the Mars bar. Gee had barely glimpsed him outside the bread shop, and momentarily wondered if this scruffy apparition could be the same person. For a beat, on a dusty track in a Russian forest, the spy and the people sent to rescue him stared at one another in indecision. The MI6 team had prepared for four people, including two small children, but PIMLICO was evidently alone. Gordievsky was expecting to be picked up by two intelligence officers. Veronica had said nothing about any women, let alone women who seemed to be laying out some sort of formal English picnic, complete with teacups. And was that a child? Could MI6 really have brought along a baby on a dangerous escape operation?

Gordievsky looked from one man to the other, and then grunted, in English: "Which car?"

Ascot pointed to the open trunk of Gee's car. Caroline hurried back from the turnout's entrance with the baby. Rachel took Gordievsky's mud-caked, malodorous, and possibly radioactive shoes, tied them in a plastic bag, and threw them under the front seat of the car. Gordievsky climbed into the trunk of the Sierra and lay down. Gee handed him water, the medical pack, and the empty bottle and indicated by hand signals that he should undress in the trunk. The aluminum space blanket was laid on top of him. The women bundled the picnic into the backseats.

Gee gently closed the trunk, and Gordievsky disappeared into darkness. With Ascot in the lead, the two cars rejoined the main road, and accelerated.

The entire pickup had taken eighty seconds.

At Kilometer Post 852, the next GIA observation post loomed into view, and with it a memorable tableau. The mustard-colored Zhiguli and the two police cars were parked, doors open, on the right side of the road. A KGB man in plainclothes was in earnest conversation with five militiamen. "They all turned swiftly to look at us as we appeared," and stared, open-mouthed, as the two British cars drove by, their faces registering a mixture of confusion and relief. "The driver ran back to his car as soon as we were past," wrote Ascot. "He had such a puzzled and incredulous look on his face that I expected to be stopped and at least questioned about our movements."

But the surveillance cars slotted in behind, just as before. Had they radioed ahead to the border, warning the guards to look out for a party of foreign diplomats? Did they file a report admitting that they had lost the British diplomats for several minutes?

Or did they, in more traditional Soviet fashion, assume that the foreigners had merely stopped off the road to relieve themselves, disguise the fact that several minutes were unaccounted for, and say nothing at all? It is impossible to know the answer to this question, but it is easy to guess it.

From the trunk, Rachel and Arthur Gee could hear muted grunts and bumps, as Gordievsky struggled to remove his clothes in the constricted space.

Then a distinctive gush, as he decanted his lunchtime beers. Rachel turned up the music: Dr. Hook's *Greatest Hits*, a compilation of the American rock band's records that included "Only Sixteen," "When You're in Love with a Beautiful Woman," and "Sylvia's Mother." The style of Dr. Hook's music is often described as "easy listening." Gordievsky did not find it easy. Even crammed into the boiling trunk of the car, fleeing for his life, he found time to be irritated by this lowbrow schmaltzy pop. "It was horrible, horrible music. I hated it."

But it was not the noise their secret passenger was making that most worried Rachel, it was the smell: a mixture of sweat, cheap soap, tobacco, and beer, rising from the rear of the car. It wasn't unpleasant exactly, but it was most distinctive, and quite strong.

"It was the smell of Russia. It's not something you would have found in an ordinary English car." The sniffer dogs would surely register that something in the back of the car smelled quite different from the passengers in the front.

By a process of contortion, Gordievsky managed to remove his shirt and trousers, but the exertion left him clutching for breath. The heat was already intense, and the air inside the trunk seemed to thicken with each gulp. He swallowed a sedative pill. Gordievsky imagined the scene that would take place if the border guards found him. The British would feign surprise, and claim that the fugitive had been planted as a provocation. They would all be hauled off. He would be taken to the Lubyanka, forced to confess, and then killed.

Back in Moscow, the KGB must have been aware that it had a problem. Yet it still did not move to close the nearest land border, or make the connection between Gordievsky's disappearance and the two British diplomats who had slipped away from an embassy function the previous evening to drive to Finland. Instead it was at first assumed that Gordievsky must have killed himself, and was probably lying at the bottom of the Moscow River, or else drunk in a bar. Weekends are lethargic times in all large bureaucracies, when the second-tier staff comes to work and the boss relaxes. The KGB began looking for Gordievsky, but without particular urgency. After all, where could he possibly run to? And if he had committed suicide, what could be clearer evidence of guilt?

On the twelfth floor of Century House, Derek Thomas, the deputy under-secretary for Intelligence from the Foreign Office, had joined the PIMLICO team in P5's office to wait for Shawford's telephone call and learn the outcome of the "fishing expedition" in Finland. At the Foreign Office, David Goodall, the permanent under-secretary, gathered his senior advisers to await word from Thomas. At 1:30 in the afternoon, 3:30 in Russia, Goodall, a devout Roman Catholic, looked at his watch and declared: "Ladies and gentlemen, they should be crossing the border around now. I think it would be appropriate to say a small prayer." The half-dozen officials bowed their heads.

The traffic crawled through Vyborg. If the KGB was going to flush them out by staging a traffic accident and ramming one of the cars, then it would take place in the center of town. The Zhiguli had vanished. Then the police cars peeled off. "If they're going to get us, they'll get us at the border," Gee thought.

Rachel remembered the training they had undergone, at Veronica Price's insistence, in Guildford woods, squeezed into a trunk under a space blanket, hearing the sounds of the engine, the music from the cassette deck, the unexpected jolts, halts, and Russian voices. "It had seemed crackers at the time."

Now it appeared inspired: "We all knew what he was going through."

Gordievsky swallowed another pill and felt his mind and body slacken a little. He pulled the space blanket over his head. Even though he was stripped to his underwear, the sweat was running down his back and pooling on the metal floor of the trunk.

Ten miles west of Vyborg, they reached the perimeter of the militarized border area, a wall of mesh fencing, topped with barbed wire. The border zone was roughly twelve miles in width. Between there and Finland were five separate barriers, three Soviet and two Finnish.

At the first border check, the frontier guard gave the party "a hard look" but then waved them through without a document check. The border authorities had clearly been told to expect the diplomatic party. At the next checkpoint Ascot scanned the faces of the guards, "but sensed no special tension in the air directed specifically at us."

In the other car, Arthur Gee was focused on a different anxiety. He was having what might be termed a "Have I left the iron on?" moment. He could not remember whether, in his haste, he had locked the trunk of the car. Indeed, he was not even sure he had closed it properly. Gee had a sudden, horrible vision of the trunk lid popping open as they passed through the border area, to reveal the spy, in fetal position, curled up inside. He stopped the car, jumped out, headed to the edge of the forest, and urinated in the bushes. On the way back he checked, as casually as he could, that the trunk was locked—which it was, just as the iron is always off. The delay had taken less than a minute.

The next checkpoint brought them to the border itself. The men parked the cars side by side in the fenced parking lot of the immigration holding area, and then joined the queue at the customs and immigration kiosk. Filling out paperwork for leaving the Soviet Union could be a time-consuming business. Rachel and Caroline prepared for a long wait. No sound came from the trunk. Rachel remained in the passenger seat, trying to look bored and in pain. The baby Florence was fractious, helpfully providing distraction and covering any noise with her wails. Caroline took her out of her car seat and stood talking to Rachel through the open door, gently rocking the baby. Border guards passed between the lines of cars, looking left and right. Rachel braced herself to "throw a wobbly" if they attempted to search the car. If they insisted, Ascot would then present his copy of the letter of protest and the terms of the Vienna Convention. If they still seemed determined to open the trunk, he would throw his own diplomatic wobbly, and insist that they were going to immediately drive back to Moscow to launch a formal protest. At that point, they would probably all be arrested.

Two tourist buses were parked nearby, the passengers asleep or staring idly out of the windows.

Around the edges of the wired enclosure, wild willow herb grew in purple profusion. The smell of fresh-cut hay wafted across the parking lot. The woman official in the customs and immigration kiosk was grumpy and slow, complaining bitterly about the extra work created by the youth festival and the influx of drunk young foreigners. Ascot made Russian small talk, fighting the urge to hurry her. The border guards were carefully searching the other cars, mostly Moscow-based businessmen and Finnish visitors returning home.

The air was hot and still. Rachel heard a low cough from the trunk, and Gordievsky shifted his weight, rocking the car very slightly. Unaware that they were already inside the border zone, he was clearing his throat, attempting to ensure there would be no involuntary spluttering. Rachel turned up the music. "Only Sixteen" by Dr. Hook echoed incongruously around the concrete lot. A dog handler appeared, and stood, eight yards away, looking intently at the British cars and stroking his Alsatian. A second sniffer dog was inspecting a container truck.

The first dog approached, eager and panting, straining at its chain. Rachel reached casually for a packet of crisps, opened it, offered a crisp to Caroline, and dropped a couple on the ground. The British cheese and onion crisp has a most distinctive aroma. Invented by the Irish potato crisp magnate Joe "Spud" Murphy in 1958, cheese and onion is a pungent artificial cocktail of onion powder, whey powder, cheese powder, dextrose, salt, potassium chloride, flavor enhancers, monosodium glutamate, 5'-sodium ribonucleotide, yeast, citric acid, and coloring. Caroline had bought her imported Golden Wonder crisps from the embassy shop, which stocked Marmite, digestive biscuits, marmalade, and other British staples impossible to obtain in Russia. The Soviet sniffer dogs had almost certainly never smelled anything like cheese and onion crisps before.

She offered a crisp to one of the dogs, which wolfed it down before being yanked away by the unsmiling handler. The other dog, however, was now snuffling at the trunk of the Sierra. Gordievsky could hear muffled Russian voices overhead.

As the dog circled the car, Caroline Ascot reached for a weapon that had never been deployed before in the Cold War, or any other. She placed Florence on the trunk directly over the hidden spy, and began changing her nappy—which the baby, with immaculate timing, had just filled. She then dropped the soiled and smelly diaper next to the inquisitive Alsatian. "The dog duly slunk off, offended." Olfactory diversion was never part of the plan. The nappy ruse had been completely spontaneous, and highly effective.

The men returned with the completed paperwork.

Fifteen minutes later a border guard appeared with their four passports, checked them against the occupants, handed them over, and politely bid them goodbye.

A queue of seven cars had formed at the last barrier, a belt of barbed wire, with two elevated lookout posts and guards armed with machine guns. For about twenty minutes they inched forward, aware that they were being closely scrutinized through binoculars from the posts. Gee was now ahead of Ascot.

"It was a nerve-racking moment."

The final Soviet hurdle was passport control itself. The Soviet officers seemed to scrutinize the British diplomatic passports for an age, before the barrier was raised.

They were now technically in Finland, but two more hurdles remained: Finnish customs and immigration, and Finnish passport control. It would require only a single telephone call from the Soviets to turn them around. The Finnish customs officer studied Gee's documents, and then pointed out that his car insurance would be out of date in a few days. Gee remonstrated that they would be returning to the Soviet Union before that. The official shrugged and stamped the document. Gordievsky felt the driver's door close, and a jolt as the car moved off again.

The cars funneled toward the final barrier. Beyond lay Finland. Gee posted the passports through the grille. The Finnish official examined them slowly, handed them back, and came out of his kiosk to raise the barrier. Then his phone rang. He returned to the kiosk. Arthur and Rachel Gee stared ahead in silence.

After what seemed like an eternity, the border guard returned, yawning, and raised the barrier. It was 4:15, Moscow time, 3:15 in Finland. Inside the trunk, Gordievsky heard the fizz of tires on warm asphalt, and felt a shudder as the Ford picked up speed.

Suddenly classical music was blasting out of the tape deck at top volume, no longer the soupy pop of Dr. Hook, but the swelling sounds of an orchestral piece he knew well. Arthur and Rachel Gee still could not tell their passenger, in words, that he was free; but they could do so in sound, with the haunting opening chords of a symphonic poem written by Finnish composer Jean Sibelius in celebration of his native land.

They were playing *Finlandia*.

[Editor's postscript: Gordievsky made it across Finland and on to England where he and his family's safety was assured and guarded. The KGB was stunned and deeply embarrassed. In November they had Gordievsky tried in absentia by a military tribunal, convicted of treason, and sentenced to death. The sentence, of course, has never been carried out.]

Chapter Two

The Morning They Shot the Spies

W. C. Heinz

Some stories are so well-written, so gripping, that they will never disappear from print and fade into obscurity as the years pass. You're about to read one of them.

For a magazine man like myself, the demise of the old True *magazine was painful to watch. During the late 1940s and through the 1950s,* True *could be counted on for strong male-oriented nonfiction on subjects ranging from cars to fishing. The rise of* Playboy *and other so-called "girlie" or "skin" magazines doomed such traditional stalwarts as* True *and* Argosy.

A fine collection of True *articles was* A Treasury of True, *edited by Charles Barnard. Long out of print, the book contains stories, cartoons, illustrations, and covers. In it Barnard points out that whenever and wherever the old* True *editors got together, "The Morning They Shot the Spies" always came up in conversation as one of the most respected pieces. The author, W. C. Heinz, went on to write the outstanding boxing novel,* The Professional.

The setting here is the Ardennes during the Battle of the Bulge in the winter of 1944–45. Part of the German plan to smash through the Allied forces in the region included using German soldiers wearing US uniforms to wreak havoc behind the lines.

We skirted Liege and turned east on the road that leads past the Belgian forts dug into the ground. It was cold. It was two days to Christmas. It was still early and the mist hung over the fields and, in some places, over the road. I remembered when we went through here with the tanks in

September. The sun shone every day and it was warm then, and the Germans were running for the Rhine. It was hard to find Germans then, and when the Americans found them the Germans quit easy and it seemed that the war would be over by Christmas and maybe we would be home.

"Stay on here," I said to the driver. "After we go through Henri Chapelle I'll tell you. I remember it's on the left-hand side of the road."

When we went through Henri Chapelle the people were just starting the day. There were a few of them on the street—a woman in a shawl pouring a pail of steaming, cloudy water into the cobblestone gutter, and a couple of workers walking along the sidewalk, their breaths showing, the collars of their old jackets turned up and their hands in their pants pockets. They paid no attention to us.

"That's the place up on the left," I said to the driver. "I can remember it."

I could remember the wall along the road, and the opening in it. I could remember the low stucco barracks on the other three sides of the dirt quadrangle, and we drove past the guard at the gate and across the frozen yard. The driver put the jeep in with some others at the far end, and we got out, stiff from the cold, and walked back across the dry, hard dirt to what looked like the office.

There were some MP personnel working in there at desks behind a guard rail. There was a pot-bellied stove at the back, and we walked over to it, standing around it and taking the heat and talking about it until a young lieutenant came over and asked us if he could help us.

"We're here for this spy thing," I said.

"Oh," he said. "Then you go across there to the messhall."

He pointed and you could see through the glass in the far door the building that he meant.

"What time is it coming off?"

"I'm afraid I don't know," the lieutenant said. "This place is in a mess. Just go over there, I'm sure that someone will tell you in plenty of time for you to see it."

We went out and walked across the quadrangle toward the building. The side showing on the quadrangle was made up almost entirely of wide sliding doors. One of them was open and, looking in, I could see some people who had driven down from the Ninth Army at Maastricht.

I judged this place had been a stable when the Germans had used it. Now the Americans were using it as a messhall, and a couple of the people from Ninth Army were sitting on the benches, their backs to the long tables, while the others moved around, stamping their feet, their hands in their pockets. There was no heat in the place.

The Ninth Army people didn't know anything. I could tell from the way they talked that they didn't know the censors had put a stop on this, that you couldn't write about it, but I wasn't going to tell them.

In a few minutes a captain came in. He was quite young and freshly shaven, and he looked cleaner than anything else around the place. He was smiling and he went around introducing himself and shaking hands. He seemed to be trying to be the perfect host, and his enthusiasm and his friendliness made me a little annoyed with him.

"I suppose," he said, "that you gentlemen understand about the censorship of all pictures."

"We know about it," one of the photographers said. "You don't have to worry about it."

"And I suppose you also understand," the captain said, "that nothing is to be written about this."

I felt a little sorry for the writers who had come down from Maastricht. It came to them as a surprise. They started to put up a real kick, but they must have known it was a waste of time to argue.

"But I thought they wanted a lot of publicity about it," one of them said. "I thought they wanted it to get back to the Germans so they'd stop this sneaking guys into our lines."

"I don't know anything about that," the captain said.

"Then why didn't they tell us?" somebody else said. "Why didn't they tell us before we wasted our time driving way down here in this cold?"

"I'm sorry," the captain said. "You know as much about it as I do."

Several of them said they would leave, talking about it among themselves, but they all stayed. To put an end to the argument someone asked the captain what he knew about the prisoners.

"All I know," he said, and you could see him thinking about what he had rehearsed, "is that they were picked up at night inside our lines in an American jeep. They were wearing American uniforms, and had a radio. They hadn't accomplished anything, as they had just entered our lines when they were picked up.

"One of them is an out-and-out Nazi. He's the short one. The other two, I believe, are innocent of any original intent of spying. One of them is a farm boy from Westphalia.

"He's quite simple and, I think, quite honest.

"The story he tells—and I'm inclined to believe it—is that several weeks ago, before this German counteroffensive started, a call went out for men who speak English. He volunteered, he said, because he thought it would be a soft job back at headquarters on propaganda or prisoner interrogation or something like that. The next thing he knew, he was in an American uniform and in an American jeep and heading for our lines. He said there was nothing he could do, and I don't suppose there was, because they always put one Nazi in with the weak ones to see that they keep in line."

We stood around the captain listening, and some of the Ninth Army people were taking notes. I thought the captain was very efficient. He was telling us all that he could.

"We've never done anything like this before," he said. "It's rather a messy thing, and we'll be glad to get it over."

"Then what are we waiting for? We were notified this thing would be at nine-thirty."

"I don't know," the captain said. "I imagine they may be waiting to see if there's any other word from Shaef. I suppose they want to be sure Shaef hasn't had a change of mind about it." *[Editor's note: "Shaef" was the Supreme Headquarters Allied Expeditionary Force.]*

"Then how long do we have to wait?"

"I haven't found out," the captain said, "but it should be within a half hour."

"How about the prisoners? Can you tell us how they're taking it?"

"All right," the captain said. "The chaplain has been seeing two of them, but the Nazi wants nothing to do with him. We have some

Wehrmacht nurses in the next cell, and last night the three asked that the nurses be allowed to sing some Christmas carols for them."

"Then they know they're going to be shot this morning?"

"Yes. The chaplain informed them last night."

"Was the request for the carols granted?"

"Of course."

"What carols did the nurses sing?"

"I don't remember exactly," the captain said, "because the only one I recognized was 'Silent Night.' We had to stop them after a while."

"Why?"

"Because they were disturbing our troops."

I wondered if the captain knew that "Silent Night" is a German carol that the rest of us borrowed.

"We can go now," he said. "Keep together and follow me.

"When you get there, keep about twenty-five or thirty feet back. There will be an MP stationed there, and you are to keep behind that line. That goes for the photographers, too. Also, once you get there you will have to stay because no one will be allowed to leave."

"In other words," one of the Ninth Army people said, "if we want to back out, we have to back out now."

"That's right," the captain said, smiling.

I thought about backing out and I wished no one had mentioned it. I was starting to be afraid, and we followed the captain out and across the quadrangle. We walked in a straggling group past the place where the jeeps were parked, and we took a path that ran along, on the left, the sidewall of a low, gray stucco building. On the right there was a field, gray with frost, and the path was rough with frozen footprints. I wondered if the prisoners knew now how close they were to it.

The path we took led down into a field behind the stucco building. The field sloped a little away from the building, running down to a barbed-wire fence. Beyond that the ground dropped rather suddenly, and you could see into a valley, filled now with the mist. We walked maybe fifty feet into the field, the captain taking us around several MPs standing at ease in the field, and then we turned and faced the back wall of the building.

The wall was about ten feet high. About three feet out from it and spaced about twenty feet apart were three squared posts painted black. The post holes were new.

We stood there in a group, an MP to our left, looking at the posts. I looked at the ground, frost-white, the grass tufts frozen, the soil hard and uneven. I wondered if it is better to die on a warm, bright day among friends, or on a day when even the weather is your enemy. I turned around and looked down into the valley. The mist still hung in the valley, but it was starting to take on a brassy tint from the sun trying to work through it. I could make out three white farm buildings on the valley floor—a little yellowed now from the weak sunlight—and I could envision this, in the spring, a pleasant valley.

This view I see now, I said to myself, will be the last thing their eyes will ever see. I looked at it intently for that reason. I thought of the human eye and of its complexity and its marvelous efficiency. I found myself thinking only of the farm boy, the Westphalian, for whom this would be the last room, the last view, and I turned back to the others.

That was when we heard the sound of marching feet. I turned and I saw them coming around the corner of the building, along the path we had taken.

There was, first, an MP officer. Behind him came the first prisoner and I knew at once that he was the one the captain had described as the farm boy from Westphalia. Behind him, in twos, marched eight MPs, then another prisoner, eight MPs, the third prisoner and eight more MPs. The boots of the MPs shone with polish and on their helmets the lettering and bands were a fresh, new white. The prisoners wore American fatigue jumpers like those that garage mechanics sometimes wear—more green than khaki—and there was a band of blue paint on each leg and each arm.

So that technically they won't be shot in American uniforms, I thought. They had to give them something to wear.

It was difficult to march well over the rough, frozen ground. You could tell this by the way the tips of the rifles wavered in the lines. I watched them, thinking that these were among the last steps these prisoners would ever take, thinking of the wonders of the walking process, of the countless steps we give away so cheaply for needless reasons until there are no more.

Now the column seemed to be marching so quickly.

They had turned off the path and now moved across in front of us, between us and the wall. When they reached a point where the Westphalian was opposite the last post, the officer at the head shouted and the column stopped, the men marking time, the feet of the prisoners a part of the rhythm. Then he shouted again and the feet stopped and the column stood at attention. Both times that he shouted I noticed that the Westphalian looked down and back nervously at the feet of the MPs behind him as he obeyed the orders.

He is a good soldier, I thought. At a time like this he is worrying about being in step, and he is afraid that he is not catching the commands. You have to give him something for that, I thought, and I looked at him carefully. He was the one all right—tall, big-boned, long-faced, with long arms and large, homely red hands that hung below the sleeves of the American fatigues. The fatigues were too small for him and made him seem all the more pathetic.

There was no doubt about the second one either. He was the one the captain had described as the Nazi. He was short, about 5 feet 4, and he had a high, bulging forehead and flat, black hair and he wore black-rimmed glasses. He stood very erect, his face set as stiffly as his body.

The third one did not impress me. He was well built—by far the best looking of the three—and he had black, curly hair. In my mind he was something between the farm boy and the Nazi, and he was not, for my purposes, important.

I saw these things quickly, for the officer was shouting again and the MPs, the prisoners a split second behind them, were facing left. They were facing the wall and the three posts in front of it, and then two MPs were leading each prisoner to a post, and the column was turning and marching back toward us, then turning back again to the wall and standing in two rows, twelve men to a row.

The prisoners standing in front of the posts looked very pale now. I looked at their thin fatigues and their bare hands. I wondered if the Westphalian felt the cold. I should have liked to have asked him.

Now, while the squad and the rest of us waited, two MPs walked to the post where the Westphalian stood, and there were strands of yellow, braided rope in their hands. You could see how new and clean the rope was, and when one of the MPs took a strand of rope and bent down at the post the other took the Westphalian by the shoulders and moved him back an inch or two. The first MP wrapped the rope around the Westphalian's ankles and around the post, and as he started to do this the Westphalian looked down, his hair falling forward, and he shuffled his feet back, watching until the MP was done. After that the second MP took the Westphalian's arms and put them back, one on each side, behind the post. Then the first MP tied them there, and the Westphalian, turning first to one side and then the other, watched intently.

He is trying to help them, I said to myself. Even now he is trying to do the right thing. I wondered how he could do this, and I knew he was brave because he was very afraid. I wondered how a man could be that brave, and then I saw a photographer, disobeying what the captain had told us, kneeling a few feet in front of the Westphalian, focusing his camera on him. I saw the Westphalian staring right back at the photographer, his eyes wide, his whole face questioning, and for that moment he seemed about to cry.

They left the Westphalian and went to the one in the middle, the one the captain had described as the Nazi. He already stood very stiffly against the post, and he did not move when they tied his feet. When they tied his arms behind his post he thrust them back there for them, and he squared his head and shoulders against the post. He was looking over the heads of all of us, and his face was very stern.

They went, then, to tie the third prisoner, the unimportant one. I looked at the other two, tied to the posts, looking out over the heads of the firing squad. I remembered the view of the valley behind my back. That is the last thing, I thought again, that the Westphalian will ever see. I looked at his long, pale face and I wondered if he was seeing anything. I knew that somewhere someone would think of him presently, as they might be thinking of him now, wondering what he was doing. I thought of a farmhouse, like so many we had passed in this war, the whitened stone cottage, the flat fields, an old woman, a turnip heap and, somewhere in the yard, a dung pile.

They had finished tying the third prisoner. The three stood rigid against the posts like woodcuts of men facing execution. There were MP officers, clean and erect and efficient, moving between them, inspecting knots and saluting one another and then a chaplain—a full colonel, helmeted, wearing a trench coat but with a black-satin stole around his neck and hanging down his front—stepped out from beside the squad and walked slowly, a small black book held in his hands in front of him, to the post where the Westphalian was tied.

I saw him say something to the Westphalian and I saw the Westphalian look to him and stare into his face and nod his head. I saw the chaplain reading from the book, and once I saw the Westphalian's lips moving, his head nodding a little, and then the chaplain was finished and the Westphalian was staring into his face as he moved away.

The chaplain stopped beside the one in the middle, the one described as the Nazi. The prisoner shook his head without looking at the chaplain, but the chaplain was saying something anyway, and then he moved on to the prisoner at the end who listened as the chaplain spoke.

When the chaplain had finished he walked back to a point behind the firing squad. Then two MPs stepped forward and walked to the Westphalian and one of them had in his hand a band of black cloth. He stood in back of the post and he reached around the head of the Westphalian to fix the cloth across his eyes.

This now, I said to myself, is that last moment that he will see anything on this earth. I wondered if the Westphalian was thinking that thought.

They fixed the bands over the eyes of the others. Then two MPs stepped forward and, starting with the prisoner on the left, pinned over the hearts of each prisoner white paper circles. The circles were about the size of a large orange. So they won't miss, I thought.

I was very cold, now, in these few gray seconds in this field. There was some saluting among the MP officers, and there were the three prisoners, each alone, their eyes bound with black and the white circles over their hearts, waiting.

I will not look, I was saying to myself. I think I am afraid to look. It is so easy to turn away, I thought, and then I said that I had come to see this when I did not have to because I had wanted to study myself.

I heard then the MP officer at the right of the firing squad give a command, and I saw the first row of twelve men drop to one knee. I heard another command and saw the rifles come up and I heard the sound of the stocks rustling against the clothing, and then I heard the Nazi in the middle shouting, guttural and loud in the morning, and I caught the end of his sentence.

"—Unser Fuehrer Adolf Hitler!"

At that moment—with the Nazi shouting—I heard the command to fire and I heard the explosion of the rifles, not quite all together and almost like a short burst from a machine gun. I was watching the Nazi, whose cry had drawn me at the last second, and I saw him stiffen in the noise and I saw the wall behind him chip and the dust come off it, and the Nazi stood flattened and rigid still against the post.

He's dead, I said to myself. They're all dead.

I looked, then, to the Westphalian, and as I looked I saw the blood on his front and I saw his head fall forward and then his shoulders and chest move out from the pole. I saw the Nazi standing rigid and the other prisoner beginning to sag out, and I was conscious again of the photographers. I remembered, now, seeing the one moving up to take pictures as they had prepared the prisoners, and now again he was kneeling in front of the Westphalian and shooting his camera at him and the others were moving about rapidly and shooting quickly, and I envied them their occupation.

I watched the weird dance, then, of the prisoners, dead but still dying. The Nazi stood firm against the post, only his head bent forward, but the one on the left sagged forward slowly, and then I saw the Westphalian go, first to his left and then, pausing, to his right, swaying. I saw him hang there for a moment, and then I saw him pitch forward, hung by his wrists, bent in the middle, his head down to his knees, his long hair hanging, the whole of him straining at the ropes around his wrists.

He's not alive, I said to myself. He's really dead.

Two medics walked up to him then and the one, bending down, looked into his eyes and, with his fingers, closed the lids. Then the second, bending down, slid his hands under the Westphalian's armpits, lifting him so that the first could put a stethoscope to his chest. In a moment they dropped him, leaving him sagging and swaying a little, and they moved on to the Nazi in the middle.

The Nazi strained a little at the ropes but his body was still rigid. I saw them pausing longer at the Nazi, the two of them looking at him more carefully. I was wondering if they were really finding the Nazi harder to kill. They stood there, talking to each other, putting the stethoscope on him for the second time, and then they finally moved on. They found the other prisoner dead and they walked back to the group beside the firing squad. They saluted the officer in charge and I heard the officer's command to the squad and saw the squad, facing about, march back across the field and up the path.

"What he said," one of the Ninth Army men was saying, "means: 'Long live our Fuehrer, Adolph Hitler.'"

We waited for the photographers to finish taking their pictures of the prisoners in their positions of death and of the two MPs cutting them from the poles. They cut the Westphalian down first and put him on a stretcher, and then two others came with a white mattress cover and they slid him, feet first, off the stretcher and into the mattress cover. They left the mattress cover in front of the post and they went on to the Nazi.

When the MPs were finished and we were ready to leave I looked for the last time at what was left. There was the wall, chipped behind each post, and among the marks the bullets had made were small splashes of blood. There were the three posts, spattered, and before each post a white mattress cover, filled with a body. There was the stretcher, blood-spattered, and on the frozen ground were strewn the things typically American—the black paper ends from the film packs, the flash bulbs, milky-white and expended, and an empty, crumpled Lucky Strike cigarette package. An MP, a rifle on his shoulder, walked up and down.

We went back to the small office near the gate. Our fingers and hands were stiff and ached from the cold, and we stood near the pot-bellied stove. There was a G.I. working at a filing cabinet near the stove and he started to talk to us.

"I'm glad it's over," he said.

"I am, too," I said.

"Not as much as us," he said. "For three days this place has been on end. We haven't been able to get anything else done."

The captain who had led us to the field came in. I thanked him and told him I thought it had all gone very well.

"We should have used combat troops," he said. "This bunch was so nervous that—just between us—there were only three bullets in one of the bull's-eyes, only three out of eight."

"Maybe one had the blank," I said. "That would be three out of seven."

"I don't know," the captain said. "I don't know if they used one blank."

The chaplain who had pronounced the last rites came in. He stood talking with another officer who was, I judged, the chaplain attached to the MP battalion.

"Well," he said, sticking out his hand, "I think it was conducted very well."

"Thank you," the other said, taking his hand. "Come and see us again. We hope next time it will be under more pleasant circumstances."

We went out and found our driver and he wanted to know how it was. We said it was all right, and we drove back. By afternoon the weather had cleared and the Germans came over. They came in so low that I could see the swastikas on the first plane and they bombed hell out of us. They killed Jack Frankish and three Belgians, and Colonel Andrews died later in the hospital.

Damn, I said to myself, I wish this war were over and I wish I were home. For such a long time in September we had all thought we might be home for Christmas.

CHAPTER THREE

The Spy

Michael Shaara

The Pulitzer Prize winner and acclaimed novel The Killer Angels *(1974), carries the banner of historical fiction. Some aspects of stories in such novels are open to interpretation. They may, or may not, have happened as the author has presented them. The main body of historical fiction is factual, and that is the case with* The Killer Angels, *including this excerpt. The lead character, a man named Harrison, actually existed. Also, as presented here in some of the finest prose you're ever read on the Civil War, Harrison was, indeed, a spy. He worked for Robert E. Lee and General James Longstreet. It was Harrison's report on the movement of the Union Army that enabled Lee to turn his Army of Northern Virginia toward Gettysburg. The timing was critical, because the eyes and ears of Lee's army, J.E.B. Stuart's Cavalry, had been absent for days. It left Lee groping his way through Pennsylvania without any idea of the location and strength of the forces in front of him. Then came Harrison's message, and the three bloodiest days of fighting on US soil in history.*

He rode into the dark of the woods and dismounted.

He crawled upward on his belly over cool rocks out into the sunlight, and suddenly he was in the open and he could see for miles, and there was the whole vast army below him, filling the valley like a smoking river. It came out of a blue rainstorm in the east and overflowed the narrow valley road, coiling along a stream, narrowing and choking at a white bridge, fading out into the yellowish dust of June but still visible on the farther road beyond the blue hills, spiked with flags and guidons like a great chopped bristly snake, the snake ending headless in a blue wall of summer rain.

The spy tucked himself behind a boulder and began counting flags. Must be twenty thousand men, visible all at once. Two whole Union Corps. He could make out the familiar black hats of the Iron Brigade, troops belonging to John Reynold's First Corps. He looked at his watch, noted the time. They were coming very fast. The Army of the Potomac had never moved this fast. The day was murderously hot and there was no wind and the dust hung above the army like a yellow veil. He thought: there'll be some of them die of the heat today. But they are coming faster than they ever came before.

He slipped back down into the cool dark and rode slowly downhill toward the silent empty country to the north. With luck he could make the Southern line before nightfall. After nightfall it would be dangerous. But he must not seem to hurry. The horse was already tired. And yet there was the pressure of that great blue army behind him, building like water behind a cracking dam. He rode out into the open, into the land between the armies.

There were fat Dutch barns, prim German orchards. But there were no cattle in the fields and no horses, and houses everywhere were empty and dark. He was alone in the heat and the silence, and then it began to rain and he rode head down into monstrous lightning. All his life he had been afraid of lightning but he kept riding. He did not know where the Southern headquarters was but he knew it had to be somewhere near Chambersburg. He had smelled out the shape of Lee's army in all the rumors and bar talk and newspapers and hysteria he had drifted through all over eastern Pennsylvania, and on that day he was perhaps the only man alive who knew the positions of both armies. He carried the knowledge with a hot and lovely pride. Lee would be near Chambersburg, and wherever Lee was Longstreet would not be far away. So finding the headquarters was not the problem. The problem was riding through a picket line in the dark.

The rain grew worse. He could not even move in under a tree because of the lightning. He had to take care not to get lost. He rode quoting Shakespeare from memory, thinking of the picket line ahead somewhere in the dark. The sky opened and poured down on him and he rode on: *It will be rain tonight: Let it come down.* That was a speech of murderers. He had been an actor once. He had no stature and a small voice and there were no big parts for him until the war came, and now he was the only one who knew how good he was. If only they could see him work, old cold Longstreet and the rest. But everyone hated spies. I come a single spy. Wet single spy. But *they* come in whole battalions. The rain began to ease off and he spurred the horse to a trot. *My kingdom for a horse.* Jolly good line. He went on, reciting *Henry the Fifth* aloud: "Once more into the breech . . ."

Late that afternoon he came to a crossroad and the sign of much cavalry having passed this way a few hours ago. His own way led north to Chambersburg, but he knew that Longstreet would have to know who these people were so close to his line. He debated a moment at the cross-roads, knowing there was no time. A delay would cost him daylight. Yet he was a man of pride and the tracks drew him. Perhaps it was only Jeb Stuart. The spy thought hopefully, wistfully: If it's Stuart I can ask for an armed escort all the way home. He turned and followed the tracks. After a while he saw a farmhouse and a man standing out in a field, in a peach orchard, and he spurred that way. The man was small and bald with huge round arms and spoke very bad English. The spy went into his act: a simple-minded farmer seeking a runaway wife, terrified of soldiers. The bald man regarded him sweatily, disgustedly, told him the soldiers just gone by were "plu" soldiers, Yankees. The spy asked: What town lies yonder? And the farmer told him Gettysburg, but the name meant nothing. The spy turned and spurred back to the crossroads. Yankee cavalry meant John Buford's column. Moving lickety-split. Where was Stuart? No escort now. He rode back again toward the blue hills. But the horse could not be pushed. He had to dismount and walk.

That was the last sign of Yankees. He was moving up across South Mountain; he was almost home. Beyond South Mountain was Lee and, of course, Longstreet. A strange friendship: grim and gambling Long-street, formal and pious old Bobby Lee. The spy wondered at it, and then the rain began again, bringing more lightning but at least some cooler air, and he tucked himself in under his hat and went back to *Hamlet.* Old

Jackson was dead. *Good night, sweet Prince, and flights of angels sing thee to thy rest.*

He rode into darkness. No longer any need to hurry. He left the roadway at last and moved out in to a field away from the lightning and the trees and sat in the rain to eat a lonely supper, trying to make up his mind whether it was worth the risk of going on. He was very close; he could begin to feel them up ahead.

There was no way of knowing when or where, but suddenly they would be there in the road stepping phantomlike out of the trees wearing those sick eerie smiles, and other men with guns would suddenly appear all around him, prodding him in the back with hard steel barrels, as you prod an animal, and he would have to be lucky, because few men rode out at night on good and honest business, not now, this night, in this invaded country.

He rode slowly up the road, not really thinking, just moving, reluctant to stop. He was weary. Fragments of *Hamlet* flickered in his brain: *If it be not now, yet it will come. Ripeness is all.* Now *there's* a good part. A town ahead. A few lights. And then he struck the picket line.

There was a presence in the road, a liquid Southern voice. He saw them outlined in lightning, black ragged figures rising around him. A sudden lantern poured yellow light. He saw one bleak hawkish grinning face; hurriedly he mentioned Longstreet's name. With some you postured and with some you groveled and with some you were imperious. But you could do that only by daylight, when you could see the faces and gauge the reaction. And now he was too tired and cold. He sat and shuddered: an insignificant man on a pale and muddy horse. He turned out to be lucky. There was a patient sergeant with a long gray beard who put him under guard and sent him along up the dark road to Longstreet's headquarters.

He was not safe even now, but he could begin to relax. He rode up the long road between picket fires, and he could hear them singing in the rain, chasing each other in the dark of the trees. A fat and happy army, roasting meat and fresh bread, telling stories in the dark. He began to fall asleep on the horse; he was home. But they did not like to see him sleep, and one of them woke him up to remind him, cheerily, that if there was no one up there who knew him, why, then, unfortunately, they'd have to hang him, and the soldier said it just to see the look on his face, and the spy shivered, wondering, Why do there have to be men like that, men who enjoy another man's dying?

Longstreet was not asleep. He lay on the cot watching the lightning flare in the door of the tent. It was very quiet in the grove and there was the sound of the raindrops continuing to fall from the trees although the rain had ended. When Sorrel touched him on the arm he was glad of it; he was thinking of his dead children.

"Sir? You asked to be awakened if Harrison came back."

"Yes." Longstreet got up quickly and put on the old blue robe and the carpet slippers. He was a very big man and he was full-bearded and wild-haired. He thought of the last time he'd seen the spy, back in Virginia, tiny man with a face like a weasel: "And where will your headquarters be, General, up there in Pennsylvania? 'Tis a big state indeed." Him standing there with cold gold clutched in a dirty hand. And Longstreet had said icily, cheerily, "It will be where it will be. If you cannot find the headquarters of this whole army you cannot be much of a spy." And the spy had said stiffly, "*Scout*, sir. I am a scout. And I am a patriot, sir." Longstreet had grinned. We are all patriots. He stepped out into the light. He did not know what to expect. He had not really expected the spy to come back at all. The little man was there: a soggy spectacle on a pale and spattered horse. He sat grinning wanly from under the floppy brim of a soaked and dripping hat. Lightning flared behind him; he touched his cap.

"Your servant, General. May I come down?"

Longstreet nodded. The guard backed off. Longstreet told Sorrel to get some coffee. The spy slithered down from the horse and stood grinning foolishly, shivering, mouth slack with fatigue.

"Well, sir—" the spy chuckled, teeth chattering "—you see, I was able to find you after all."

Longstreet sat at the camp table on a wet seat, extracted a cigar, lighted it. The spy sat floppily, mouth still open, breathing deeply.

"It has been a long day. I've ridden hard all this day."

"What have you got?"

"I came through the pickets at night, you know. That can be very touchy."

Longstreet nodded. He watched, he waited. Sorrel came with steaming coffee; the cup burned Longstreet's fingers. Sorrel sat, gazing curiously, distastefully at the spy.

The spy guzzled, then sniffed Longstreet's fragrant smoke, wistfully: "I say, General, I don't suppose you've got another of those? Good Southern tobacco?"

"Directly," Longstreet said. "What have you got?"

"I've got the position of the Union Army."

Longstreet nodded, showing nothing. He had not known the Union Army was on the move, was within two hundred miles, was even this side of the Potomac, but he nodded and said nothing. The spy asked for a map and began pointing out the positions of the corps.

"They're coming in seven corps. I figure at least eighty thousand men, possibly as much as a hundred thousand. When they're all together they'll outnumber you, but they're not as strong as they were; the two-year enlistments are running out. The First Corps is here. The Eleventh is right behind it. John Reynolds is in command of the lead elements, I saw him at Taneytown this morning."

"Reynolds," Longstreet said.

"Yes, sir."

"You saw him yourself?"

The spy grinned, nodded, rubbed his nose, chuckled. "So close I could touch him. It was Reynolds all right."

"This morning. At Taneytown."

"Exactly. You didn't know any of that, now did you, General?" The spy bobbed his head with delight. "You didn't even know they was on the move, did ye? I thought not. You wouldn't be spread out so thin if you knowed they was comin'."

Longstreet looked at Sorrel. The aide shrugged silently. If this was true, there would have been some word. Longstreet's mind moved over it slowly. He said: "How did you know we were spread out?"

"I smelled it out." The spy grinned, foxlike, toothy. "Listen, General, I'm good at this business."

"Tell me what you know of our position."

"Well, now I can't be too exact on this, 'cause I ain't scouted you myself, but I gather that you're spread from York up to Harrisburg and then back to Chambersburg, with the main body around Chambersburg and General Lee just 'round the bend."

It was exact. Longstreet thought: if this one knows it, *they* will know it. He said slowly, "We've had no word of Union movement."

The spy bobbed with joy. "I knew it. Thass why I hurried. Came through that picket line in the dark and all. I don't know if you realize, General—"

Sorrel said coldly, "Sir, don't you think, if this man's story was true, that we would have heard *something*?"

Sorrel did not approve of spies. The spy grimaced, blew.

"You ain't exactly on friendly ground no more, Major. This ain't Virginia no more."

True, Longstreet thought. But there would have been something. Stuart? Longstreet said, "General Stuart's cavalry went out a few days back. He hasn't reported any movement."

The spy shrugged, exasperated, glooming at Sorrel. Sorrel turned his back, looked at his fingernails.

Longstreet said, "What have you heard of Stuart?"

"Not much. He's riding in the north somewhere. Stirring up headlines and fuss, but I never heard him do any real damage."

Longstreet said, "If the Union Army were as close as you say, one would think—"

"Well, I'm damned," the spy said, a small rage flaming. "I come through that picket line in the dark and all. Listen, General, I tell you this: I don't know what old Stuart is doing and I don't care, but I done my job and this is a fact. This here same afternoon of this here day I come on the tracks of Union cavalry thick as fleas, one whole brigade and maybe two, and them bluebellies weren't no four hours hard ride from this here now spot, and that, by God, is the Lord's truth." He blew again, meditating.

Then he added, by way of amendment, "Buford's column, I think it was. To be exact."

Longstreet thought: can't be true. But he was an instinctive man, and suddenly his brain knew and his own temper boiled. Jeb Stuart was joy-riding. God *damn* him. Longstreet turned to Sorrel.

"All right, Major. Send to General Lee. I guess we'll have to wake him up. Get my horse."

Sorrel started to say something, but he knew that you did not argue with Longstreet. He moved.

The spy said delightedly, "General Lee? Do I get to see General Lee? Well now." He stood up and took off the ridiculous hat and smoothed wet plastered hair across a balding skull. He glowed. Longstreet got the rest of the information and went back to his tent and dressed quickly.

If the spy was right the army was in great danger. They could be cut apart and cut off from home and destroyed in detail, piece by piece. If the spy was right, then Lee would have to turn, but the old man did not believe in spies nor in any information you had to pay for, had not approved of the money spent or even the idea behind it. And the old man had faith in Stuart, and why in God's name had Stuart sent nothing, not even a courier, because even Stuart wasn't fool enough to let the whole damned Army of the Potomac get this close without word, not one damned lonesome word. Longstreet went back out into the light. He had never believed in this invasion. Lee and Davis together had overruled him. He did not believe in offensive warfare when the enemy outnumbered you and outgunned you and would come looking for you anyway if you waited somewhere on your own ground. He had not argued since leaving home, but the invasion did not sit right in his craw; the whole scheme lay edgewise and raspy in his brain, and treading here on alien ground, he felt a cold wind blowing, a distant alarm. Only instinct. No facts as yet. The spy reminded him about the cigar. It was a short way through the night to Lee's headquarters, and they rode past low sputtering campfires with the spy puffing exuberant blue smoke like a happy furnace.

"'Tis a happy army you've got here, General," the spy chatted with approval. "I felt it the moment I crossed the picket line. A happy army, eager for the fight. Singing and all. You can feel it in the air. Not like them bluebellies. A desperate tired lot. I tell you, General; this will be a factor.

The bluebellies is almost done. Why, do you know what I see everywhere I go? Disgraceful, it is. On every street in every town, able-bodied men. Just *standing* there, by the thousands, reading them poor squeaky piti-ful newspapers about this here mighty invasion and the last gasp of the Union and how every man must take up arms, haw." The spy guffawed. "Like a bunch of fat women at church. The war's almost over. You can feel it, General. The end is in the air."

Longstreet said nothing, He was beginning to think of what to do if the spy was right. If he could not get Lee to turn now there could be disaster. And yet if the Union Army was truly out in the open at last there was a great opportunity: a sudden move south, between Hooker and Washington, cut *them* off from Lincoln.

Yes. Longstreet said, "What do you hear of Hooker? Where is he?"

The spy stopped, mouth sagging. "Oh by Jesus. Forgive me." He gri-maced, shook his head. I done forgot. There was an item in the newspaper this morning. Saying that Hooker was replaced. They gave the command to Meade, I think it was."

"George Meade?"

"Yes, sir. I think."

"You're sure?"

"Well, it was Meade the newspaper said, but you know them damn newspapers."

Longstreet thought: new factor. He spurred the horse, but he couldn't move fast because of the dark. Lee must listen. God bless the politicians. Reynolds was their best man. Why did they go to Meade? But I'm sorry to see Hooker go. Old Fighting Joe.

Longstreet said, "It was Meade, then, and not Reynolds?"

"Rumor was that Reynolds was offered the job but wouldn't have it on a plate. That's what the paper said."

Old John's too smart to take it. Not with that idiot Halleck pulling the strings. But Meade? Fussy. Engineer. Careful. No genius for sure. But a new factor. A Pennsylvania man. He will know this country.

The spy chatted on amiably. He seemed to need to talk. He was say-ing, "Strange thing about it all, thing that bothers me is that when you do this job right nobody knows you're doing it, nobody ever watches you work, do you see? And sometimes I can't help but wish I had an audience. I've played some scenes, ah, General, but I've been lovely."

The spy sighed, puffed, sighed again. "This current creation, now, is marvelous. I'm a poor half-witted farmer, do you see, terrified of soldiers, and me lovely young wife has run off with a drummer and I'm out a-scourin' the countryside for her, a sorrowful pitiful sight I am. And people lookin' down their noses and grinnin' behind me back and all the time tellin' me exactly what I want to know about who is where and how many and how long ago, and them not even knowin' they're doin' it, too busy feelin' contemptuous. There are many people, General, that don't give a damn for a human soul, do you know that? The strange thing is, after playing this poor fool farmer for a while I can't help but feel sorry for him. Because nobody cares."

They came to Lee's camp, in the grove just south of Chambersburg.

By the time they got there Longstreet knew that the spy was telling the truth. Young Walter Taylor was up, annoyed, prissy, defending General Lee's night's rest even against Longstreet, who glowed once with the beginning of rage, and sent Taylor off to get the old man out of bed. They dismounted and waited. The spy sat under an awning, grinning with joy at the prospect of meeting Lee. Longstreet could not sit down. He disliked getting the old man up: Lee had not been well. But you could lose the war up here. Should have gone to Vicksburg. News from there very bad. It will fall, and after that ... we must win here if we are to win at all, and we must do it soon. The rain touched him; he shivered. Too damn much rain would muck up the roads.

Lee came out into the light. The spy hopped to attention.

Lee bowed slightly, stiffly.

"Gentlemen."

He stood bareheaded in the rain: regal, formal, a beautiful white-haired, white-bearded old man in a faded blue robe. He looked haggard. Longstreet thought: He looks older every time you see him. For a moment the spy was silent, enraptured, then he bowed suddenly from the waist, widely, formally, gracefully, plucking the floppy hat from the balding head and actually sweeping the ground with it, dandy, ridiculous, something off a stage somewhere designed for a king.

"General," the spy said grandly, "*a votre service.*" He said something else in a strange and Southern French. Longstreet was startled at the transformation.

Lee glanced at Longstreet: a silent question. Longstreet said, "Beg pardon, sir. I thought this urgent. The man has information."

Lee looked at the spy silently. His face showed nothing.

Then he said formally, "Sir, you must excuse me, I do not know your name."

"The name is *Harrison*, sir, at present." The spy grinned toothily. "The name of an ex-President, ex-general. A small joke, sir. One must keep one's sense of humor."

Lee glanced again at Longstreet. Longstreet said, "The man has the position of the Union Army. He says they are very close. I have a map."

He moved to the map table under the awning. The spy followed with reproach. Lee came slowly to the table, watching the man. After a moment he said to Harrison, "I understand that you are General Long-street's—" a slight pause "—'scout.'" Lee would not use the word *spy*. "I believe we saw you last back in Virginia."

"That's a fact," the spy worshipped. "I been kind of circulatin' since, amongst the bluebellies, and I tell you, General, sir, that it's an honor and a priv—"

Longstreet said, "He claims their lead elements are here. He says there is a column of strong Union cavalry not four hours off."

Lee looked at the map. Then he sat down and looked more closely. Longstreet gave the positions, the spy fluttering mothlike behind him with numbers and names and dates. Lee listened without expression.

Longstreet finished. "He estimates perhaps one hundred thousand men."

Lee nodded. But estimates meant nothing. He sat for a moment staring at the map and then bowed his head slightly.

Longstreet thought: he doesn't believe. Then Lee raised his eyes and regarded the spy.

"You appear to have ridden hard. Have you come a long way?"

"Sir, I sure have."

"And you came through the picket line after dark?"

"Yes, sir—" the spy's head bobbed "—I did indeed."

"We are in your debt." Lee stared at the map. "Thank you. Now I'm sure General Longstreet will see to your accommodations."

The spy was dismissed, had sense enough to know it. He rose reluctantly. He said, "It has been my pleasure, sir, to have served such a man as yourself. God bless you, sir."

Lee thanked him again. Longstreet instructed Sorrel to see that the man was fed and given a tent for the night and to be kept where Longstreet could find him if he needed him, which meant: keep an eye on him. The spy went out into the dark. Longstreet and Lee sat alone at the table in the rain.

Lee said softly, "Do you believe this man?"

"No choice."

"I suppose not." Lee rubbed his eyes, leaned forward on the table. With his right hand he held the muscle of his left arm. He shook his head slowly. "Am I to move on the word of a paid spy?"

"Can't afford not to."

"There would have been something from Stuart."

"There should have been."

"Stuart would not have left us blind."

"He's joyriding again," Longstreet said, "This time you ought to stomp him. Really stomp him."

Lee shook his head. "Stuart would not leave us blind."

"We've got to turn," Longstreet said. His heart was beating strongly. It was bad to see the indomitable old man weak and hatless in the early morning, something soft in his eyes, pain in his face, the right hand rubbing the pain in the arm. Longstreet said, "We can't risk it. If we don't concentrate they'll chop us up."

Lee said nothing. After a moment Longstreet told him about Meade. Lee said, "They should have gone to Reynolds."

"Thought so too. I think he turned it down."

Lee nodded. He smiled slightly. "I would have preferred to continue against General Hooker."

Longstreet grinned. "Me too."

"Meade will be . . . cautious. It will take him some time to take command, to organize a staff. I think . . . perhaps we should move quickly. There may be an opportunity here."

"Yes. If we swing in behind him and cut him off from Washington . . ."

"If your man is correct."

"We'll find out."

Lee bent toward the map. The mountains rose like a rounded wall between them and the Union Army. There was one gap east of Chambersburg and beyond that all the roads came together, web-like, at a small town. Lee put his finger on the map.

"What town is that?"

Longstreet looked. "Gettysburg," he said.

Lee nodded. "Well—" He was squinting. "I see no reason to delay. It's their army I'm after, not their towns." He followed the roads with his finger, all converging on that one small town. "I think we should concentrate in this direction. This road junction will be useful."

"Yes." Longstreet said.

Lee looked up with black diamond eyes. "We'll move at first light."

Longstreet felt a lovely thrill. Trust the old man to move.

"Yes, sir."

Lee started to rise. A short while ago he had fallen from a horse onto his hands, and when he pushed himself up from the table Longstreet saw him wince. Longstreet thought: Go to sleep and let me do it. Give the order and I'll do it all. He said, "I regret the need to wake you, sir."

Lee looked past him into the soft blowing dark. The rain had ended. A light wind was moving in the tops of the pines—cool sweet air, gentle and clean. Lee took a deep breath.

"A good time of night. I have always liked this time of night."

"Yes,"

"Well." Lee glanced once almost shyly at Longstreet's face, then looked away. They stood for a moment in awkward silence.

They had been together for a long time in war and they had grown very close, but Lee was ever formal and Longstreet was inarticulate, so they stood for a long moment side by side without speaking, not looking at each other, listening to the raindrops fall in the leaves. But the silent moment was enough. After a while Lee said slowly, "When this is over, I shall miss it very much."

"Yes."

"I do not mean the fighting."

"No."

"Well," Lee said. He looked to the sky. "It is all in God's hands."

They said good night. Longstreet watched the old man back to his tent. Then he mounted and rode alone back to his camp to begin the turning of the army, all the wagons and all the guns, down the narrow mountain road that led to Gettysburg. It was still a long dark hour till dawn. He sat alone on his horse in the night and he could feel the army asleep around him, all those young hearts beating in the dark. They would need their rest now. He sat alone to await the dawn, and let them sleep a little longer.

Chapter Four

The Wolves at the Door: The True Story of America's Greatest Female Spy

Judith L. Pearson

The story of how a young woman from Baltimore, Maryland, became one of the Gestapo's most-wanted spies in World War II is told with searing realism in The Wolves at the Door. *While in France to join the diplomatic corps, Virginia Hall saw Hitler roll into Poland, then into France itself. She joined a British Special Operations unit and began espionage activities that put her in the sights of the Gestapo, which had tortured many of her fellow spies to death. In May, 1942, she fled France via a dangerous hike through the Pyrenees Mountains into neutral Spain. Upon her return to England, she was recruited by the OSS and sent back to France disguised as an elderly peasant woman. This excerpt from* The Wolves at the Door *describes Hall's return to France in the months prior to D-Day, June 6, 1944, and how her daring operations led to the death of 150 German soldiers and the capture of 500 others, the sabotage of communication and transport lines, and ongoing resistance activities.*

When Buckmaster had told Virginia in his letter to her in Spain that "the Gestapo are pulling in everything they can," he had hard evidence to back his statement. The Nazis were furious about the acts of French Resistance and carried out reprisals in every part of the country. In Paris, the Nazis murdered fifty people a day for five days after German government officials were gunned down. The murders stopped only after the Nazis were satisfied they had the culprits in custody, the latter having been ratted out by "helpful" collaborators. In Nantes, two hundred and fifty miles southwest of Paris, forty-eight citizens were executed for killing a German colonel. And in Tours, two hundred miles south of Paris, a grenade was tossed into a column of German soldiers on their way to a movie. More than half the city was burned to the ground, and a great many of the young men were taken away, never to be seen again.

A great deal more had changed since Virginia left France. The Resistance found themselves no longer fighting just against the German army and the Gestapo. A new organization had entered the picture. It was called the Milice.

Shortly after France had fallen to the Germans, World War I veteran Joseph Darnand was made head of the *Légion Française des Combattants*, the Legion of French Veterans. The organization consisted of chivalrous gentlemen hoping to recoup honor for the defeated French army. But the group was too staid for Darnand's taste and a year later he developed a faction within the legion called the *Service de l'Ordre Légionnaire*, which supported Pétain's Vichy France. In January 1943, he reorganized once again, and the Milice was the result.

This Vichy secret police force was a paramilitary organization that swore an oath against "Jewish leprosy," democracy, and individualism. The Milice was really a Fascist gang, half fanatics, half thugs. Their ranks swelled to thirty-five thousand and included the dregs of French society: former criminals, gangsters, and the depraved. The Milice worked in the areas where they lived, familiar areas, making them much more effective than the Gestapo in that regard. And unlike the Police Nationale, which sought out "enemies of the state," the Milice hunted, tortured, and killed for personal gain and satisfaction. Those with grudges against former lovers or business associates found the Milice the perfect outlet for their revenge. The populace hated its members and it quickly became the most dangerous enemy of the Resistance.

Buckmaster had also been right when he told Virginia, "What was previously a picnic, comparatively speaking, is now real war." The France she was about to reenter in March 1944 was more starving, more dangerous, and more desperate.

—◦—

Monday, March 20, was a gray day in London. The city's trees and flowers had no confidence that spring was coming anytime soon. Consequently, new growth and buds were nowhere to be found on any of them. Virginia took a noon train out of Victoria Station, heading south for the English Channel. She lugged two suitcases. One was soft-sided and bulging like a cow about to calve. It carried the items she would use to change her identity. The other suitcase was smaller, about two feet long, but at thirty pounds, heavier than the first. It contained a Type 3 Mark II transceiver, a combination radio transmitter and receiver.

While many OSS agents were infiltrating France by parachute, Virginia's wooden leg would prevent her from jumping. Rather, she was returning to France by sea. Two hours and sixty-six miles from London, Virginia's train arrived at the port city of Portsmouth. She took a cab from the station to a pub, where she met a young British naval officer. After a quick lunch, he took her to the Devonshire Royal Navy Base, a blur of British and American naval uniforms, and dropped her off at a small building set apart from the others.

Inside, Lieutenant Paul Williams welcomed Virginia and immediately offered her a cup of tea. Her companion hadn't arrived yet, Lieutenant Williams told her, so in the meantime, he would give her a quick rundown on their operation. She would be crossing on a Motor Gun Boat, officially MGB 502, under the lieutenant's command. The mahogany-skinned vessel was 117 feet long, fast, and safe. The trip to the French coast would probably take no more than six hours.

And Lieutenant Williams told Virginia she shouldn't worry about the Germans. MGB 502 was fitted with a two-pounder Vickers antiaircraft gun, a couple of twin-mount .50-caliber machine guns, and a semi-automatic two-pounder gun.

Virginia wasn't really interested in the details of the armaments; only that the boat had them.

Although strong tides formed along the Breton coast, Lieutenant Williams continued, there were plenty of deserted beaches that suited the operation perfectly. She and her companion would be landing at a point called Beg an Fry. His crew was familiar with the waters there, no shoals or offshore reefs. When they were close to shore, the boat would slow down considerably, running quieter and with less wake. Virginia and her companion would go ashore in a camouflaged rubber dinghy.

This is it, Virginia thought. I'm finally going back to France. Lieutenant Williams told her they'd be leaving at twenty-two hundred hours. A knock at the door ended their conversation. The door opened at his command and Virginia turned to see a stocky, balding man with spectacles. He announced that his name was Aramis and offered Virginia his hand. He had a slight French accent, which Virginia took as a good sign. It meant he was probably of French parentage and could compensate for her decidedly Anglo accent.

She introduced herself as Diane, the code name she and Major van der Strict had decided upon before she left London. Lieutenant Williams had some other business to attend to and suggested that perhaps Aramis and Virginia would like a private office to discuss business. After that, they would all meet again in the officer's mess for dinner and make their final preparations for departure.

As soon as they were alone, Aramis was very anxious to get to know his new working companion and began by telling Virginia all about himself. In no time at all, he had told her that he was a commercial artist from Pittsburgh, was sixty-two years old and was a civilian. This would be his first mission in the field, but he felt confident that he was up to any challenge that came their way.

Virginia was concerned about Aramis immediately. It wasn't his age or his inexperience; it was his willingness to open up so completely with a relative stranger. Never mind the fact that they would be partners. The number one rule for agents at the OSS and the SOE was never to tell the truth about themselves. New recruits were taught they could only abandon their cover if they were in a closed room with a staff member who took the initiative to say, "We are now talking under X conditions." Then, and only then, could an agent divulge the truth about himself.

Failure to adhere to that rule had gotten recruits thrown out. They were cleverly tested on it. Regardless of their performance on a particularly grueling day of physical trials, intelligence tests, and "Gestapo-style" questioning, the hopeful students were told one by one that they had failed. They were then sent individually to a room where a sympathetic staff member would offer them a cigarette and ask what had happened, hinting that perhaps something could be done about it. Recruits were often so relieved at a friendly face that they forgot the basic requirement of secrecy and divulged everything that had happened to them that day, without the staff member telling them they were talking under "X conditions." And that became their demise.

Virginia was not willing to put herself or their mission in jeopardy by saying anything more than was absolutely necessary. She told Aramis that she had done a significant amount of wireless training at the SOE classes in London, avoiding any mention that she, herself, had been an SOE agent. Their circuit would be a joint operation with the Brits, who would call it Saint. The Americans would refer to their circuit as Heckler. She would be the wireless operator. It was her understanding, she said, that their objective was to gather as much information as possible about German troop installations and movements in central France, and to locate potential reception fields for parachute drops. In addition, she had been told that Aramis would spend most of his time working in Paris, developing safe houses there, and that he should have any necessary outgoing messages couriered to her. She would transmit them along with her own findings.

Finally, Virginia disclosed that she would be disguising herself as much older for their mission and would don her costume after dinner. Once they'd covered those topics, Virginia had very little more to say to Aramis and their conversation dwindled to a discussion of weather and how it might affect their trip that night.

Their dinner with Lieutenant Williams was a much brighter event, as he regaled them with stories about his experiences in the Navy. At eight o'clock, Virginia excused herself to begin preparations for her disguise. She returned to a small room where she had dropped off her belongings earlier. The room had a sink and running water, necessary for the first part of her disguise. Pulling the hairpins from the carefully formed bun at the nape of her neck, she wet her hair in the sink and applied the dye she'd brought with her from London. By the time she'd finished, her soft brown hair was a dull gray color that she would eventually pull into a severe bun and cover with a large babushka.

Next, Virginia remade herself into a plump, elderly woman. First she donned a starched peplum to make her hips appear broader, and over it she pulled on two heavy woolen skirts. To increase the bulk on her torso, she put on a man's shirt and sweater, and stuffed all of that under a ratty woman's pullover. Brown woolen stockings and scuffed sabots completed the look.

The entire outfit had been provided courtesy of agents and refugees coming out of France. Both the British and American governments wanted to make sure everything about the people they infiltrated into occupied territories was authentic, so they developed a wardrobe department that would rival any in Hollywood. And as other agents had done, Virginia had also spent several days the previous week in a dentist's chair, having her fillings changed to resemble those done by French dentists.

The final part of her transformation was to change the way she moved. The "Limping Lady" nickname the Gestapo had given her was insulting. Virginia had assumed all along she walked in a fairly normal manner. Evidently she had not concealed her limp over the years as well as she thought she had. Under the present circumstances, it was vital that she master a new gait. In keeping with her disguise, a shuffle was appropriate, combined with the kind of stoop brought on by old age. She had practiced and perfected this demeanor over the past months. It had to pass muster.

———

When Virginia reappeared in Lieutenant Williams's office after her transformation, neither Aramis nor the lieutenant recognized her at first. Williams said afterward that his immediate thought was the chewing out he was going to give the guard post for allowing civilians on the base. Once they realized it was Virginia, the men assured her that she in no way resembled the woman they had just dined with.

The next hour or so, the lieutenant and several sailors gave Virginia and Aramis lessons on how to get out of the dinghy that would put them on the French shore. It was essential that they do it quickly and quietly. Their lesson came to an abrupt end when a sailor appeared to tell them it was time to board the boat. Virginia and Aramis were seated inside the cabin area, where they were protected from the wind and the spray. They faced a strong head wind, but the speed at which the boat was traveling compensated for it and the ride was not quite as bumpy as Virginia had expected. About five hours later, she felt the engine slow, which of course increased the effect the waves had on the vessel. The crew got the dinghy ready, and with a hearty handshake from Lieutenant Williams, Virginia and Aramis set off for the Breton coast.

OSS instructions for Virginia and Aramis's mission were divided into three parts. First, they were to establish themselves in an "accessible place not more than 100 kilometers to the south or southeast of Paris." Second, they were to "proceed to find three safe houses, one in Paris, the second in a small town within easy reach of Paris, and the third somewhere in the country." The final stage of their mission was to consist of "setting up in each of these three houses one large and one small wireless set, ready to operate as quickly as possible should a wireless operator arrive."

They were also both carrying cash. Virginia had five hundred thousand francs and Aramis had a million francs. The London office expected them to be in contact for any other needs as soon as possible.

Brittany is the French province that juts out into the channel and is frequently referred to as the "*nez rouge de France*," the red nose of France. The double entendre refers to the shape of the province, similar to that of a nose, and the fact that the frequent harsh winds cause some elder inhabitants' noses to be permanently reddened from broken blood vessels. The coastline is unfriendly, craggy, and often very steep. But the independent Breton people were the antithesis of their harsh homeland: cordial, loyal to the Allied cause, and eager to organize into Resistance groups.

Aramis and Virginia's landing was less than ideal. Aramis stumbled getting out of the dinghy and fell onto the rocks. He tore his pants, cut his leg, and was drenched. They were to walk to a small barn just a mile inland, which was owned by a member of the local Resistance. A cold rain had started to fall and with Aramis limping badly, a walk that should have taken them fifteen minutes, took almost an hour. It was about 4:00 a.m. when they arrived at the barn and settled against some straw bales for a quick nap. When the farmer woke them an hour later, Virginia asked him for a bandage for Aramis's leg and a needle and thread to patch his trousers. When the man left, she told Aramis that since his disguise was that of an elderly man, his new limp was a great asset. He was not amused, however.

They left the farmer's barn an hour later, looking like any other elderly couple, and walked along the rutted road that led to the town of Morlaix.

Aramis's identity papers showed that his name was Henri Lassot. Virginia's read Mlle. Marcelle Montagne. In Morlaix, they went to the train station and bought two second-class tickets for Paris. They hobbled up into the car and sat in near silence the entire four-hour trip. Aramis even dozed on and off. But Virginia's eyes were glued to the French countryside. It had been eighteen months since she'd left, and the country now appeared even more chained to the Nazi boot. German soldiers with dogs often patrolled the passing train platforms. Bomb damage was evident in the fields and pastures from craters and upheaved earth. In the towns, it could be seen in the rubble of burned-out buildings.

When they arrived at the Montparnasse station in Paris and walked out into the city, what Virginia saw devastated her and she struggled to maintain her composure. The once beautiful City of Lights was now a wretched-looking ghost town. While it had not been heavily bombed, as had London and other French cities, it had received its share. Virginia saw half-destroyed buildings and piles of rubble and burned-out automobiles.

Fortunately none of the city's treasures had been touched: the Eiffel Tower, the Arc de Triomphe, and Notre-Dame still stood proudly. But they now wore flags of the Third Reich. German street signs had been posted everywhere directing drivers and pedestrians to Nazi military establishments. And to keep the Parisians up to date on news, the German-controlled newspapers posted clippings on buildings for those passing by on the sidewalks of major thoroughfares.

The French men and women Virginia saw were a sorry lot. Their hollow eyes stared straight ahead, yet didn't seem to see. They especially avoided eye contact with the Germans, who had begun calling Paris "*la ville sans regard*" (the city that never looks at you). Some Parisians sat dejectedly on the sidewalk, begging for food with outstretched hands, but not speaking. Others tried to sell anything they could find for a few francs, from broken pieces of furniture to shoelaces. Aramis and Virginia proceeded at their slow pace, not saying a word to anyone they passed, nor to one another. When they finally arrived at their destination, 59 rue de Babylone, to their great relief the door opened after the first knock. The owner of the home, Mme. Long, was someone Virginia knew from her prewar days in Paris, and whose activities in the

Resistance she had learned about from Philippe Vomécourt when she was still in Lyon.

Mme. Long's welcome of the two weary travelers was genuine. She told them she had secured a room for Aramis at a nearby boarding house whose owner was an avid Gaullist. Then she sat them down in her kitchen and boiled water for tea.

Again Aramis chatted about himself and gave hints about their mission and his clumsy landing on the coast the night before. His candor irked Virginia, not because she didn't trust Mme. Long with the information, but because he was so willing to divulge it. When he limped off toward the boarding house two doors down, Mme. Long expressed concern to Virginia. She said her home was open to Virginia, but that she didn't want Aramis to return. Virginia told her she understood completely and promised Mme. Long that since they were leaving first thing in the morning, he wouldn't have to come back. She said she would tell him that Mme. Long thought she was being watched and that he'd better not contact her when he came back to Paris.

The next morning, March 22, Virginia and Aramis left Paris by train for Châteauroux, and then changed trains, arriving in the town of Crozant in the midafternoon. They walked to a little village just down the road called Maidou, where Virginia found M. Eugène Lopinat, a farmer she had orders to contact. Lopinat wasn't terribly active in the Resistance, but could be counted on to find lodging for those who needed it. He took Virginia to a one-room cottage he owned at the opposite end of the village from his little farm. The cottage had no electricity and no running water.

Virginia would work for Lopinat, tending to his cows, cleaning his house, and preparing meals for him, his elderly mother, and their hired hand. The arrangement was that she would eat her meals with them as well.

Shortly after they had arrived, Aramis said he was tired and wanted to get started for Paris. But before he left, Virginia brought up the subject of his talking too much. She insisted that he tell only those he had taken into his confidence exactly as much as they needed to know, and no more. And she was particularly insistent that he not tell anyone about her. Furthermore, he was to send a courier when he needed to communicate with her, and the same one each time. They had already agreed on a code phrase for the courier to identify himself to Virginia.

Aramis was insulted by the reproach and huffed off down the road toward Crozant. Virginia wasn't worried that she had hurt his feelings, only that he wouldn't take her words to heart. But there was work to do. She wanted to explore her surroundings before she had to go make dinner for the Lopinats.

The whole setup appeared to be perfect. The cottage was at the end of an isolated dirt path that no one would travel without the distinct purpose of coming to see her. The house had a loft with a window, accessed by a ladder. She could make her radio transmissions from there, spreading her antennae out the window and down the backside of the house without fear of it being seen.

As the days passed, Virginia decided cooking meals at Lopinat's house was an adventure. There was no stove, so she had to cook on an open fire. The country-dwelling French had fared better in the area of food thus far in the occupation than had their city-dwelling counterparts. And the Lopinats were no exception. There was always an ample supply of vegetables to make soups and stews, and even an occasional slab of meat. There were eggs from the Lopinats' chickens, when they weren't stolen, and usually ingredients to make bread.

Lopinat's mother assumed Virginia was near her own age, and often tried to engage her in conversation. Virginia would nod and smile and say, "Oui," but tried to avoid her as much as possible. The time she spent with Lopinat's livestock, however, was a different matter. The cows needed to be taken to pasture every day, which gave Virginia the perfect excuse to take in the countryside in search of fields for the receptions of landings and parachute drops. There were precious few areas that would work, but for those she thought had possibilities, she made note of the coordinates.

It was all going well except for Aramis. He was proving to be a disappointment. Rather than using couriers, he insisted on coming to Virginia in Maidou himself with his news. Having him around made her nervous, and she was never confident that he hadn't talked too much in Paris or on his journey. Furthermore, he could easily be followed. Her brief sojourn in the Spanish prison was more than enough of a taste for Virginia. The last thing she wanted was to spend any time under German guard. Furthermore, despite his robust appearance, Aramis wasn't very hardy. On each trip, he would tell her how exhausted he was and how he'd had to go to bed for several days when he'd returned to Paris after the previous journey.

He did bring good news on occasion, however. He reported that he had located several safe houses in Paris. They could be used as stopovers for agents or hiding places for pilots in need. In fact, he told her, one of the houses was already harboring seven Allied airmen, five of them American. The safe houses needed code phrases for entry, so the two of them devised phrases and Virginia radioed the information to London. Herein lay her second disappointment in the mission thus far: radio contact was spotty at best.

It had all started out well. Her first message to London had been on April 4, letting them know that she was temporarily installed and that Aramis was in Paris. When she radioed the message about the safe houses, London replied, asking the number they could accommodate. She told them on her next "sked" and gave them the pass phrases for each house. But then things began to go south. She would send a message, only to have them reply they weren't able to copy her.

They suggested she extend the aerial, which she did. They suggested perhaps the weather was bad, but it wasn't. They suggested that it was the Germans, scrambling the signals and wondered if they were honing in on her with their direction finder. This, she agreed, was a distinct possibility, making Aramis's unnecessary trips to her house even more nerve-racking. An old woman would not be receiving visitors and suspicions could easily be aroused.

But Virginia was determined to make the most of her situation and gather as much intelligence as she could. The Allies needed to know the location of German troops and their movements. How could a little old lady who tended cows get information from the German army? The answer was right in front of her: cheese.

Lopinat's mother made cheese for their own use. Why not make more of it to sell? Virginia had learned to make cheese on Box Horn Farm, and whether the cows were American or French didn't matter, the process was still the same. She was fluent in German from her days at the academy in Vienna, so when she came into close proximity to sell her cheese to the Germans, she might be able to eavesdrop on their conversations. She'd then relay the useful information back to London, presuming, of course, it was a day when the radio was working properly.

Lopinat and his mother thought the idea of making a little extra money from the Nazis was a good idea, and loaded Virginia up with a basket of cheese the next day. Once she had taken the cows to the field, she started walking toward Crozant. It wasn't long before she came across a small German convoy on the road. She took a deep breath and hobbled up to one of the officers. He asked her what she was peddling, to which she responded in an old crone's voice. He wanted to know the price. She had figured this out ahead of time, thinking ten francs was reasonable. Another officer walked up then to add his opinion. They discussed the worth of the cheese in German and the first officer finally gave Virginia the money, took his cheese, and waved her off.

It had worked! Although she'd not gleaned any information on her first foray, it was a perfect dress rehearsal. She had multiple performances over the next several weeks. And although her radio was still not functioning perfectly, it was good enough for her to pass on overheard information about troop movements and weapons depots to OSS in London. She had just finished her "sked" one day and was putting her radio away in the loft when she heard the sound of a truck engine. Her first thought was that Aramis was now driving to see her. She closed the radio's suitcase and slid it among the crates and disused furniture stored in the loft. Once she'd descended the ladder, she resumed her character and shuffled to the door. Standing in front of her cottage was a truck full of Germans.

The ranking officer in the group asked her what she was doing in the middle of nowhere by herself. Virginia explained in a raspy voice that she took care of M. Lopinat's cows and cooked for him and his mother.

The officer wasn't satisfied with her response and ordered three soldiers to go into the cottage. She stood frozen, her mind racing. Had she sufficiently hidden the radio? She heard her few pieces of furniture crash to the floor. Simultaneous ripping sounds told her that her bed was being torn apart. And then she heard the ladder being set up against the loft.

Tense seconds ticked past. Not a sound came from the cottage interior. She began to think about how far she could get on foot before the Germans fired at her. No, she decided, running wouldn't be the answer. It would be better to talk her way out of trouble, declaring she had no idea what was in the loft. She was an old woman and couldn't climb the ladder. As long as she could plead her case here, she had a chance. But if this truckload of Boches turned her over to the Gestapo, they'd soon find out she wasn't who she was pretending to be.

Virginia leaned against a post supporting the porch roof. It was something an old woman would do, but she needed steadying as well. She was certain the German officer could see her heart pounding beneath her clothing. The soldiers finally came out and marched directly to their officer. One of them carried something, although Virginia could not see what it was. The officer looked over the soldier's shoulder at Virginia and walked slowly toward her. He stopped and peered at her.

The officer recognized her as the old woman who peddled cheese up and down the road. And it was cheese that his men had found, good cheese they told him. Certainly she wouldn't mind if soldiers of the Third Reich helped themselves to some. The officer looked hard at her for a few seconds and then reached into his pocket and threw some coins on the ground in front of her.

The men piled in and the truck turned around and rumbled away. Virginia tottered back into the cottage, but her unsteadiness was not feigned. That encounter had been too close. A week later, the Germans picked up four citizens of Maidou and shot them. Their bodies were spiked through the neck on an iron fence in the center of town as a warning to those who might think about joining the Resistance. Two days later, Aramis came back with a message for Virginia. A newly arrived OSS agent had not made his radio checks. The London office feared that he had been arrested. That was enough for Virginia. At her appointed sked, she radioed London, *wolves are at the door. stop. will be in contact soon. stop.*

Virginia and Aramis left for Paris immediately. The next day, he invited her to meet two old family friends of his, Mme. Rabut and her grown son, Pierre. Theirs was one of the safe houses he had procured. Virginia liked Mme. Rabut immediately and felt at ease with her and confident in her. Three days later, when Virginia was ready to depart for her new location, she asked Mme. Rabut to accompany her. She envied those agents whose accents were as perfect as native French people. But she couldn't take chances. She had decided never to travel without a French chaperone, someone who would reduce her need to speak.

The two women took the morning train to Cosne, a city about five hours southeast of Paris. Virginia went directly to the home of Colonel Vessereau, chief of police for the department of Creuse. His position made him a valuable member of the Resistance, and Virginia had been apprised of his work by OSS in London. The colonel and his wife were expecting Virginia and couldn't have been more accommodating. They had a room for her and told her that their attic would be perfect for transmitting. Mme. Rabut stayed the night and before she left the next day, Virginia asked her to keep her new location in Cosne a secret. And if Aramis had any messages for her, Virginia suggested, perhaps Mme. Rabut could bring them to her. Mme. Rabut was thrilled to play an even greater role in the Resistance.

Colonel Vessereau was anxious to introduce Virginia to the Resistance group he'd been building. He had developed ties with several local gendarmes who were military men, seen action before the armistice, and hated the Nazis. They, in turn, knew of a group of about a hundred men who were ready for action. The men were members of the Maquis.

The theme of the Maquis was a reflection of the refrain from the French national anthem, "La Marseillaise." Written in 1792, the refrain begins with the lines *"Aux armes, citoyens! Formez vos bataillons"* (To arms, citizens, form your battalions). And that was exactly what they did. They were the perfect fighting force: strapping young men, albeit undernourished, with an ax to grind against the Nazis.

Over time, the Maquis grew to include a variety of refugees from justice, including German deserters, anti-Franco Spaniards, and urban resisters. Whenever possible, the peasantry provided the Maquis with food, shelter, and clothing. Their guerrilla tactics against the German military became widely known, and the citizens of occupied France silently applauded these anonymous freedom fighters. But what they lacked was arms. An Allied spy like Virginia was someone they were anxious to meet.

❦

In a top-secret document prepared on May 19, 1944, by American Military Intelligence, the Cosne area Resistance was described as "fairly well organised. Big possibilities, guerilla experience." The document concluded that the area had "very good potential strategic and morale value, subject to further development in outlying districts."

Virginia knew all about the area's potential. She and Colonel Vessereau had decided the best route to take was to split the Maquis in Cosne into four groups of twenty-five men each. These men had dreamed about resistance, but hadn't had sufficient means to carry it out. Getting someone from London who was arranging to arm them was a dream come true. And it was a clear indication that the world had not forgotten them.

Virginia arranged a parachute drop for the night of May 15. To facilitate agents' requests for supplies, OSS had created groups of like items that agents could order by code name, depending on their need. "Dough" contained general demolition items, "maggots" included magnets and explosive supplies, and "yeast" was a container full of incendiary materials.

For the Cosne Maquis, Virginia requested "dough" and "maggot" containers, plus additional containers of "sten" guns, weapons that were cheap to manufacture, easy to assemble and disassemble, and tough enough to endure the drops. Best of all, they could be fired with German 9 mm ammunition, a plus for anyone who could capture any. Virginia had already trained the colonel, his wife, and several others on how to signal arriving planes, and they recruited half a dozen Maquis to help them haul away and conceal the supplies. The eleven of them arrived at the designated field at 11 o'clock to wait for the plane and its twelve containers. As soon as they heard the plane, Virginia flashed an M, the night's code letter, in Morse with a white light. The plane signaled back and Virginia re-illuminated her light. The colonel, his wife, and another Resistance member then lit their red lights. The four of them made a diamond shape with Virginia nearest to the incoming plane. If the flight crew drew lines from one light to another, the point where the lines crossed would be the desired point of the drop. Of course to figure out their positions, Virginia had to take into account the wind speed, which could cause the containers to drift. Looking for wayward containers in the dark was like searching for the proverbial needle. Not to mention the pressure of trying not to arouse suspicions of neighbors and passersby.

This night's drop came off without a hitch. The containers floated to almost the exact spot Virginia had envisioned. With difficulty, the Maquis members concealed their excitement at the array of supplies now at their fingertips. Of course there was still work to do, since the parachutes had to be disconnected and buried in holes they had to dig, and the containers had to be loaded onto the waiting hay wagon and carted back to town. Once they had accomplished that, the group split up with only two men riding on the hay wagon. The other eight left in pairs, taking separate routes back to their homes.

By this time, Virginia had actually left the home of the colonel and was living in the nearby town of Sury-près-Léré, in the garret of a farmhouse owned by Jules Juttry. It was best for her to move around so as not to jeopardize herself, or her hosts, by transmitting from the same location all the time. M. Juttry was elderly; Virginia guessed him to be in his mid-eighties. He was not at all pleased to have Virginia living in his house, and suspected she was a German spy. His widowed daughter, Estelle Bertrand, had made the arrangements.

Estelle was nearing fifty and had come to live with her father after her husband was killed during the fighting in 1940. She had been a part of the Resistance for several years and was inspired by the fact that an American would give up so much for the cause of France. She had accompanied Virginia to that night's parachute drop, having learned the reception procedures, and would be setting them up once Virginia moved on to her next destination.

On Tuesday, May 28, Virginia received a radio message from OSS headquarters in London:

happy to have received your contact of the 25th. stop. period of activity is commencing. stop. please communicate before next friday all information gathered since your arrival concerning large movements by train or road. stop.

Virginia pondered the words "period of activity" and wondered what that might be. But her job was to report, not to question. For whatever reason, headquarters needed this information before Friday, June 2, 1944.

———

The spring of 1944 was one of the worst in the history of Europe. Torrential rains, powerful winds, and raging seas pounded the shorelines of both Great Britain and the European continent. The violent weather bolstered the members of the Third Reich. It appeared that even Mother Nature was on their side as she stalled what they were sure was the imminent Allied invasion of Europe.

———

Hearing that strangers had been asking questions about her in Sury-près-Léré, Virginia knew it was time to move again to another safe house. She relocated to Sury-ès-Bois, nine miles to the west, again finding herself living in a farmhouse.

She had radioed London, as she'd been requested to do, with information about German troop movements. There had been some, but nothing out of the ordinary. The area she was in was just about dead center in France and important rail lines ran throughout it. She reported on the trains too, their times and what they appeared to be carrying. But again, nothing was out of the ordinary.

As she had done for nearly three months, Virginia played the part of an old peasant woman. This time she was moving a herd of goats from field to field, all the while keeping a lookout for those who would work for parachute drops. She delivered goats' milk to members of the Resistance, giving her the perfect cover to pass messages as well. And the donkey cart she borrowed from the farmer provided ideal transportation for moving the goods that floated to earth in cylinders. She arranged for two parachute drops from Sury-ès-Bois. The Resistance needed more arms and supplies, therefore a radio set, battery chargers, soap, and money arrived.

These two drops proved to be the highlight of the late spring days, and Virginia became edgy, as there was very little else to do.

Of all the elements that made up her job, this was the most difficult: the tension-filled calm before the next storm. And if an Allied invasion of France was the next storm, it would be of tornadic proportions. A person of action, Virginia craved striding forward to attain a goal. Incessant waiting was unnerving. It gave her too much time to think, and not about the obvious danger her work entailed.

—◆—

Sometimes Virginia's isolation bothered her. She was a people person who loved being in the center of a crowd. But for about three years, she had lived lies. She could never completely confide in anyone, get close, or let her guard down. That was her only regret about her chosen path. But when she stepped back to consider the whole picture, reflecting on the vital nature of accomplishing her duties, it was a small sacrifice.

A thick tension enveloped the Resistance members in early June 1944 as well. They knew an invasion was imminent, just as the Germans did. And like a great many French people, they had hoped that it would occur months earlier. Thoughts of liberation even permeated the churches as priests prayed from their pulpits, urgently asking God for deliverance from the evil occupiers. They cautioned their parishioners to be patient and not to act out unilaterally against the Germans. These rogue attacks almost always brought severe reprisals by the Nazis.

Some French had become disenchanted, grumbling that the Allies had promised to send help, but hadn't delivered. Virginia took a more pragmatic approach, explaining to those around her that launching an attack before preparations had been finalized would be suicidal. There was no sense in trying to pull off something half-baked. It would destroy the element of surprise and could prove lethal to many of those involved. There was no time for complaining, Virginia told them. Far too much work had yet to be done in preparation.

She and the members of Heckler, like other combined SOE and OSS circuits throughout France, had been directed to follow a well-laid-out plan, code-named Plan Vert. For the last month, while they continued to recruit and train new members, they also gradually increased their acts of sabotage. Armed with the supplies from London, they had made attacks against local Nazi headquarters and vehicles. They had taken out essential roads and telephone stations, and had successfully removed German explosives from bridges the Allies would need in their advance across France.

When the invasion did occur, Virginia told her circuit members, their advance work would prove to be invaluable to the Allies. And she assured them that they were not alone. Groups such as theirs were being trained all over France, all ready to aid the Allies.

On day 1,452 of the German occupation of France, Virginia sat on the floor in her room in the farmhouse, along with M. Juttry's daughter-in-law, Estelle, and several other members of their circuit. There were only thirty-two other Americans in France on this day. But that was to change soon.

Virginia and her group were listening to the BBC's French broadcast for that evening.

"*Ici Londres. Les français parlent aux français. Veuillez écouter quelques messages personnels.*" (This is London. The French speaking to the French. First, please listen to a few personal messages.)

The broadcast included, as always, a number of personal messages. From wine cellars to hay barns, Resistance members and Allied agents gathered in secret to listen for the code phrase that would signal the day they had long awaited.

The first half of the code had been broadcast at 9:00 p.m. on June 1: "*Les sanglots longs des violins de l'automne*" (The long sobs of the violins of autumn), was the first line of poet Paul Verlaine's work "Chanson d'Automne." To those who understood, the words meant that the invasion would begin soon, sometime in the first half of the month. When the second line of the poem was broadcast, those listening would be alerted that the invasion would begin within the next forty-eight hours.

That had been four days ago, and this group of five had listened intently every night since. The room was small, with only a tiny window to let in fresh air. Virginia's bed and washstand took up most of the space. The small table where the radio sat was rickety, and every time someone bumped it in the process of getting closer to hear more clearly, the signal flickered in and out. The Germans had gotten very adept at scrambling the BBC's transmissions, but could only do so one wave band at a time. The broadcasts were actually made on several bands, so if one was unintelligible, another could be tried. And cutting the electricity, which the Nazis did frequently, was not a deterrent either, as Virginia's radio worked on a battery.

Finally, at 8:15 p.m., listening to the 261-meter wave band, they heard the second half of the code: "*Blessent mon coeur d'une langueur monotone*" (Wound my heart with a monotonous languor.)

That was it: *le jour J*. D-Day.

❧

Once the second half of the message signaling the invasion had been broadcast, myriad other messages were sent to circuits and Resistance groups across France. These prearranged code phrases notified the groups that it was time to put into action all of their preplanned acts of sabotage. Like other circuit heads, Virginia had been told to attack roads, railways, and telecommunications, and harass occupation troops by whatever means she and her circuit could. The Allies were certain that the first thing the Germans would do at the onset of the invasion would be to flood Normandy with additional men and supplies. The rail lines were the Nazis' lifeline and had to be taken out.

Virginia had organized small groups within Heckler that would be ready to leap into action once the invasion was announced. Their job was to lay the explosives on the rail lines around Cosne. Under cover of darkness, the groups went to work on the night of June 6.

Virginia, accompanied by two young Frenchmen, Robert and Gilles, arrived at their designated location around midnight. She had chosen this particular spot after carefully surveying the area in daylight a week earlier. It was a meadow, midway between Cosne and Sury-près-Léré with a nice hedge nearby they could use for cover if they needed it. It seemed unlikely, though, since there were no lights and no sign of life anywhere around.

Robert carried the rucksack with their necessary materials: two three-quarter-pound packs of plastic explosives connected to one another by a double Cordtex lead, two igniters known as "fog signals," two detonators, and extra Cordtex, which they'd use for the fuse. Robert was to set up the fog signals and detonators while Gilles's job was to affix the plastic explosive packs to the rail with their attached webbed straps. Armed with a sten gun, Virginia would stand guard.

They had only been working a short time when Virginia heard voices down the track. Peering into the darkness, she saw two German soldiers walking, or rather weaving, between the rails about fifty meters away, singing at the top of their lungs. They were obviously drunk. She and the two men grabbed their materials and dove behind the hedge. The three of them flattened themselves against the coarse grass. The magazine of Virginia's sten could accommodate thirty-two rounds of ammunition, which was what she had with her. She was not at all apprehensive at the thought of emptying it into the Germans, but the noise might bring more soldiers than she would be able to hold off.

The three of them waited, holding their breath. The noise from the soldiers continued, but didn't come any closer. In fact, it seemed to Virginia that it began to grow more distant, until it was no longer audible. Cautiously the three crept back to the train track, but saw no one in either direction. Satisfied the threat was gone, they resumed the work.

While Gilles went back to work on the plastic explosive units, Robert labored with the fog signals. He loaded them with detonators, and placed them about two meters from the explosives. Then he taped Cordtex fuse to the adapters on the signals and handed it off to Gilles who attached the other end to the plastic explosive units. The train would crush the fog signals, which would explode, setting off the detonators, whose fire would travel up the Cordtex and ignite the plastic explosive units, all within the space of a few seconds. The end result would be a derailed locomotive engine and a meter of unusable rail, both of which would take days to repair.

Job completed, the three of them hurried back to their homes. The next train wasn't expected for two hours, and it was never wise for saboteurs to hang around after an explosion anyway. But a smile spread across

Virginia's face the next morning when she heard that not only had her team been successful, but so had the other four. That meant four different sets of tracks had been rendered useless for several days, delaying matériel vital to the German defense of the Allies' invasion.

Altogether in those first days after the Normandy landings, 571 rail targets were sabotaged. In addition, Resistance members with ties to the *Syndicat de la société nationale des chemins de fer*, the train workers union, urged their friends to be as uncooperative as possible. The ensuing chaos resulting from the work of the Resistance caused the Nazis disruption, disorganization, and delays.

CHAPTER FIVE

The Thirty-Nine Steps

John Buchan

The English writer John Buchan (1875–1940) wrote so many good novels that listing them all would take too much time. One of his finest novels, a thriller, was The Thirty-Nine Steps. *It eventually became a British TV drama, and was made into three separate feature films, including one by Alfred Hitchcock. This is the story of an English spy tangling with German agents in the summer of 1914, just prior to World War I. The German agents are in England. At the same time Richard Hannay—Buchan's protagonist—is chasing them, local authorities are chasing him. A corpse found in his flat deepens the suspense and complications of the tale. This excerpt from the novel includes scenes of Hannay on the run, and you get a real taste of the drama that has caught the attention of so many readers and filmmakers over the years since the book was first published in 1915.*

I sat down on the very crest of the pass and took stock of my position.

Behind me was the road climbing through a long cleft in the hills, which was the upper glen of some notable river. In front was a flat space of maybe a mile, all pitted with bog-holes and rough with tussocks, and then beyond it the road fell steeply down another glen to a plain whose blue dimness melted into the distance. To left and right were round-shouldered green hills as smooth as pancakes, but to the south—that is, the left hand—there was a glimpse of high heathery mountains, which I remembered from the map as the big knot of hill which I had chosen for my sanctuary. I was on the central boss of a huge upland country, and could see everything moving for miles. In the meadows below the road half a mile back a cottage smoked, but it was the only sign of human life. Otherwise there was only the calling of plovers and the tinkling of little streams.

It was now about seven o'clock, and as I waited I heard once again that ominous beat in the air. Then I realized that my vantage-ground might be in reality a trap. There was no cover for a tomtit in those bald green places.

I sat quite still and hopeless while the beat grew louder. Then I saw an airplane coming up from the east. It was flying high, but as I looked it dropped several hundred feet and began to circle round the knot of hill in narrowing circles, just as a hawk wheels before it pounces. Now it was flying very low, and now the observer on board caught sight of me. I could see one of the two occupants examining me through glasses.

Suddenly it began to rise in swift whorls, and the next I knew it was speeding eastward again till it became a speck in the blue morning.

That made me do some savage thinking. My enemies had located me, and the next thing would be a cordon round me. I didn't know what force they could command, but I was certain it would be sufficient. The airplane had seen my bicycle, and would conclude that I would try to escape by the road. In that case there might be a chance on the moors to the right or left. I wheeled the machine a hundred yards from the high-way, and plunged it into a moss-hole, where it sank among pond-weed and water-buttercups. Then I climbed to a knoll which gave me a view of the two valleys. Nothing was stirring on the long white ribbon that threaded them.

I have said there was not cover in the whole place to hide a rat. As the day advanced it was flooded with soft fresh light till it had the fragrant sunniness of the South African veld. At other times I would have liked the place, but now it seemed to suffocate me. The free moorlands were prison walls, and the keen hill air was the breath of a dungeon.

I tossed a coin—heads right, tails left—and it fell heads, so I turned to the north. In a little I came to the brow of the ridge which was the containing wall of the pass. I saw the highroad for maybe ten miles, and far down it something that was moving, and that I took to be a motor-car.

Beyond the ridge I looked on a rolling green moor, which fell away into wooded glens.

Now my life on the veld has given me the eyes of a kite, and I can see things for which most men need a telescope. ... Away down the slope, a couple of miles away, several men were advancing, like a row of beaters at a shoot.

I dropped out of sight behind the sky-line. That way was shut to me, and I must try the bigger hills to the south beyond the highway. The car I had noticed was getting nearer, but it was still a long way off with some very steep gradients before it. I ran hard, crouching low except in the hollows, and as I ran I kept scanning the brow of the hill before me. Was it imagination, or did I see figures—one, two, perhaps more—moving in a glen beyond the stream?

If you are hemmed in on all sides in a patch of land there is only one chance of escape. You must stay in the patch, and let your enemies search it and not find you. That was good sense, but how on earth was I to escape notice in that table-cloth of a place? I would have buried myself to the neck in mud or lain below water or climbed the tallest tree. But there was not a stick of wood, the bog-holes were little puddles, the stream was a slender trickle. There was nothing but short heather, and bare hill bent, and the white highway.

Then in a tiny bight of road, beside a heap of stones, I found the roadman.

He had just arrived, and was wearily flinging down his hammer. He looked at me with a fishy eye and yawned.

"Confoond the day I ever left the herdin'!" he said, as if to the world at large. "There I was my ain maister. Now I'm a slave to the Goavernment, tethered to the roadside, wi' sair een, and a back like a suckle."

He took up the hammer, struck a stone, dropped the implement with an oath, and put both hands to his ears. "Mercy on me! My heid's burstin'!" he cried.

He was a wild figure, about my own size but much bent, with a week's beard on his chin, and a pair of big horn spectacles.

"I canna dae't," he cried again. "The Surveyor maun just report me. I'm for my bed."

I asked him what was the trouble, though indeed that was clear enough.

"The trouble is that I'm no sober. Last nicht my dochter Merran was waddit, and they danced till fower in the byre. Me and some ither chiels sat down to the drinkin', and here I am. Peety that I ever lookit on the wine when it was red!"

I agreed with him about bed.

"It's easy speakin'," he moaned. "But I got a postcard yestreen sayin' that the new Road Surveyor would be round the day. He'll come and he'll no find me, or else he'll find me fou, and either way I'm a done man. I'll awa' back to my bed and say I'm no weel, but I doot that'll no help me, for they ken my kind o' no-weel-ness."

Then I had an inspiration. "Does the new Surveyor know you?" I asked.

"No him. He's just been a week at the job. He rins about in a wee motor-cawr, and wad speir the inside oot o' a whelk."

"Where's your house?" I asked, and was directed by a wavering finger to the cottage by the stream.

"Well, back to your bed," I said, "and sleep in peace. I'll take on your job for a bit and see the Surveyor."

He stared at me blankly; then, as the notion dawned on his fuddled brain, his face broke into the vacant drunkard's smile.

"You're the billy," he cried. "It'll be easy eneuch managed. I've finished that bing o' stanes, so you needna chap ony mair this forenoon. Just take the barry, and wheel eneuch metal frae yon quarry doon the road to mak anither bing the morn. My name's Alexander Turnbull, and I've been seeven year at the trade, and twenty afore that herdin' on Leithen Water. My freens ca' me Ecky, and whiles Specky, for I wear glesses, being waik i' the sicht. Just you speak the Surveyor fair, and ca' him Sir, and he'll be fell pleased. I'll be back or midday."

I borrowed his spectacles and filthy old hat; stripped off coat, waistcoat, and collar, and gave him them to carry home; borrowed, too, the foul stump of a clay pipe as an extra property. He indicated my simple tasks, and without more ado set off at an amble bedwards. Bed may have been his chief object, but I think there was also something left in the foot of a bottle. I prayed that he might be safe under cover before my friends arrived on the scene.

Then I set to work to dress for the part. I opened the collar of my shirt—it was a vulgar blue-and-white check such as ploughmen wear—and revealed a neck as brown as any tinker's. I rolled up my sleeves, and there was a forearm which might have been a blacksmith's, sunburnt and rough with old scars. I got my boots and trouser-legs all white from the dust of the road, and hitched up my trousers, tying them with string below the knee. Then I set to work on my face. With a handful of dust I made a water-mark round my neck, the place where Mr. Turnbull's Sunday ablutions might be expected to stop. I rubbed a good deal of dirt also into the sunburn of my cheeks. A roadman's eyes would no doubt be a little inflamed, so I contrived to get some dust in both of mine, and by dint of vigorous rubbing produced a bleary effect.

The sandwiches Sir Harry had given me had gone off with my coat, but the roadman's lunch, tied up in a red handkerchief, was at my disposal. I ate with great relish several of the thick slabs of scone and cheese and drank a little of the cold tea. In the handkerchief was a local paper tied with string and addressed to Mr. Turnbull—obviously meant to solace his midday leisure. I did up the bundle again, and put the paper conspicuously beside it.

My boots did not satisfy me, but by dint of kicking among the stones I reduced them to the granite-like surface which marks a roadman's footgear. Then I bit and scraped my finger-nails till the edges were all cracked and uneven. The men I was matched against would miss no detail. I broke one of the bootlaces and retied it in a clumsy knot, and loosed the other so that my thick grey socks bulged over the uppers. Still no sign of anything on the road. The motor I had observed half an hour ago must have gone home.

My toilet complete, I took up the barrow and began my journeys to and from the quarry a hundred yards off.

I remember an old scout in Rhodesia, who had done many queer things in his day, once telling me that the secret of playing a part was to think yourself into it. You could never keep it up, he said, unless you could manage to convince yourself that you were *it*. So I shut off all other thoughts and switched them on to the road-mending. I thought of the little white cottage as my home, I recalled the years I had spent herding on Leithen Water, I made my mind dwell lovingly on sleep in a box-bed and a bottle of cheap whisky. Still nothing appeared on that long white road.

Now and then a sheep wandered off the heather to stare at me. A heron flopped down to a pool in the stream and started to fish, taking no more notice of me than if I had been a milestone. On I went, trundling my loads of stone, with the heavy step of the professional. Soon I grew warm, and the dust on my face changed into solid and abiding grit. I was already counting the hours till evening should put a limit to Mr. Turnbull's monotonous toil.

Suddenly a crisp voice spoke from the road, and looking up I saw a little Ford two-seater, and a round-faced young man in a bowler hat.

"Are you Alexander Turnbull?" he asked. "I am the new County Road Surveyor. You live at Blackhopefoot, and have charge of the section from Laidlawbyres to the Riggs? Good! A fair bit of road, Turnbull, and not badly engineered. A little soft about a mile off, and the edges want cleaning. See you look after that. Good morning. You'll know me the next time you see me."

Clearly my get-up was good enough for the dreaded Surveyor. I went on with my work, and as the morning grew towards noon I was cheered by a little traffic. A baker's van breasted the hill, and sold me a bag of ginger biscuits which I stowed in my trouser-pockets against emergencies. Then a herd passed with sheep, and disturbed me somewhat by asking loudly, "What had become o' Specky?"

"In bed wi' the colic," I replied, and the herd passed on. ...

Just about midday a big car stole down the hill, glided past and drew up a hundred yards beyond. Its three occupants descended as if to stretch their legs, and sauntered towards me.

Two of the men I had seen before from the window of the Galloway inn—one lean, sharp, and dark, the other comfortable and smiling. The third had the look of a countryman—a vet, perhaps, or a small farmer. He was dressed in ill-cut knickerbockers, and the eye in his head was as bright and wary as a hen's.

"Morning," said the last. "That's a fine easy job o' yours."

I had not looked up on their approach, and now, when accosted, I slowly and painfully straightened my back, after the manner of roadmen; spat vigorously, after the manner of the low Scot; and regarded them steadily before replying. I confronted three pairs of eyes that missed nothing.

"There's waur jobs and there's better," I said sententiously. "I wad rather hae yours, sittin' a' day on your hinderlands on thae cushions. It's you and your muckle cawrs that wreck my roads! If we a' had oor richts, ye sud be made to mend what ye break."

The bright-eyed man was looking at the newspaper lying beside Turnbull's bundle.

"I see you get your papers in good time," he said.

I glanced at it casually. "Aye, in gude time. Seein' that that paper cam' out last Setterday I'm just sax days late."

He picked it up, glanced at the superscription, and laid it down again. One of the others had been looking at my boots, and a word in German called the speaker's attention to them.

"You've a fine taste in boots," he said. "These were never made by a country shoemaker."

"They were not," I said readily. "They were made in London. I got them frae the gentleman that was here last year for the shootin'. What was his name now?" And I scratched a forgetful head. Again the sleek one spoke in German. "Let us get on," he said. "This fellow is all right."

They asked one last question.

"Did you see anyone pass early this morning? He might be on a bicycle or he might be on foot."

I very nearly fell into the trap and told a story of a bicyclist hurrying past in the grey dawn. But I had the sense to see my danger. I pretended to consider very deeply.

"I wasna up very early," I said. "Ye see, my dochter was merrit last nicht, and we keepit it up late. I opened the house door about seeven and there was naebody on the road then. Since I cam up here there has just been the baker and the Ruchill herd, besides you gentlemen."

One of them gave me a cigar, which I smelt gingerly and stuck in Turnbull's bundle. They got into their car and were out of sight in three minutes.

My heart leaped with an enormous relief, but I went on wheeling my stones. It was as well, for ten minutes later the car returned, one of the occupants waving a hand to me. Those gentry left nothing to chance.

I finished Turnbull's bread and cheese, and pretty soon I had finished the stones. The next step was what puzzled me. I could not keep up this roadmaking business for long. A merciful Providence had kept Mr. Turnbull indoors, but if he appeared on the scene there would be trouble. I had a notion that the cordon was still tight round the glen, and that if I walked in any direction I should meet with questioners. But get out I must. No man's nerve could stand more than a day of being spied on.

I stayed at my post till five o'clock. By that time I had resolved to go down to Turnbull's cottage at nightfall and take my chance of getting over the hills in the darkness. But suddenly a new car came up the road, and slowed down a yard or two from me. A fresh wind had risen, and the occupant wanted to light a cigarette.

It was a touring car, with the tonneau full of an assortment of baggage. One man sat in it, and by an amazing chance I knew him. His name was Marmaduke Jopley, and he was an offense to creation. He was a sort of blood stockbroker, who did his business by toadying eldest sons and rich young peers and foolish old ladies. "Marmie" was a familiar figure, I understood, at balls and polo-weeks and country houses. He was an adroit scandal-monger, and would crawl a mile on his belly to anything that had a title or a million. I had a business introduction to his firm when I came to London, and he was good enough to ask me to dinner at his club. There he showed off at a great rate, and pattered about his duchesses till the snobbery of the creature turned me sick. I asked a man afterwards why nobody kicked him, and was told that Englishmen reverenced the weaker sex.

Anyhow there he was now, nattily dressed, in a fine new car, obviously on his way to visit some of his smart friends. A sudden daftness took me, and in a second I had jumped into the tonneau and had him by the shoulder.

"Hullo, Jopley," I sang out. "Well met, my lad!" He got a horrid fright. His chin dropped as he stared at me. "Who the devil are you?" he gasped.

"My name's Hannay," I said. "From Rhodesia, you remember."

"Good God, the murderer!" he choked.

"Just so. And there'll be a second murder, my dear, if you don't do as I tell you. Give me that coat of yours. That cap, too."

He did as he was bid, for he was blind with terror. Over my dirty trousers and vulgar shirt I put on his smart driving-coat, which buttoned high at the top and thereby hid the deficiencies of my collar. I stuck the cap on my head, and added his gloves to my get-up. The dusty roadman in a minute was transformed into one of the neatest motorists in Scotland. On Mr. Jopley's head I clapped Turnbull's unspeakable hat, and told him to keep it there.

Then with some difficulty I turned the car. My plan was to go back the road he had come, for the watchers, having seen it before, would probably let it pass unremarked, and Marmie's figure was in no way like mine.

"Now, my child," I said, "sit quite still and be a good boy. I mean you no harm. I'm only borrowing your car for an hour or two. But if you play me any tricks, and above all if you open your mouth, as sure as there's a God above me I'll wring your neck. *Savez?*"

I enjoyed that evening's ride. We ran eight miles down the valley, through a village or two, and I could not help noticing several strange-looking folk lounging by the roadside. These were the watchers who would have had much to say to me if I had come in other garb or company. As it was, they looked incuriously on. One touched his cap in salute, and I responded graciously.

As the dark fell I turned up a side glen which, as I remember from the map, led into an unfrequented corner of the hills. Soon the villages were left behind, then the farms, and then even the wayside cottage. Presently we came to a lonely moor where the night was blackening the sunset gleam in the bog pools. Here we stopped, and I obligingly reversed the car and restored to Mr. Jopley his belongings.

"A thousand thanks," I said. "There's more use in you than I thought. Now be off and find the police."

As I sat on the hillside, watching the tail-light dwindle, I reflected on the various kinds of crime I had now sampled. Contrary to general belief, I was not a murderer, but I had become an unholy liar, a shameless impostor, and a highwayman with a marked taste for expensive motor-cars.

I spent the night on a shelf of the hillside, in the lee of a boulder where the heather grew long and soft. It was a cold business, for I had neither coat nor waistcoat. These were in Mr. Turnbull's keeping, as was Scudder's little book, my watch and—worst of all—my pipe and tobacco pouch. Only my money accompanied me in my belt, and about half a pound of ginger biscuits in my trousers pocket.

I supped off half those biscuits, and by worming myself deep into the heather got some kind of warmth. My spirits had risen, and I was beginning to enjoy this crazy game of hide-and-seek. So far I had been miraculously lucky. The milkman, the literary innkeeper, Sir Harry, the roadman, and the idiotic Marmie, were all pieces of undeserved good fortune. Somehow the first success gave me a feeling that I was going to pull the thing through.

My chief trouble was that I was desperately hungry. When a Jew shoots himself in the City and there is an inquest, the newspapers usually report that the deceased was "well-nourished." I remember thinking that they would not call me well-nourished if I broke my neck in a bog-hole. I lay and tortured myself—for the ginger biscuits merely emphasized the aching void—with the memory of all the good food I had thought so little of in London. There were Paddock's crisp sausages and fragrant shavings of bacon, and shapely poached eggs—how often I had turned up my nose at them! There were the cutlets they did at the club, and a particular ham that stood on the cold table, for which my soul lusted. My thoughts hovered over all varieties of mortal edible, and finally settled on a porterhouse steak and a quart of bitter with a welsh rabbit to follow. In longing hopelessly for these dainties I fell asleep.

I woke very cold and stiff about an hour after dawn. It took me a little while to remember where I was, for I had been very weary and had slept heavily. I saw first the pale blue sky through a net of heather, then a big shoulder of hill, and then my own boots placed neatly in a blueberry bush. I raised myself on my arms and looked down into the valley, and that one look set me lacing up my boots in mad haste.

For there were men below, not more than a quarter of a mile off, spaced out on the hillside like a fan, and beating the heather. Marmie had not been slow in looking for his revenge.

I crawled out of my shelf into the cover of a boulder, and from it gained a shallow trench which slanted up the mountain face. This led me presently into the narrow gully of a burn, by way of which I scrambled to the top of the ridge. From there I looked back, and saw that I was still undiscovered. My pursuers were patiently quartering the hillside and moving upwards.

Keeping behind the skyline I ran for maybe half a mile, till I judged I was above the uppermost end of the glen. Then I showed myself, and was instantly noted by one of the flankers, who passed the word to the others. I heard cries coming up from below, and saw that the line of search had changed its direction. I pretended to retreat over the skyline, but instead went back the way I had come, and in twenty minutes was behind the ridge overlooking my sleeping place. From that viewpoint I had the satisfaction of seeing the pursuit streaming up the hill at the top of the glen on a hopelessly false scent.

I had before me a choice of routes, and I chose a ridge which made an angle with the one I was on, and so would soon put a deep glen between me and my enemies. The exercise had warmed my blood, and I was beginning to enjoy myself amazingly. As I went I breakfasted on the dusty remnants of the ginger biscuits.

I knew very little about the country, and I hadn't a notion what I was going to do. I trusted to the strength of my legs, but I was well aware that those behind me would be familiar with the lie of the land, and that my ignorance would be a heavy handicap. I saw in front of me a sea of hills, rising very high towards the south, but northwards breaking down into broad ridges which separated wide and shallow dales. The ridge I had chosen seemed to sink after a mile or two to a moor which lay like a pocket in the uplands. That seemed as good a direction to take as any other.

My stratagem had given me a fair start—call it twenty minutes—and I had the width of a glen behind me before I saw the first heads of the pursuers. The police had evidently called in local talent to their aid, and

the men I could see had the appearance of herds or gamekeepers. They
hallooed at the sight of me, and I waved my hand. Two dived into the glen
and began to climb my ridge, while the others kept their own side of the
hill. I felt as if I were taking part in a schoolboy game of hare and hounds.

But very soon it began to seem less of a game. Those fellows behind
were hefty men on their native heath. Looking back I saw that only three
were following direct, and I guessed that the others had fetched a circuit
to cut me off. My lack of local knowledge might very well be my undo-
ing, and I resolved to get out of this tangle of glens to the pocket of moor
I had seen from the tops. I must so increase my distance as to get clear
away from them, and I believed I could do this if I could find the right
ground for it. If there had been cover I would have tried a bit of stalking,
but on these bare slopes you could see a fly a mile off. My hope must be in
the length of my legs and the soundness of my wind, but I needed easier
ground for that, for I was not bred a mountaineer. How I longed for a
good Afrikander pony!

I put on a great spurt and got off my ridge and down into the moor
before any figures appeared on the skyline behind me. I crossed a burn,
and came out on a highroad which made a pass between two glens. All
in front of me was a big field of heather sloping up to a crest which was
crowned with an odd feather of trees. In the dyke by the roadside was a
gate, from which a grass-grown track led over the first wave of the moor.

I jumped the dyke and followed it, and after a few hundred yards—
as soon as it was out of sight of the highway—the grass stopped and it
became a very respectable road, which was evidently kept with some care.
Clearly it ran to a house, and I began to think of doing the same. Hitherto
my luck had held, and it might be that my best chance would be found
in this remote dwelling. Anyhow there were trees there, and that meant
cover.

I did not follow the road, but the burnside which flanked it on the right,
where the bracken grew deep and the high banks made a tolerable screen. It
was well I did so, for no sooner had I gained the hollow than, looking back,
I saw the pursuit topping the ridge from which I had descended.

After that I did not look back; I had no time. I ran up the burnside,
crawling over the open places, and for a large part wading in the shallow

stream. I found a deserted cottage with a row of phantom peat-stacks and an overgrown garden. Then I was among young hay, and very soon had come to the edge of a plantation of wind-blown firs. From there I saw the chimneys of the house smoking a few hundred yards to my left. I forsook the burnside, crossed another dyke, and almost before I knew was on a rough lawn. A glance back told me that I was well out of sight of the pursuit, which had not yet passed the first lift of the moor.

The lawn was a very rough place, cut with a scythe instead of a mower, and planted with beds of scrubby rhododendrons. A brace of black game, which are not usually garden birds, rose at my approach. The house before me was the ordinary moorland farm, with a more pretentious whitewashed wing added. Attached to this wing was a glass veranda, and through the glass I saw the face of an elderly gentleman meekly watching me.

I stalked over the border of coarse hill gravel and entered the open veranda door. Within was a pleasant room, glass on one side, and on the other a mass of books. More books showed in an inner room. On the floor, instead of tables, stood cases such as you see in a museum, filled with coins and queer stone implements.

There was a knee-hole desk in the middle, and seated at it, with some papers and open volumes before him, was the benevolent old gentleman. His face was round and shiny, like Mr. Pickwick's, big glasses were stuck on the end of his nose, and the top of his head was as bright and bare as a glass bottle. He never moved when I entered, but raised his placid eyebrows and waited on me to speak.

It was not an easy job, with about five minutes to spare, to tell a stranger who I was and what I wanted, and to win his aid. I did not attempt it. There was something about the eye of the man before me, something so keen and knowledgeable, that I could not find a word. I simply stared at him and stuttered.

"You seem in a hurry, my friend," he said slowly.

I nodded towards the window. It gave a prospect across the moor through a gap in the plantation, and revealed certain figures half a mile off straggling through the heather.

"Ah, I see," he said, and took up a pair of field-glasses through which he patiently scrutinized the figures.

"A fugitive from justice, eh? Well, we'll go into the matter at our leisure. Meantime I object to my privacy being broken in upon by the clumsy rural policeman. Go into my study, and you will see two doors facing you. Take the one on the left and close it behind you. You will be perfectly safe."

And this extraordinary man took up his pen again.

I did as I was bid, and found myself in a little dark chamber which smelt of chemicals, and was lit only by a tiny window high up in the wall. The door had swung behind me with a click like the door of a safe. Once again I had found an unexpected sanctuary.

All the same I was not comfortable. There was something about the old gentleman which puzzled and rather terrified me. He had been too easy and ready, almost as if he had expected me. And his eyes had been horribly intelligent.

No sound came to me in that dark place. For all I knew the police might be searching the house, and if they did they would want to know what was behind this door. I tried to possess my soul in patience, and to forget how hungry I was.

Then I took a more cheerful view. The old gentleman could scarcely refuse me a meal, and I fell to reconstructing my breakfast. Bacon and eggs would content me, but I wanted the better part of a flitch of bacon and half a hundred eggs. And then, while my mouth was watering in anticipation, there was a click and the door stood open.

I emerged into the sunlight to find the master of the house sitting in a deep armchair in the room he called his study, and regarding me with curious eyes.

"Have they gone?" I asked.

"They have gone. I convinced them that you had crossed the hill. I do not choose that the police should come between me and one whom I am delighted to honor. This is a lucky morning for you, Mr. Richard Hannay."

As he spoke his eyelids seemed to tremble and to fall a little over his keen grey eyes. In a flash the phrase of Scudder's came back to me, when he had described the man he most dreaded in the world. He had said that he "could hood his eyes like a hawk." Then I saw that I had walked straight into the enemy's headquarters.

My first impulse was to throttle the old ruffian and make for the open air. He seemed to anticipate my intention, for he smiled gently, and nodded to the door behind me. I turned, and saw two men-servants who had me covered with pistols.

He knew my name, but he had never seen me before. And as the reflection darted across my mind I saw a slender chance.

"I don't know what you mean," I said roughly. "And who are you calling Richard Hannay? My name's Ainslie."

"So?" he said, still smiling. "But of course you have others. We won't quarrel about a name."

I was pulling myself together now, and I reflected that my garb, lacking coat and waistcoat and collar, would at any rate not betray me. I put on my surliest face and shrugged my shoulders.

"I suppose you're going to give me up after all, and I call it a damned dirty trick. My God, I wish I had never seen that cursed motor-car! Here's the money and be damned to you," and I flung four sovereigns on the table.

He opened his eyes a little. "Oh no, I shall not give you up. My friends and I will have a little private settlement with you, that is all. You know a little too much, Mr. Hannay. You are a clever actor, but not quite clever enough."

He spoke with assurance, but I could see the dawning of a doubt in his mind.

"Oh, for God's sake stop jawing," I cried. "Everything's against me. I haven't had a bit of luck since I came on shore at Leith. What's the harm in a poor devil with an empty stomach picking up some money he finds in a bust-up motor-car? That's all I done, and for that I've been chivvied for two days by those blasted bobbies over those blasted hills. I tell you I'm fair sick of it. You can do what you like, old boy! Ned Ainslie's got no fight left in him."

I could see that the doubt was gaining.

"Will you oblige me with the story of your recent doings?" he asked.

"I can't, guv'nor," I said in a real beggar's whine. "I've not had a bite to eat for two days. Give me a mouthful of food, and then you'll hear God's truth."

I must have showed my hunger in my face, for he signaled to one of the men in the doorway. A bit of cold pie was brought and a glass of beer, and I wolfed them down like a pig—or rather, like Ned Ainslie, for I was keeping up my character. In the middle of my meal he spoke suddenly to me in German, but I turned on him a face as blank as a stone wall.

Then I told him my story—how I had come off an Archangel ship at Leith a week ago, and was making my way overland to my brother at Wigtown. I had run short of cash—I hinted vaguely at a spree—and I was pretty well on my uppers when I had come on a hole in a hedge, and, looking through, had seen a big motor-car lying in the burn. I had poked about to see what had happened, and had found three sovereigns lying on the seat and one on the floor. There was nobody there or any sign of an owner, so I had pocketed the cash. But somehow the law had got after me. When I had tried to change a sovereign in a baker's shop, the woman had cried on the police, and a little later, when I was washing my face in a burn, I had been nearly gripped, and had only got away by leaving my coat and waistcoat behind me.

"They can have the money back," I cried, "for a fat lot of good it's done me. Those perishers are all down on a poor man. Now, if it had been you, guv'nor, that had found the quids, nobody would have troubled you."

"You're a good liar, Hannay," he said.

I flew into a rage. "Stop fooling, damn you! I tell you my name's Ainslie, and I never heard of anyone called Hannay in my born days. I'd sooner have the police than you with your Hannays and your monkey-faced pistol tricks. ... No, guv'nor, I beg pardon, I don't mean that. I'm much obliged to you for the grub, and I'll thank you to let me go now the coast's clear."

It was obvious that he was badly puzzled. You see he had never seen me, and my appearance must have altered considerably from my photographs, if he had got one of them. I was pretty smart and well dressed in London, and now I was a regular tramp.

"I do not propose to let you go. If you are what you say you are, you will soon have a chance of clearing yourself. If you are what I believe you are, I do not think you will see the light much longer."

He rang a bell, and a third servant appeared from the veranda.

"I want the Lanchester in five minutes," he said. "There will be three to luncheon."

Then he looked steadily at me, and that was the hardest ordeal of all.

There was something weird and devilish in those eyes, cold, malignant, unearthly, and most hellishly clever. They fascinated me like the bright eyes of a snake. I had a strong impulse to throw myself on his mercy and offer to join his side, and if you consider the way I felt about the whole thing you will see that that impulse must have been purely physical, the weakness of a brain mesmerized and mastered by a stronger spirit. But I managed to stick it out and even to grin.

"You'll know me next time, guv'nor," I said.

"Karl," he spoke in German to one of the men in the doorway, "you will put this fellow in the storeroom till I return, and you will be answerable to me for his keeping."

I was marched out of the room with a pistol at each ear.

The storeroom was a damp chamber in what had been the old farmhouse. There was no carpet on the uneven floor, and nothing to sit down on but a school form. It was black as pitch, for the windows were heavily shuttered. I made out by groping that the walls were lined with boxes and barrels and sacks of some heavy stuff. The whole place smelt of mold and disuse. My jailers turned the key in the door, and I could hear them shifting their feet as they stood on guard outside.

I sat down in that chilly darkness in a very miserable frame of mind. The old boy had gone off in a motor to collect the two ruffians who had interviewed me yesterday. Now, they had seen me as the roadman, and they would remember me, for I was in the same rig. What was a roadman doing twenty miles from his beat, pursued by the police? A question or two would put them on the track. Probably they had seen Mr. Turnbull, probably Marmie too; most likely they could link me up with Sir Harry, and then the whole thing would be crystal clear. What chance had I in this moorland house with three desperadoes and their armed servants?

I began to think wistfully of the police, now plodding over the hills after my wraith. They at any rate were fellow-countrymen and honest men, and their tender mercies would be kinder than these ghoulish aliens. But they wouldn't have listened to me. That old devil with the eyelids had not taken long to get rid of them. I thought he probably had some kind of graft with the constabulary. Most likely he had letters from Cabinet Ministers saying he was to be given every facility for plotting against Britain. That's the sort of owlish way we run our politics in this jolly old country.

The three would be back for lunch, so I hadn't more than a couple of hours to wait. It was simply waiting on destruction, for I could see no way out of this mess. I wished that I had Scudder's courage, for I am free to confess I didn't feel any great fortitude. The only thing that kept me going was that I was pretty furious. It made me boil with rage to think of those three spies getting the pull on me like this. I hoped that at any rate I might be able to twist one of their necks before they downed me.

The more I thought of it the angrier I grew, and I had to get up and move about the room. I tried the shutters, but they were the kind that lock with a key, and I couldn't move them. From the outside came the faint clucking of hens in the warm sun. Then I groped among the sacks and boxes. I couldn't open the latter, and the sacks seemed to be full of things like dog-biscuits that smelt of cinnamon. But, as I circumnavigated the room, I found a handle in the wall which seemed worth investigating.

It was the door of a wall cupboard—what they call a "press" in Scotland—and it was locked. I shook it, and it seemed rather flimsy. For want of something better to do I put out my strength on that door, getting some purchase on the handle by looping my braces round it. Presently the thing gave with a crash which I thought would bring in my warders to inquire. I waited for a bit, and then started to explore the cupboard shelves.

There was a multitude of queer things there. I found an odd vesta or two in my trouser pockets and struck a light. It was out in a second, but it showed me one thing. There was a little stock of electric torches on one shelf. I picked up one, and found it was in working order.

With the torch to help me I investigated further. There were bottles and cases of queer-smelling stuffs, chemicals no doubt for experiments, and there were coils of fine copper wire and yanks and yanks of thin oiled silk. There was a box of detonators, and a lot of cord for fuses. Then away at the back of the shelf I found a stout brown cardboard box, and inside it a wooden case. I managed to wrench it open, and within lay half a dozen little grey bricks, each a couple of inches square.

I took up one, and found that it crumbled easily in my hand. Then I smelt it and put my tongue to it. After that I sat down to think. I hadn't been a mining engineer for nothing, and I knew lentonite when I saw it.

With one of these bricks I could blow the house to smithereens. I had used the stuff in Rhodesia and knew its power. But the trouble was that my knowledge wasn't exact. I had forgotten the proper charge and the right way of preparing it, and I wasn't sure about the timing. I had only a vague notion, too, as to its power, for though I had used it I had not handled it with my own fingers.

But it was a chance, the only possible chance. It was a mighty risk, but against it was an absolute black certainty. If I used it the odds were, as I reckoned, about five to one in favor of my blowing myself into the tree-tops; but if I didn't I should very likely be occupying a six-foot hole in the garden by the evening. That was the way I had to look at it. The prospect was pretty dark either way, but anyhow there was a chance, both for myself and for my country.

The remembrance of little Scudder decided me. It was about the beastliest moment of my life, for I'm no good at these cold-blooded resolutions. Still I managed to rake up the pluck to set my teeth and choke back the horrid doubts that flooded in on me. I simply shut off my mind and pretended I was doing an experiment as simple as Guy Fawkes fireworks.

I got a detonator, and fixed it to a couple of feet of fuse. Then I took a quarter of a lentonite brick, and buried it near the door below one of the sacks in a crack of the floor, fixing the detonator in it. For all I knew half those boxes might be dynamite. If the cupboard held such deadly explosives, why not the boxes? In that case there would be a glorious skyward journey for me and the German servants and about an acre of surrounding country. There was also the risk that the detonation might set off the other bricks in the cupboard, for I had forgotten most that I knew about lentonite. But it didn't do to begin thinking about the possibilities. The odds were horrible, but I had to take them.

I ensconced myself just below the sill of the window, and lit the fuse. Then I waited for a moment or two. There was dead silence—only a shuffle of heavy boots in the passage, and the peaceful cluck of hens from the warm out-of-doors. I commended my soul to my Maker, and wondered where I would be in five seconds....

A great wave of heat seemed to surge upwards from the floor, and hang for a blistering instant in the air. Then the wall opposite me flashed into a golden yellow and dissolved with a rending thunder that hammered my brain into a pulp. Something dropped on me, catching the point of my left shoulder.

And then I think I became unconscious.

My stupor can scarcely have lasted beyond a few seconds. I felt myself being choked by thick yellow fumes, and struggled out of the debris to my feet. Somewhere behind me I felt fresh air. The jambs of the window had fallen, and through the ragged rent the smoke was pouring out to the summer noon. I stepped over the broken lintel, and found myself standing in a yard in a dense and acrid fog. I felt very sick and ill, but I could move my limbs, and I staggered blindly forward away from the house.

A small mill-lade ran in a wooden aqueduct at the other side of the yard, and into this I fell. The cool water revived me, and I had just enough wits left to think of escape. I squirmed up the lade among the slippery green slime till I reached the mill-wheel. Then I wriggled through the axle hole into the old mill and tumbled on to a bed of chaff. A nail caught the seat of my trousers, and I left a wisp of heather-mixture behind me.

The mill had been long out of use. The ladders were rotten with age, and in the loft the rats had gnawed great holes in the floor. Nausea shook me, and a wheel in my head kept turning, while my left shoulder and arm seemed to be stricken with the palsy. I looked out of the window and saw a fog still hanging over the house and smoke escaping from an upper window. Please God I had set the place on fire, for I could hear confused cries coming from the other side.

But I had no time to linger, since this mill was obviously a bad hiding-place. Anyone looking for me would naturally follow the lade, and I made certain the search would begin as soon as they found that my body was not in the storeroom. From another window I saw that on the far side of the mill stood an old stone dovecot. If I could get there without leaving tracks I might find a hiding-place, for I argued that my enemies, if they thought I could move, would conclude I had made for open country, and would go seeking me on the moor.

I crawled down the broken ladder, scattering chaff behind me to cover my footsteps. I did the same on the mill floor, and on the threshold where the door hung on broken hinges. Peeping out, I saw that between me and the dovecot was a piece of bare cobbled ground, where no footmarks would show. Also it was mercifully hid by the mill buildings from any view from the house. I slipped across the space, got to the back of the dovecot and prospected a way of ascent.

That was one of the hardest jobs I ever took on. My shoulder and arm ached like hell, and I was so sick and giddy that I was always on the verge of falling. But I managed it somehow. By the use of out-jutting stones and gaps in the masonry and a tough ivy root I got to the top in the end. There was a little parapet behind which I found space to lie down. Then I proceeded to go off into an old-fashioned swoon.

I woke with a burning head and the sun glaring in my face. For a long time I lay motionless, for those horrible fumes seemed to have loosened my joints and dulled my brain. Sounds came to me from the house—men speaking throatily and the throbbing of a stationary car. There was a little gap in the parapet to which I wriggled, and from which I had some sort of prospect of the yard. I saw figures come out—a servant with his head bound up, and then a younger man in knickerbockers. They were looking for something, and moved towards the mill. Then one of them caught sight of the wisp of cloth on the nail, and cried out to the other. They both went back to the house, and brought two more to look at it. I saw the rotund figure of my late captor, and I thought I made out the man with the lisp. I noticed that all had pistols.

For half an hour they ransacked the mill. I could hear them kicking over the barrels and pulling up the rotten planking. Then they came outside, and stood just below the dovecot arguing fiercely. The servant with the bandage was being soundly rated. I heard them fiddling with the door of the dovecote and for one horrid moment I fancied they were coming up. Then they thought better of it, and went back to the house.

All that long blistering afternoon I lay baking on the rooftop. Thirst was my chief torment. My tongue was like a stick, and to make it worse I could hear the cool drip of water from the mill-lade. I watched the course of the little stream as it came in from the moor, and my fancy followed it to the top of the glen, where it must issue from an icy fountain fringed with cool ferns and mosses. I would have given a thousand pounds to plunge my face into that.

I had a fine prospect of the whole ring of moorland. I saw the car speed away with two occupants, and a man on a hill pony riding east. I judged they were looking for me, and I wished them joy of their quest.

But I saw something else more interesting. The house stood almost on the summit of a swell of moorland which crowned a sort of plateau, and there was no higher point nearer than the big hills six miles off. The actual summit, as I have mentioned, was a biggish clump of trees—firs mostly, with a few ashes and beeches. On the dovecot I was almost on a level with the tree-tops, and could see what lay beyond. The wood was not solid, but only a ring, and inside was an oval of green turf, for all the world like a big cricket-field.

I didn't take long to guess what it was. It was an aerodrome, and a secret one. The place had been most cunningly chosen. For suppose anyone were watching an airplane descending here, he would think it had gone over the hill beyond the trees. As the place was on the top of a rise in the midst of a big amphitheater, any observer from any direction would conclude it had passed out of view behind the hill. Only a man very close at hand would realize that the airplane had not gone over but had descended in the midst of the wood. An observer with a telescope on one of the higher hills might have discovered the truth, but only herds went there, and herds do not carry spy-glasses. When I looked from the dovecot I could see far away a blue line which I knew was the sea, and I grew furious to think that our enemies had this secret conning-tower to rake our waterways.

Then I reflected that if that airplane came back the chances were ten to one that I would be discovered. So through the afternoon I lay and prayed for the coming of darkness, and glad I was when the sun went down over the big western hills and the twilight haze crept over the moor.

The airplane was late. The gloaming was far advanced when I heard the beat of wings and saw it volplaning downward to its home in the wood. Lights twinkled for a bit and there was much coming and going from the house. Then the dark fell, and silence.

Thank God it was a black night. The moon was well on its last quarter and would not rise till late. My thirst was too great to allow me to tarry, so about nine o'clock, so far as I could judge, I started to descend. It wasn't easy, and half-way down I heard the back door of the house open, and saw the gleam of a lantern against the mill wall. For some agonizing minutes I hung by the ivy and prayed that whoever it was would not come round by the dovecot. Then the light disappeared, and I dropped as softly as I could on to the hard soil of the yard.

I crawled on my belly in the lee of a stone dyke till I reached the fringe of trees which surrounded the house. If I had known how to do it I would have tried to put that airplane out of action, but I realized that any attempt would probably be futile. I was pretty certain that there would be some kind of defense round the house, so I went through the wood on hands and knees, feeling carefully every inch before me. It was as well, for presently I came on a wire about two feet from the ground. If I had tripped over that, it would doubtless have rung some bell in the house and I would have been captured.

A hundred yards farther on I found another wire cunningly placed on the edge of a small stream. Beyond that lay the moor, and in five minutes I was deep in bracken and heather. Soon I was round the shoulder of the rise, in the little glen from which the mill-lade flowed. Ten minutes later my face was in the spring, and I was soaking down pints of the blessed water.

But I did not stop till I had put half a dozen miles between me and that accursed dwelling.

CHAPTER SIX

OSS: The Secret History of America's First Intelligence Agency

Richard Harris Smith

In his introduction to OSS, *author Richard Harris Smith reveals many tangled knots of government operations that made his book difficult to write. Thankfully, he prevailed in his quest into a labyrinth of files previously closed as "secret." The result of his labors, including his time with the CIA, is this "no-files-barred" account of the organization that led our nation's intelligence-gathering activities into World War II and the beginning of the Cold War years beyond. This excerpt from the first chapter of* OSS *focuses on the man called "Wild Bill." That would be William Joseph Donovan. In Smith's words from the book's opening chapter called "Donovan's Dreamers":*

"COI was the Office of the Coordinator of Information and at its helm was William Joseph Donovan, known since his youth as 'Wild Bill.' A stocky, gray-haired man of fifty-eight, Donovan was anything but wild—he was a Hoover Republican, an Irish Catholic, and a millionaire Wall Street lawyer. Yet Roosevelt had chosen him to direct the New Deal's excursion into espionage, sabotage, 'black' propaganda, guerrilla warfare, and other 'un-American' sub- versive practices."

Formed prior to WWII, a division of COI quickly morphed into the Office of Strategic Services (OSS) after Pearl Harbor, creating daring and dangerous new chapters in the history of American espionage.

Five months before the Japanese attack on Pearl Harbor precipitated America's entry into the World War, Franklin Roosevelt christened a mysterious addition to his New Deal alphabet bureaucracy. What, asked the Washington rumor-mongers, was this new agency called COI? A "staff of Jewish scribblers," shrilled Herr Goebbels' propaganda machine in Berlin. "Full of politics, ballyhoo, and controversy," chimed in isolationist crusader Charles Lindbergh. At the War Department, uncomprehending generals soon scoffed at a "fly-by-night civilian outfit headed up by a wild man who was trying to horn in on the war."

COI was the Office of the Coordinator of Information and at its helm was William Joseph Donovan, known since his youth as "Wild Bill." A stocky, gray-haired man of 58, Donovan was anything but wild—he was a Hoover Republican, an Irish Catholic, and a millionaire Wall Street lawyer. Yet Roosevelt had chosen him to direct the New Deal's excursion into espionage, sabotage, "black" propaganda, guerrilla warfare, and other "un-American" subversive practices. The President had been impressed by Donovan's impassioned advocacy of American involvement in the European conflict, by his prediction that Britain would not collapse under the pressure of the Luftwaffe, and by his personal audacity and imagination. Donovan had observed the ruthless success of the fascist "fifth column" in Europe and the Balkans, and he longed to create an international secret service for the United States that could prove equal to the Nazi challenge. Roosevelt liked Donovan's organizational vision and was intrigued by his "blend of Wall Street orthodoxy and sophisticated American nationalism."

In every respect, OSS was Donovan's child. He nourished the agency in its infancy, and it bore the stamp of his personality. Donovan was a "civilian general"—an eminently successful corporate attorney as well as a World War I hero who held America's three highest military decorations. OSS also existed in a twilight zone of civilian-military identity that displeased the old-line West Pointers, who derided "Donovan's dragoons."

Like most officers who served in his burgeoning organization, Donovan possessed "indefatigable energy and wide-ranging enthusiasm combined with great resourcefulness," to quote his colleague Allen Dulles. He frequently traveled to lines of combat without concern for his personal safety. "My place is in the field, as well as in Washington," he would often say. "To help my men I must see their problems firsthand." His dynamism and constant movement was the mainstay of an agency that eventually enlisted over thirteen thousand Americans.

His mobility and activism were not the qualities of a conventional administrator. Some said he "ran OSS like a country editor." But the exigencies of war called for unconventional methods, and the absence of a rigid organizational hierarchy enabled an exceptional group of men and women to work with great effectiveness under Donovan's leadership. The agency's psychological staff proudly noted that "OSS undertook and carried out more different types of enterprises calling for more varied skills than any other single organization of its size in the history of our country."

Donovan was an irrepressible optimist. Air Force General "Hap" Arnold remembers him as the "one man who never told me that such and such was not available. He was incapable of a defeatist intelligence answer. . . . He would say 'What do you want? When do you want it? I'll get it for you.' To out-of-the-way places he would send details, or scouts, spies, or small detachments, to secure the information we needed, and would always give us that data in time."

"Woe to the officer," wrote OSS colonel (and later ambassador) David Bruce, "who turned down a project because, on its face, it seemed ridiculous, or at least unusual." Every eccentric schemer with a harebrained plan for secret operations (from phosphorescent foxes to incendiary bats) would find a sympathetic ear in Donovan's office. One aged American businessman devised a scheme for the establishment of clandestine air bases behind the Japanese lines in China. It reached the desk of Adlai Stevenson, then special assistant to the Secretary of the Navy. Stevenson passed it on to Donovan with the comment, "Fearful that your mail may be declining, I enclose another plan for winning the war! You need not tell me how grateful you are." Donovan promptly replied, "Thank you very much for your memorandum. We will work this out together. I ignore nothing—you never can tell."

Inevitably, activism also meant waste. Donovan procured for OSS an unlimited (and largely unvouchered) budget that ran into the hundreds of millions during the four years of the war. Critics later spoke of the funds "squandered by OSS agents who bought or hired planes, automobiles, office equipment, houses, printing plants—anything they needed or thought they did." The mysterious valise of one OSS officer stationed at the American embassy in Vichy France was opened by curious State Department officials who found the case filled with some $200,000 in small bills. Another OSS man was to be assigned to a post on one of the Canary Islands. "But," remembers a Donovan aide, "no commercial steamships called there during wartime. No matter! Buy a ship! One was bought for a million dollars or so. Only after the purchase was made was it realized that it would not be the most secret way to plant an undercover agent to have a special steamship arrive to land him. I never learned what happened to the ship."

Though all wartime agencies operated in disarray, OSS had its own unique brand of administrative confusion. Young officers recruited under the most secret conditions would report for duty to a well-guarded Washington headquarters only to be asked, "Do you have any idea what OSS might have hired you for?"

The general, assistants protectively explained, promoted "the appearance of chaos as a screen to the increasing potency and effectiveness of his organization." But, in fact, Donovan simply refused to be bothered with organizational detail. Such harried administrative officers as Louis Ream (a US Steel executive), Atherton Richards (an Hawaiian pineapple magnate), or James Grafton Rogers (a Yale law professor) "would walk into Donovan's office with dozens of charts; charts for the budget, charts for the administration, charts for the various divisions.... Donovan would glance at them, smile at them, approve them with a mild wave of the hand, and then he would have another idea, and he would forget them completely." Standard operating procedures were almost taboo in OSS. Effective action was the sole objective. His own military status notwithstanding, Donovan had little use for West Point formalities. An apocryphal tale that made the rounds at OSS headquarters had it that during the Anzio landing in Italy, Donovan found himself standing on the deck of the command ship beside Major General Mark Clark, the commander of the operation and his superior in rank. According to this story, Donovan put his arm around the gangly General Clark in paternal fashion and asked, "Well, son, what are we going to do next?" It was an appropriate parable for an agency where one out of every four of the 9,000 military personnel was a commissioned officer. Rank was bestowed with an ease dictated almost entirely by ad hoc operational requirements; traditional military protocol was superfluous. One captain who led an OSS team behind the Japanese lines in China remembered, "All officers were quite junior, and as long as everybody did his work few of us bothered with military regulations. High brass was unlikely to inspect. There was no saluting, and the men could dress as they pleased. . . . Some men let their hair and beards grow, others favored long walrus mustaches and shaved skulls."

Insubordination became a way of life for OSS officers, but Donovan was unconcerned. He often said, "I'd rather have a young lieutenant with guts enough to disobey an order than a colonel too regimented to think and act for himself." He was frequently called upon to defend the actions of his over-eager subordinates, and it was rarely a simple task. Unaware that a top-secret naval intelligence team had broken the Japanese military code, OSS men in Portugal secretly entered the Japanese embassy and stole a copy of the enemy's codebook. The Japanese discovered the theft and promptly changed their ciphers. Washington was left without a vital source of information, and the Joint Chiefs of Staff were irate. There were other high-level flaps. Donovan's men in Italy smuggled arms to Tito's Communist guerrillas in Yugoslavia without the approval of the British theater commander. And OSS men in Morocco sent Communist agents to Franco's Spain without notifying the American embassy in Madrid. In every case, Donovan supported his officers. He had given his men their freedom of action and he would not allow them to be punished for exercising it with enthusiasm.

OSS officers soon realized that their superiors avoided disciplinary action, even in cases of incompetence or corruption. Operational funds disappeared mysteriously in the hills of Greece, France, and Italy, only to reappear in the bank accounts of a few OSS veterans after the war. Many OSS men also found mistresses, both foreign and domestic, compatible with their clandestine existence. Joining the thieves and Don Juans were the mentally unstable. "We were working with an unusual type of individual," wrote an OSS captain who sent hundreds of agents into occupied France. "Many had natures that fed on danger and excitement. Their appetite for the unconventional and spectacular was far beyond the ordinary. It was not unusual to find a good measure of temperament thrown in." There was often a thin line between unconventionality and instability. Donovan's psychological chief, Dr. Henry Murray of Harvard, noted: "The whole nature of the functions of OSS were particularly inviting to psychopathic characters; it involved sensation, intrigue, the idea of being a mysterious man with secret knowledge."

Safeguards were virtually nonexistent. When Donovan finally decided to court-martial two overseas officers (one an incompetent drunkard who was living with his WAC secretary, the other an industrious manager of black market operations in the vicinity of his Neapolitan base), aides protested that court-martial proceedings against *any* officer for *any* reason would be damaging to the secrecy and the morale of the organization.

There was little in the OSS structure to promote respect for formal channels of authority. One civilian liberal who resigned from OSS after objecting, unsuccessfully, to Washington's support of the Italian monarchy, later reflected: "I should have stayed under anyone, however incapable, made whatever promises were necessary about oaths to the House of Savoy, and then used my ingenuity in circumventing both." In Yugoslavia, an OSS lieutenant in Donovan's mission to Tito, a playwright by profession, was told by his colonel to encode a message for radio transmission. "That," replied the lieutenant, "can wait till tomorrow." The colonel reasoned gently, "I'll admit it's not much fun coding, but that's true of lots of things in the army." "Army?" asked the startled lieutenant. "Did you say army? Hell, man, we're not in the army. We're in the OSS." And in China, an OSS captain received an order to report on the attitude of the local populace in his operational area toward the contending Nationalist and Communist forces. He and his teammates suspected that the information was to be passed along to the Chinese government and they had no sympathy for the Chiang Kai-shek regime. Besides, they felt that the internal struggle in China should be just that, a domestic Chinese affair. "Let's put it to a vote," suggested the officer to his fellows. The order "lost" and was disregarded. That was the OSS way.

Donovan himself was sometimes the victim of his own scorn for authority. The young Harvard historian H. Stuart Hughes was serving in an OSS research post in North Africa when Donovan stopped off while on one of his world tours. Convinced that Hughes spoke Italian admirably, the general ordered him to prepare for a parachute jump into German-occupied Italy. Lacking both language fluency and parachute training, the bewildered Hughes asked his local OSS commander for advice. "Disappear till the general leaves," was the reply. Hughes kept out of sight until Donovan's departure and the assignment was quickly forgotten.

The confusion created by the freedom given OSS officers was abetted by status conflicts within the organization. OSS men who carried out dangerous espionage and sabotage missions behind enemy lines felt an estrangement from their superiors who issued directives from the rear-echelon havens of Washington, London, Algiers, Cairo, New Delhi, and Kunming. Most of the executives at these headquarters were civilians with high military rank but no military training. Field operators scoffed at "bourbon whiskey colonels" with "cellophane commissions" (you could see through them, but they kept the Draft off). This was not simply traditional military resentment of civilian direction. OSS field officers Thomas Braden and Stewart Alsop observed that while "the great majority of the operational men had gone through the Army the hard way, and those who were commissioned had come up through the ranks, a very large proportion of the administrative officers in OSS had received direct commissions in the early days. They had bought uniforms, and put them on, and there they were, soldiers, just like that. Some of these men were excellent executives, and good soldiers, but the operational men often resented their higher rank." Considering the OSS officers' contempt for military hierarchy, tension between desk colonels and field agents was hardly surprising.

It worked both ways. One decidedly conservative OSS executive— the chief of the organization's scientific Research and Development Branch—castigated "many of the personnel I met at a lower level ... who seemed to be rah-rah youngsters to whom OSS was perhaps an escape from routine military service and a sort of lark." On the other hand, each member of the OSS higher echelons "risked his future status as a banker or trustee or highly placed politician in identifying himself with illegality and unorthodoxy."

Mutual antipathy plagued all aspects of OSS operations. An OSS major working with the Norwegian resistance asked his London headquarters for permission to take and hold a town as a fort from which to waylay the Germans. Relaying a decision of the Supreme Command, OSS headquarters denied the request. But the major tried again. "I am here," he said. "I know what I am doing. I know I can do it; the resistance wants me to do it, and I intend to do it." That made OSS headquarters angry: "You have your orders. Disobedience will be subject to disciplinary action upon your return." Was headquarters bluffing? Probably, but the incident suggests the flavor of "normal" relations with men in the field. Certainly the drive for operational autonomy was no fluke of erratic behavior, nor even a sign of youthful exuberance. A sedate and mature civilian intelligence operator like Allen Dulles, chief of the OSS mission in neutral Switzerland (and postwar Director of the CIA) was equally wary of working too closely with Washington. Writing after the war of his negotiations for the surrender of the German forces in North Italy, Dulles cautiously suggested: "An intelligence officer in the field is supposed to keep his home office informed of what he is doing. That is quite true, but with some reservations, as he may overdo it. If, for example, he tells too much or asks too often for instructions, he is likely to get some he doesn't relish, and what is worse, he may well find headquarters trying to take over the whole conduct of the operation. Only a man on the spot can really pass judgment on the details as contrasted with the policy decisions, which, of course, belong to the boss at headquarters." Dulles added, "It has always amazed me how desk personnel thousands of miles away seem to acquire wisdom and special knowledge about local field conditions which they assume goes deeper than that available to the man on the spot." Almost without exception, Dulles and other OSS operators feared the burden of a high-level decision that might "cramp" their freedom of action.

To the amazement of his executives, General Donovan personally supported the field viewpoint. He made no secret of the fact that his heart was with the officers on the firing line. He proudly assured the Allied commander in Southeast Asia, British Admiral Louis Mountbatten, that "if at any time he wanted something done for which he could not spare two or three thousand men," he should simply "call on OSS and we would send in twenty or thirty men to do the job." And Donovan meant it.

General Donovan possessed the "power to visualize an oak when he saw an acorn," in the words of the OSS Psychological Staff. "For him the day was never sufficient unto itself; it was always teeming with the seeds of a boundless future" and "every completed project bred a host of new ones." As Donovan traversed the globe on frequent world tours, "at every stop, brief as it might be, he would leave a litter of young schemes to be reared and fashioned by his lieutenants and translated into deeds of daring."

Under the general's prodding, OSS grew and expanded—and aroused the resentment of other official bureaucracies. From the moment of the COI's creation, a host of predatory government agencies "forgot their internecine animosities and joined in an attempt to strangle this unwanted newcomer at birth." The grumbling against the new organization became such a deafening roar that President Roosevelt loaned his son James to the COI as a liaison officer to prevent other departments from devouring Donovan's upstarts before they had even set to work.

The Federal Bureau of Investigation looked particularly askance at this newcomer to the clandestine world. J. Edgar Hoover's agents were already entrenched in South America when OSS began to contemplate this FBI preserve with interest. Hoover objected. The dispute became so heated that Roosevelt was forced to intervene. The President awarded Hoover sole responsibility for secret operations south of the border (a decision OSS later disregarded).

This first clash left Hoover with a fear of OSS encroachment that undoubtedly strengthened his natural paranoia about sinister conspiracies. Representatives of the British secret services in the United States were amazed to find that "Hoover keenly resented Donovan's organization from the moment it was established," and his resentment "was inevitably extended towards its British collaborators. . . . It took a long while to convince him that he could not succeed in his determination to exclude the British organization from contact with other US intelligence agencies."

OSS also had running bouts with the Department of State. The COI had just acquired a few temporary rooms in the State Department Annex in its very early days, when Cordell Hull's assistants first became worried about competition with the new agency. When COI requested access to some State files, Foreign Service officers nervously jibed that Donovan was "a man who could tell you the time if you loaned him your watch." State officials had good cause for anxiety; the helter-skelter but brilliant achievements of Donovan's officers would stand in sharp contrast to the tradition-bound, sluggish actions of the diplomatic service.

To novitiates of the foreign affairs bureaucracy, the contrast came as something of a shock. In 1944, an astute specialist in African affairs left the Research and Analysis Branch of OSS for a new position at the State Department. He was amazed by the change of atmosphere. His OSS environment had been free-wheeling, intellectually stimulating, and politically liberal. In contrast, he found his new Foreign Service colleagues burdened by the restraints of career ambition and the conservatism of a rigid hierarchy. He even encountered instances of racial prejudice that would have seemed anathema to his fellow analysts in OSS. The bewildered professor was Ralph Bunche.

The disappointment Bunche experienced was shared by others who found the State Department hopelessly hamstrung by bureaucratic inertia, a "spirit of smug self-satisfaction," as David Bruce put it. State thus proved an easy prey for OSS dynamism. If for no other reason than the quality of its people, OSS was destined to enter the arena of international diplomacy. Men who had served in top diplomatic posts before the war—such as the American ambassadors to Germany and Italy, the minister to Lithuania, and the deputy governor-general of the Philippines—were quickly tapped by Donovan for top OSS positions. America's first intelligence agency also served as a breeding ground for future statesmen. Since the war, former OSS officers have represented the United States as ambassadors in over twenty countries. The commander of OSS in the European theater, David Bruce, served as ambassador to England, France, and Germany, and as American representative to the Vietnam peace negotiations in Paris. General Donovan was himself named ambassador to Thailand by President Eisenhower. The exclusive "club" of COI and OSS veterans also included Presidential advisors Arthur Schlesinger, Jr., Walt Rostow, Carl Kaysen, Douglass Cater, Clark McGregor, former UN ambassador Goldberg, former Treasury Secretary C. Douglas Dillon, and CIA Directors Allen Dulles and Richard Helms. Most of these men received their first governmental experience in OSS.

⌐⌐

"The oppressed peoples must be encouraged to resist and to assist in Axis defeat, and this can be done by inciting them, by assisting them, and by training and organizing them." Sabotage alone would not suffice. "It must be accompanied by efforts to promote revolution." Those words were not written by Stalin. They were found in an October 1941 memorandum to General Donovan from his first Special Operations chief, Robert Solborg, a steel corporation executive and Russian émigré who had once been an officer of the Czar's army.

"The undercover agent must set up his machinery for building up an organization dedicated in the beginning to passive resistance. If his task is successful, passive resistance will lead by natural steps to open violence and even—at the proper time—to armed rebellion." Mao Tse-tung was not the author of these instructions for subversion. They were set forth in December 1943 by another Donovan assistant, J. Freeman Lincoln, a freelance writer who later became an editor of *Fortune* and *Time* magazines.

Even Donovan's executives realized that OSS was confronted with the task of political revolution. There could be no American embassies and no Foreign Service officers in enemy-occupied territory. Yet the competing drives for power in the occupied nations were only intensified by Axis domination and the chaos of war. New social and ideological forces were clamoring for the overthrow of old regimes in Europe, and Asian nationalists were plotting the destruction of colonial rule. It was the "liaison" officers of OSS to whom these revolutionaries often turned in hopeful anticipation.

Robert Welch, founder of the John Birch Society, charged that OSS "frequently threw the weight of American supplies, arms, money, and prestige behind the Communist terrorist organizations of Europe and Asia." There was some truth in this statement. But the full story of OSS relations with the resistance was a complex product of organizational structure, the nature of guerrilla warfare, the ideologies of the men behind the lines, and the competing political interests of America's allies.

OSS had taken its organizational cue from the British, who at the outset of World War II were considered masters of clandestine warfare. The Secret Intelligence Service (known as SIS, MI-6, or "Broadway") had been charged with overseas espionage since the late sixteenth century. An offshoot of SIS, the Special Operations Executive (SOE), was created in 1940 to assist guerrilla movements in the war against Hitler, or, in Churchill's poetic phrase, to "set Europe ablaze."

General Donovan similarly established a Secret Intelligence Branch (SI) and a Special Operations Branch (SO). Like their independent British counterparts, these divisions looked at operational problems from entirely different perspectives. SI was charged with espionage—the secret collection of intelligence information—and SO was given responsibility for sabotage and liaison with underground movements. The operational objectives of these two divisions were not always compatible. The SO principle was to work with resistance groups of any political coloration provided that they were militarily effective against the enemy. The SI branch was interested only in the collection of useful information, not in tactical raids or sabotage. Could an underground group supply valuable intelligence? If so, argued the SI men, OSS must maintain contact with that group.

"An intelligence officer," wrote Allen Dulles, summarizing the SI position, "should be free to talk to the devil himself if he could gain any useful knowledge for the conduct or the termination of the war." That was the theory of espionage. But American officers soon discovered that their conversations with particular political devils were often interpreted as implying Washington's recognition and support. OSS faced this same problem in the caves of Mao Tse-tung's headquarters in north China and in the Swiss cafés where American officers met the conservative German militarists who were plotting Hitler's assassination. Since formal organizational divisions in OSS were rarely respected, Special Operations men sometimes collected intelligence and Secret Intelligence officers occasionally fought with the underground. If this was not sufficient to confuse "operational principles" beyond recognition, General Donovan proceeded to create a third branch, the Operational Group Command, in which SI and SO activities were merged. The new Operational Groups were organized by target countries (Italian OG, French OG, and so on) and consisted of 32 men with language qualifications dropped behind the lines in uniform with directives to carry out both espionage and sabotage operations in concert with the resistance.

Regardless of their specific assignments, OSS men who parachuted into enemy territory assumed a very special role in the war. There was nothing particularly romantic about World War II for the American infantry soldier. He saw the death, misery, greed, and brutality that always accompanies armed conflict. But a select group of Donovan's men fought a different war.

Living and working behind the lines with dedicated guerrillas who fought to free their countries from fascist domination, these OSS officers found real meaning in the Roosevelt slogans of the Atlantic Charter. And few American (or British) officers failed to develop a passionate admiration for their partisan friends. The enemy was evil, the resistance was heroic. For lonely Americans hiding on a cold mountain or in a torrid jungle under constant threat of attack, there could be no other truth.

Actor Sterling Hayden was one Donovan officer who served with Tito's guerrillas in Yugoslavia. "We established a tremendously close personal feeling with these people," he later recalled. "We had enormous, I would say unlimited respect for the way they were fighting. . . . We got quite steamed up by it. I myself was steamed up considerably by it. I had never experienced anything quite like that, and it made a tremendous impression on me."

It is not surprising that most OSS field operators were idealists. A majority were under thirty years old and had received their college education during the Depression years. Also, the OSS Psychological Staff, dominated by such young academicians as 30-year-old John Gardner of Mount Holyoke, deliberately sought out potential SO and SI officers who possessed an "ability to get along with other people" and a "freedom from disturbing prejudices." The psychologists similarly shunned the selection of men for overseas service who were burdened by "feelings of national superiority or racial intolerance." This policy proved effective. One admiring war correspondent observed that "race, color, and previous condition of servitude cut no ice whatever" in OSS "so long as one actually wanted to get into the fray and help to win it."

The resistance forces naturally assumed that these young idealists were official representatives of their nation's foreign policy. "Here, I was America," wrote an OSS colonel who served with the Yugoslav royalist guerrillas. "I had a message, perhaps merely words of courage and encouragement to a long—suffering people." Behind enemy lines, the most casual word that fell from the unguarded lips of the youngest second lieutenant in the American army—he might have been a writer, lawyer, corporation executive, or artist in peacetime—would be considered holy writ by leaders of the resistance. His views had no importance in the eyes of State Department representatives thousands of miles away, but for the fighters of the underground, they were taken as inspired declarations of Washington's policy.

The British certainly recognized that their secret agents would work as unofficial diplomats and London insisted (frequently without success) that officers of the Special Operations Executive who parachuted into enemy territory should execute the political objectives of the Foreign Office. Like their Soviet allies, the British were determined to pursue their own interests as a world power in the course of the battle against the Axis. In Washington, some State Department and OSS executives had similar plans for the establishment of America's postwar imperium, but the rank-and-file of Donovan's secret service had no patience with such grand designs; they believed that Machiavellian power politics were always played at the expense of smaller nations and powerless peoples, and the underdogs of the world were the objects of OSS affection.

Many OSS men began to operate on the general principle that "in intelligence, the British are just as much the enemy as the Germans." They believed that London's secret services were more concerned with expanding England's empire than with defeating the enemy. OSS impatience with Whitehall's political maneuvers was particularly intense in the Far East, where traditional American opposition to colonialism permeated OSS operations. When General Douglas MacArthur refused to permit OSS to operate in the South Pacific, Donovan quickly convinced the British to accept OSS "cooperation" in Southeast Asia. From the standpoint of Allied unity, this was an unfortunate technical arrangement because it established India as a base point for clandestine operations in Burma, Thailand, Malaya, and Indochina. OSS men flew to Calcutta or New Delhi to begin their tours of duty in the Far East only to be "culture-shocked" by ugly manifestations of British imperialism. The OSS representative to the Anglo-American South East Asia Command wrote his wife: "Working with our Cousins has made me cynical about ideals—if we really believe our own propaganda, we would have to declare war on the British, for they have set themselves up as the master-race in India. British rule in India is fascism, there is no dodging that."

At least on the colonial issue, the OSS was in full accord with State Department officers in the Far East, and Donovan's organization became the "faithful secular arm" of the diplomats' "anti-colonialist fundamentalism." Long before the Japanese surrender, OSS planners had suggested that "American cooperation with patriotic, subversive revolutionary groups of southeastern Asia would appreciably increase our offensive power against Japan." When the task of American representation in southern Asia in the immediate postwar period later fell to OSS, Ho Chi Minh and other anticolonial crusaders received their first spiritual impetus from the unauthorized American diplomats of Donovan's band.

In early 1941, before the formation of COI, Ian Fleming, the future creator of "James Bond," then a ranking officer in British Naval Intelligence, suggested to Donovan that he should select as intelligence officers men who possessed the qualities of "absolute discretion, sobriety, devotion to duty, languages, and wide experience." Their age, Fleming added, should be "about 40 to 50." Donovan declined Fleming's advice. Instead, he promised Franklin Roosevelt an international secret service staffed by young officers who were "calculatingly reckless" with "disciplined daring" and "trained for aggressive action." In Rome, Peking, Bangkok, Paris, and Algiers, those were the operatives of OSS.

CHAPTER SEVEN

The Spies Who Stole a Train

William Pittenger

During America's great Civil War in 1862, a military clash took place that was so exciting, so dramatic and action-packed, that over a hundred years later Hollywood would turn the event into a major feature film. The courage of the event's Union heroes was so profound that a grateful nation had to come up with some new and distinct way to honor such bravery: The Medal of Honor was created. One of the first recipients was William Pittenger, who eventually became Rev. William Pittenger and penned the book Capturing a Locomotive, *the detailed account of how a band of Union soldiers, led by civilians J.J. Andrews and William Campbell, penetrated the Confederate rail complex, captured a train, and raced it toward glory. A furious chase resulted in the capture of the raiders. The citation includes this description of Pittenger:*

"One of the 19 of 22 men who penetrated nearly 200 miles south into enemy territory and captured a railroad train at Big Shanty, Georgia, in an attempt to destroy the bridges and track between Chattanooga and Atlanta."

Tried as spies, Andrews and seven of the Union soldiers were hanged. The soldiers were later awarded the Medal of Honor posthumously (as a civilian Andrews did not qualify). Some of the surviving soldiers were honored with the Medal by Secretary of War Edwin Stanton. Some had escaped the Confederate prisons; others, including Pittenger, had been freed in prisoner-of-war exchanges. The movie was The Great Locomotive Chase, *released by Walt Disney Studios in 1956.*

(Editor's note: In the first part of this excerpt, Pittenger describes meeting Andrews and hearing the details of the audacious raid he and fellow members of the Union Army had volunteered to undertake.)

We formed a close circle around Mr. Andrews while he revealed to us his daring plans. In a voice as soft and low as a woman's, but tremulous with suppressed enthusiasm, he painted the greatness of the project we were to attempt, the sublimity of rushing through a hostile country at the full speed of steam, leaving flaming bridges and raging but powerless foes behind. But he did not disguise the dangers to be encountered.

"Soldiers," he said, "if you are detected while engaged in this business, the great probability is that you will be put to death,—hung as spies, or massacred by a mob. I want you to clearly understand this, and if you are not willing to take the risk, return to camp, and keep perfectly quiet about it."

A murmur all around the circle conveyed the assurance that we would follow him to the last extremity. "Our plan," he continued, "is simply this: you are to travel on foot, or by any conveyance you can hire, either to Chattanooga or some station not far from that point on the Memphis and Charleston Railroad; then you can take passage on the cars down to Marietta; that will be our next place of assembling, and not Atlanta. You must be there by Thursday evening, ready to take passage on the cars northward again by Friday morning. I will be there as soon as you, and tell you what more is to be done." One of the soldiers asked, "If any of us are suspected, and find we can't get away, what would you advise us to do?"

"Enlist without hesitation in the rebel army," was the response. "You are fully authorized to do that, and no one of this party will be accused of desertion, even if captured among the rebels. I would be sorry to lose any one of you, but it will be far better that you should serve awhile with the enemy than to acknowledge who you are, and thus risk the disclosure of the enterprise."

"But is it likely that we could get the chance thus to enlist?" it was further asked.

"Most certainly," said Andrews. "They are taking all the prisoners out of the jails and enlisting them. They are picking up men who have run away from the conscription wherever they can find them, and serving them in the same manner. If you tell your story and stick to it, even if they are not satisfied that you are telling the truth, they will put you into the service. You can stay until some dark night on picket. But I hope you will escape all trouble, and all meet me at Marietta safely. Break this party up into squads of three or four, and don't recognize each other on the way. I will ride along the same country you are travelling, and give you any help or direction in my power. But you must not recognize me unless sure that we are not observed."

There was but one subject on which I cared to ask any questions, and that related to a distant contingency. I was well informed as to the first part of the intended enterprise.

"Suppose we succeed in capturing the train," I said, "and in burning the bridges, are we then to leave the train, and try to steal back to our lines in the same way we are now going South?"

"By no means," replied Mr. Andrews. "We will run the train right through Chattanooga, and westward until we meet Mitchel, who by that time will be coming eastward on the road from Memphis. If we should not quite reach him, we will get so close that we can dash through in a body."

This was satisfactory as far as it went, but there was still another contingency. More than anything else I dreaded being left alone in an unknown country.

"If we fail to run the captured train through Chattanooga, will we then disperse or stick together?"

"After we meet at Marietta, we will keep together, and, if necessary, cut our way back to our own lines. Form your squads now, and I will give out the money."

Swiftly we selected our companions. There was little time for choice. Most of the men were strangers. The darkness was intense, and the thunder-peals almost overhead. In a moment we formed six or seven little groups. My former comrade, Ross, stood with another man or two beside Andrews. Two men from Captain Mitchel's company and one from the next company to that in the regimental line stood by my side. Andrews went from group to group, giving out the money freely, and answering questions that were still asked. When this was accomplished, he addressed himself once more to the whole number, and we crowded around to listen to his parting words. They gave us the fullest insight into the whole plan we had yet received.

[Editor's note: Now Pettinger's text, excerpted from the book, shifts to his description of what happened on the fateful day of "The Great Locomotive Chase."]

War has a secret as well as a public story. Marches and battles are open to the popular gaze; but enterprises of another class are in their very nature secret, and these are scarcely less important and often much more interesting than the former. The work of spies and scouts, the enterprises that reach beyond the lines of an army for the purpose of surprise, the councils of officers, the intrigues by means of which great results often flow from apparently insignificant causes, and all the experiences of hospitals and prisons—these usually fill but a small place on the historian's page, though they are often of romantic interest, and not infrequently decide the course and fate of armies.

The enterprise described in these pages possesses all the unity of a drama, from the first plunge of the actors into the heart of the enemy's country, through all their adventures and changing fortunes, until the few survivors stood once more under the old flag! No single story of the war combines so many of the hidden, underground elements of the contest against rebellion as this. Disguise and secrecy, the perils of a forlorn hope, the exultation of almost miraculous success, the sufferings of prisoners, and the gloom of despair are all mingled in a varied and instructive war-picture.

In telling the story all fictitious embellishments have been rejected. No pains have been spared to ascertain the exact truth, and the reader will find names, dates, and localities so fully given that it will be easy to verify the prominent features of the account. In narrating those events which fell under his own eye, the writer has waived all scruples of delicacy, and used the first personal pronoun. This is far more simple and direct, while an opposite course would have savored of affectation.

This is not a revision or new edition of the little volume published by the present writer during the rebellion. "Daring and Suffering," like a number of similar sketches published in newspapers, maga-zines, and pamphlets, was a hasty narrative of personal adventure, and made no pretense of completeness. Capturing a Locomotive *is*

broader and more historic; a large amount of valuable material is now
employed for the first time; and the story is approached in an entirely
different manner. No paragraph of the old book is copied into the new.
—Woodbury, New Jersey, January 1882

The greater number of us arranged to pass the night at a small hotel
adjoining the Marietta depot. Before retiring we left orders with the hotel
clerk to rouse us in time for the northward-bound train, due not long
after daylight. Notwithstanding our novel situation, I never slept more
soundly. Good health, extreme fatigue, and the feeling that the die was
now cast and further thought useless, made me sink into slumber almost
as soon as I touched the bed. Others equally brave and determined were
affected in a different way. Alfred Wilson says:

No man knows what a day may bring forth, and the very uncer-
tainty of what that day's sun would bring forth in our particular cases
was the reason that some of us, myself at least of the number, did not
sleep very much. Our doom might be fixed before the setting of another
sun. We might be hanging to the limbs of some of the trees along the
railroad, with an enraged populace jeering and shouting vengeance
because we had no more lives to give up; or we might leave a trail of
fire and destruction behind us, and come triumphantly rolling into
Chattanooga and Huntsville, within the Federal lines, to receive the
welcome plaudits of comrades left behind, and the thanks of our gen-
eral, and the praises of a grateful people. Such thoughts as these passed
in swift review, and were not calculated to make one sleep soundly.

As the hotel was much crowded, we obtained a few rooms in close
proximity, and crowded them to their utmost capacity. Andrews noted our
rooms before retiring, that he might, if necessary, seek any one of us out
for consultation before we rose. Porter and Hawkins were unfortunately
overlooked; they had arrived on an earlier train and obtained lodging at
some distance from the depot. The clerk failed to have them called in time
for the morning train, as they had ordered, and, greatly to their regret and
chagrin, they were left behind. This was a serious loss, as they were both

cool, brave men, and Hawkins was the most experienced railway engineer of our company. W. F. Brown, who took his place in this work, was, however, fully competent, though possibly somewhat less cautious.

Long before the train was due, Andrews, who had slept little, if at all, that night, glided from room to room silently as a ghost, the doors being purposely left unfastened, and aroused the slumberers. It seemed to some of us scarcely a moment from the time of retiring until he came thus to the bedside of each sleeper in turn, and cautiously wakening him, asked his name, to prevent the possibility of mistake, and then told each one exactly the part he was expected to take in the enterprise of the day. There was hasty dressing, and afterwards an informal meeting held in Andrews's room, at which nearly one-half of the whole number were present, and plans were more fully discussed.

Then Marion A. Ross, one of the most determined of the whole number, took the bold step of advising and even urging the abandonment, for the present, of the whole enterprise. He reasoned with great force that under present circumstances, with the Rebel vigilance fully aroused by Mitchel's rapid advance, with guards stationed around the train we were to capture, as we had learned would be the case at Big Shanty, and with the road itself obstructed by numerous trains, the enterprise was sure to fail, and would cost the life of every man engaged in it. Andrews very gently answered his arguments and strove to show that the objections urged really weighed in favor of the original plan. No such attempt as we purposed had ever been made, and consequently would not be guarded against; the presence of a line of sentinels and of so many troops at Big Shanty would only tend to relax vigilance still further; and the great amount of business done on the road, with the running of many unscheduled trains, would screen us from too close inquiry when we ran our train ahead of time.

This reasoning was not altogether satisfactory, and some of the others joined Ross in a respectful but firm protest against persisting in such a hopeless undertaking. But Andrews, speaking very low, as was his wont when thoroughly in earnest, declared that he had once before postponed the attempt, and returned to camp disgraced. "Now," he continued, "I will accomplish my purpose or leave my bones to bleach in Dixie. But I do not wish to control any one against his own judgment. If any of you think it too hazardous, you are perfectly at liberty to take the train in the opposite direction and work your way back to camp as you can."

This inflexible determination closed the discussion, and as no man was willing to desert his leader, we all assured him of our willingness to obey his orders to the death. I had taken no part in the discussion, as I was not in possession of sufficient facts to judge of the chance of success, and I wished the responsibility to rest upon the leader, where it properly belonged.

The train was now nearly due, and we proceeded to the station for the purchase of tickets. By the time they had been procured—not all for one place, as we wished to lessen the risk of suspicion—the train swept up to the platform. Hastily glancing at it in the early morning light, and seeing only that it was very long and apparently well filled, the twenty adventurers entered by different doors, but finally took their places in one car.

From Marietta to Big Shanty the railroad sweeps in a long bend of eight miles around the foot of Kennesaw Mountain, which lies directly between the two stations. This elevation is now scarred all over with Rebel entrenchments, and was the scene of one of the severest contests of the war. This, however, as well as the whole of the three months' struggle from Chattanooga to Atlanta, came a year and a half later. At this time the nearest Federal soldiers were more than two hundred miles away. When the train moved on and the conductor came to take our tickets, we observed him carefully, as we knew not how closely his fate and ours might be linked together in the approaching struggle. The most vivid anticipation fell far short of the reality. Upon the qualities of that one man our success or failure hinged. He was quite young—not more than twenty-three or -four—and looked like a man of resolution and energy. We noticed that he was also scrutinizing us and the other passengers very closely, and naturally feared that he had in some manner been put on his guard. In fact, as we learned long afterwards, he had been warned that some of the new conscripts who were reluctant to fight for the Confederacy were contemplating an escape, and might try to get a ride on the cars. His orders were to watch for all such and arrest them at once. But he did not think that any of the men who got on at Marietta looked in the least like conscripts or deserters.

The train ran slowly, stopping at several intervening points, and did not reach Big Shanty until it was fully daylight. This station had been selected for the seizure, because the train breakfasted there, and it was probable that many of the employees and passengers would leave it for their meal, thus diminishing the opposition we might expect. Another most important reason for the selection was the absence of any telegraph office. But, on the other hand, Camp McDonald had been lately located here, and a large body of soldiers—some accounts said as many as ten thousand men—were already assembled. Their camp included the station within the guard-line. When Andrews and the first party had been at Atlanta, three weeks earlier, few troops had yet arrived at this point. The capture of a train in the midst of a camp of the enemy was not a part of the original plan, but subsequently became necessary. It was certainly a great additional element of danger, but it was not now possible to substitute any other point.

The decisive hour had arrived. It is scarcely boastful to say that the annals of history record few enterprises more bold and novel than that witnessed by the rising sun of Saturday morning, April 12, 1862. Here was a train, with several hundred passengers, with a full complement of hands, lying inside a line of sentinels, who were distinctly seen pacing back and forth in close proximity, to be seized by a mere score of men, and to be carried away before the track could be obstructed, or the intruding engineer shot down at his post. Only the most careful calculation and prompt execution, concentrating the power of the whole band into a single lightning-like stroke, could afford the slightest prospect of success.

In the bedroom conference every action was predetermined with the nicest accuracy. Our engineer and his assistant knew the signal at which to start; the brakesmen had their work assigned; the man who was to uncouple the cars knew just the place at which to make the separation; the remainder of the number constituted a guard, in two divisions, who were to stand with ready revolvers abreast of the cars to be seized, and shoot down without hesitation anyone who attempted to interfere with the work. Andrews was to command the whole, and do any part of the work not otherwise provided for. Should there be any unexpected hindrance, we were to fight until we either overcame all opposition and

THE SPIES WHO STOLE A TRAIN

captured the train or perished in a body. If we failed to carry off our prize we were inevitably lost; if any man failed to be on board when the signal was given, his fate also was sealed. A delay of thirty seconds after our designs became clearly known would have resulted in the slaughter of the whole party.

When our train rolled up to the platform, the usual announcement was shouted: "Big Shanty; twenty minutes for breakfast!" Most fortunately for us, the conductor, engineer, firemen, and train-hands generally, with many of the passengers, poured out, and hurried to the long, low eating-room which gave its name to the station. The engine was utterly unguarded. This uncommon carelessness was the result of perfect security, and greatly favored our design. Yet it was a thrilling moment! Victory or death hung on the next minute! There was no chance for drawing back, and I do not think any of us had the disposition. A little while before, a sense of shrinking came over the writer like that preceding a plunge into ice-water; but with the next breath it passed away, and left me as calm and quiet as if no enemy had been within a hundred miles. Still, for a moment, we kept our seats. Andrews went forward to examine the track and see if there was any hindrance to a rapid rush ahead. Almost immediately he returned, and said, very quietly, "All right, boys; let us go now." There was nothing in this to attract special observation; but whether it did or not was now a matter of indifference. The time of concealment was past.

We rose, left the cars, and walked briskly to the head of the train. With the precision of machinery, every man took his appointed place. Three cars back from the tender the coupling-pin was drawn out, as the load of passenger-cars would only have been an encumbrance. Wilson W. Brown, who acted as engineer, William Knight as assistant, Alfred Wilson as fireman, together with Andrews, mounted the engine, Knight grasping the lever, and waiting the word for starting. The appointed brakesmen threw themselves flat on the top of the cars. At a signal from Andrews, the remainder of the band, who had kept watch, climbed with surprising quickness into a boxcar which stood open. All was well! Knight, at Andrews's orders, jerked open the steam-valve, and we were off! Before the camp-guards or the bystanders could do more than turn a curious eye upon our proceedings, the train was under way, and we were safe from interruption.

The writer was stationed in the boxcar, and as soon as all were in, we pulled the door shut to guard against any stray musket-balls. For a moment of most intense suspense after we were thus shut in, all was still. In that moment a thousand conflicting thoughts swept through our minds. Then came a pull, a jar, a clang, and we were flying away on our perilous journey. Those who were on the engine caught a glimpse of the excited crowd, soldiers and citizens, swarming and running about in the wildest confusion. It has been said that a number of shots were fired after us, but those in the boxcar knew nothing of it, and it is certain that no one was injured. A widely circulated picture represented us as waving our hats and shouting in triumph. Nothing so melodramatic took place. The moment was too deep and earnest, and we had too many perils still to encounter for any such childish demonstration.

Yet it was a grand triumph, and having nothing of a more practical character for the moment to do, I realized it to the fullest extent. There are times in life when whole years of enjoyment are condensed into a single experience. It was so with me then. I could comprehend the emotion of Columbus when he first beheld through the dim dawn the long-dreamed-of shores of America, or the less innocent but no less fervent joy of Cortez when he planted the Cross of Spain on the halls of Montezuma. My breast throbbed fast with emotions of joy and gladness that words labor in vain to express. A sense of ethereal lightness ran through my veins, and I seemed [to be] ascending higher, higher, with each pulsation of the engine. Remember, I was but twenty-two then, full of hope and ambition. Not a dream of failure shadowed my rapture. We had always been told that the greatest difficulty was to reach and take possession of the engine, after which success was certain. But for unforeseen contingencies it would have been.

Away we rushed, scouring past field and village and woodland. At each leap of the engine our hearts rose higher, and we talked merrily of the welcome that would greet us when we dashed into Huntsville a few hours later, our enterprise done, and the brightest laurels of the war eclipsed!

We found the railroad, however, to be of the roughest and most difficult character. The grades were very heavy and the curves numerous and sharp. We seemed to be running toward every point of the compass. The deep valleys and steep hills of this part of the country had rendered the building of the road difficult and costly. There were numerous high embankments where an accident would be of deadly character. The track was also uneven and in generally bad condition, for the war had rendered railroad iron scarce and high-priced, besides diverting all attention and resources into other channels. This unfavorable character of the road very greatly increased the difficulty experienced by an engineer unfamiliar with the route in making rapid time, or in avoiding the varied difficulties incident to our progress. But we trusted implicitly that the farsighted plans of Andrews, the skill of our engineers, and our own willing efforts would overcome all hindrances.

Our first run was short. There was a sudden checking of speed and a halt. When those of us who were in the boxcar pushed open our door and asked the reason for stopping so soon, we were told that the fire was low and the steam exhausted. This was startling intelligence, and caused a moment of consternation. If our "General"—the name of the locomotive we had captured—failed us at the beginning of the race, we too well knew what the end would be. For hundreds of miles on every side of us were desperate and daring foes. A hundred times our number on horse and on foot could be gathered against us in a few hours. The most timid bird pursued by hounds feels safe, for its wings can bear it above their jaws. But if those wings should be broken! This engine gave us wings; but if it should be disabled, no valor of ours could beat back the hosts about us, no skill elude their rage.

But we found a less threatening explanation of our premature halt. The schedule time of our train was very slow—only about sixteen miles an hour—and the fires had been allowed to run down because of the expected stop of twenty minutes for breakfast at Big Shanty—a stop that we had reduced to less than two minutes. Then the valve being thrown wide open, the little steam in the boiler was soon exhausted. But this difficulty was of short duration. A rest of three minutes, with plenty of wood thrown into the furnace, wrought a change, and we again glided rapidly forward.

But when viewed soberly, and in the light of all the facts since developed, what were the chances of success and escape possessed by the flying party? Was the whole attempt, as has been frequently asserted, rash and foolhardy? Or had it that character of practicability which is ever the stamp of true genius? Historical accuracy, as well as justice to the memory of a brave but unfortunate man, compels me to pronounce the scheme almost faultless. In this estimate I have the full concurrence of all who were engaged on the opposite side. It is hard to see how the plan could have been improved without allowing its projector to have had a knowledge of the precise condition of the enemy such as no commander at the beginning of an important enterprise ever has. No one of the plans by which Generals Grant and Sherman finally overthrew the Rebellion presented a clearer prospect of success.

These are the elements of the problem upon which Andrews based his hopes. Big Shanty is twenty-eight miles north of Atlanta and thirty-two south of Kingston. Short of these places he was convinced that no engine could be obtained for pursuit. He could obstruct the road so that no train would reach Big Shanty for hours. Pinch-bars and other instruments for lifting track might be found on the captured engine, or obtained from some station or working-party. His force of twenty men was counted ample to overcome resistance at any switch or passing train. One irregular train only was expected to be on the road, and that would soon be met—certainly at Kingston or before—after which it would be safe to run at the highest speed to the first bridge, burn it, and pass on to the next, which, with all other large bridges, could be served in the same manner. Each bridge burnt would be an insuperable barrier to pursuit by an engine beyond that point. Thus, every part of the scheme was fair and promising. Only those critics who are wise after the event can pronounce the attempt rash and hopeless. The destruction of the telegraph would also be necessary; but this was not difficult. It seemed as if every contingency was provided for, and then there was the additional fighting power of twenty chosen men to guard against any possible emergency. We were now embarked on this most perilous but hopeful voyage. Coolness, precision of work, and calm effort could scarcely fail to sever the chief military communications of the enemy before the setting of the sun, and convince him that no enterprise was too audacious for the Union arms.

After the fire had been made to burn briskly Andrews jumped off the engine, ran back to the boxcar, about the door of which we were standing, and clasped our hands in an ecstasy of congratulation. He declared that all our really hard work was done and that our difficulties were nearly passed; that we had the enemy at such a disadvantage that he could not harm us; and exhibited every sign of joy. Said he, "Only one train to meet, and then we will put our engine to full speed, burn the bridges that I have marked out, dash through Chattanooga, and on to Mitchel at Huntsville. We've got the upper hand of the Rebels now, and they can't help themselves!" How glad we all were! When, three years later, the capture of Richmond set all the bells of the North ringing out peals of triumph, the sensation of joy was more diffused but less intense than we then experienced. Almost everything mankind values seemed within our grasp. Oh, if we had met but one unscheduled train!

This reference of Andrews to one train which he expected to meet before we began to burn bridges has been quoted in many public sketches, and has led to some misapprehension. He did expect to meet three trains before reaching Chattanooga; but two of these were regular trains, and being also farther up the road, were not supposed to present any serious difficulty. Their position at any given time could be definitely ascertained, and we could avoid collision with them, no matter how far we ran ahead of time. But so long as there were any irregular trains on the road before us, our only safety was in keeping the regular time of the captured train. This was, unfortunately, very slow; but if we exceeded it we lost the right-of-way, and were liable to a collision at any moment.

This risk was greatly increased by our inability to send ahead telegraphic notifications of our position. The order of southward-bound trains, according to the information we then had, was as follows: First, a way-freight, which was very uncertain as to time, but which we expected to meet early in the morning, and felt sure that it would be at Kingston or south of that point. This was the only real hindrance according to our program, and it was to this train that Andrews referred. Behind this were the regular freight train, and still farther north, the regular passenger train.

As a matter of fact, we did meet these trains at Adairsville and Calhoun, the latter being somewhat behind time; but we might have met them farther north had it not been for unforeseen hindrances. There is considerable discrepancy in the many published accounts of the following chase, which the writer has not in every case been able to perfectly reconcile. In the intense excitement and novel situations involved men were not likely to observe or remember every event accurately. But no pains have been spared to combine fullness and completeness in the following account. Using the best of my own recollections, consulting my comrades, reading carefully all published accounts, and especially going over the whole route years after, with Fuller and Murphy, two of the pursuing party, who kindly gave me all the information in their power, it is hoped that substantial accuracy has been obtained. Some of the incidents of the chase, such as the number of times the track was torn up, and whether we were fired upon by pursuing soldiers, allow some room for a conflict of memory. But the variations are not material. Side by side with the road ran the telegraph-wires, which were able, by the flashing of a single lightning message ahead, to arrest our progress and dissipate our fondest hopes. There was no telegraph station where we had captured the train, but we knew not how soon our enemies might reach one, or whether they might not have a portable battery at command. Therefore we ran but a short distance, after replenishing the furnace, before again stopping to cut the wire.

John Scott, an active young man of the Twenty-first Ohio, scrambled up the pole with the agility of a cat, and tried to break the wire by swinging upon it; but failing in this, he knocked off the insulating box at the top of the pole and swung with it down to the ground. Fortunately, a small saw was found on the engine, with which the wire was severed in two places, and the included portion, many yards in length, was taken away with us, in order that the ends might not be readily joined. While one or two of the party were thus engaged, others worked with equal diligence in taking up a rail from the track. No good track-raising instruments had been found on the train, and we had not yet procured them from any other source. A smooth iron bar, about four feet long, was the only instrument yet found, and with this some of the spikes were slowly and painfully battered out. After a few had thus been extracted, a lever was got under the rail and the remainder were pried loose. This occupied much more time than cutting the wire, and it required no prophet to foretell that if we did not procure better tools, rail-lifting would have to be used very sparingly in our program. In the present instance, however, the loss of time was no misfortune, as we were ahead of the schedule time, which we still felt bound to observe.

After another rapid but brief run, we paused long enough to chop down a telegraph-pole, cut the wire again, and place the pole, with many other obstructions, on the track. We did not here try to lift a rail; indeed, we had little serious fear of any pursuit at this time, and merely threw on these obstructions because of having spare time to employ. We thus continued—running a little ahead of time, then stopping to obstruct the track and cut the wire—until Cass Station was reached, where we took on a good supply of wood and water. At this place we also obtained a complete time schedule of the road. Andrews told the tank-tender that we were running a powder-train through to the army of General Beauregard at Corinth, which was almost out of ammunition, and that the greatest haste was necessary. He further claimed to be a Confederate officer of high rank, and said that he had impressed this train for the purpose in hand, and that Fuller, with the regular passenger train, would be along shortly. The whole story was none too plausible, as General Mitchel was now interposed between our present position and Beauregard, and we would never have been able to get a train to the army of the latter on this route; but the tender was not critical and gave us his schedule, adding that he would willingly send his shirt to Beauregard if that general needed it. When this man was afterwards asked if he did not suspect the character of the enemy he thus aided, he answered that he would as soon have suspected the President of the Confederacy himself as one who talked so coolly and confidently as Andrews did!

Keeping exactly on regular time, we proceeded without any striking adventures until Kingston was reached. This place—thirty-two miles from Big Shanty—we regarded as marking the first stage of our journey. Two hours had elapsed since the capture of the train, and hitherto we had been fairly prosperous. No track-lifting instruments had yet been obtained, notwithstanding inquiries for them at several stations. We had secured no inflammable materials for more readily firing the bridges, and the road was not yet clear before us. But, on the other hand, no serious hindrance had yet occurred, and we believed ourselves far ahead of any possible pursuit.

But at Kingston we had some grounds for apprehending difficulty. This little town is at the junction with the road to Rome, Georgia. Cars and engines were standing on the side track. Here we fully expected to meet our first train, and it would be necessary for us to get the switches properly adjusted before we could pass it to go on our way. When we drew up at the station there was handed to Andrews our first and last communication from the management of the road, in the shape of a telegram, ordering Fuller's train—now ours—to wait at Kingston for the local freight, which was considerably behind time. The order was not very welcome, but we drew out on the side track, and watched eagerly for the train. Many persons gathered around Andrews, who here, as always, personated the conductor of our train, and showered upon him many curious and somewhat suspicious questions. Ours was an irregular train, but the engine was recognized as Fuller's. The best answers possible were given. A red flag had been placed on our engine, and the announcement was made that Fuller, with another engine, was but a short way behind. The powder story was emphasized, and every means employed to avoid suspicion. Andrews only, and the usual complement of train-hands, were visible, the remainder of the party being tightly shut up in the car, which was designated as containing Beauregard's ammunition. The striking personal appearance of Andrews greatly aided him in carrying through his deception, which was never more difficult than at this station. His commanding presence, and firm but graceful address, marked him as a Southern gentleman—a member of the class from which a great proportion of the Rebel officers were drawn. His declarations and orders were therefore received with the greater respect on this account. But all these resources were here strained to the utmost.

At length the anxiously expected local freight train arrived, and took its place on another side track. We were about to start on our way, with the glad consciousness that our greatest obstacle was safely passed, when a red flag was noticed on the hindmost freight-car. This elicited immediate inquiry, and we were informed that another very long freight train was just behind, and that we would be obliged to wait its arrival also. This was most unfortunate, as we had been already detained at Kingston much longer than was pleasant.

There were many disagreeable elements in the situation. A crowd of persons was rapidly assembling. The train from Rome was also nearly due, and though it only came to the station and returned on its own branch, yet it was not agreeable to notice the constant increase of force that our enemies were gaining. If any word from the southward arrived, or if our true character was revealed in any other way, the peril would be imminent. But we trusted that this second delay would be brief. Slowly the minutes passed by. To us, who were shut up in the boxcar, it appeared as if they would never be gone. Our soldier comrades on the outside kept in the background as much as possible, remaining at their posts on the engine and the cars, while Andrews occupied attention by complaining of the delay, and declaring that the road ought to be kept clear of freight trains when so much was needed for the transportation of army supplies, and when the fate of the whole army of the West might depend upon the celerity with which it received its ammunition.

There was plausibility enough in his words to lull suspicion in all minds except that of the old switch-tender of the place, who grumbled out his conviction "that something was wrong with that stylish-looking fellow, who ordered everybody around as if the whole road belonged to him." But no one paid any attention to this man's complaints, and not many minutes after a distant whistle sounded from the northward, and we felt that the crisis had passed. As there was no more room on the side track, Andrews ordered the switch-tender to let this train run by on the main track. That worthy was still grumbling, but he reluctantly obeyed, and the long succession of cars soon glided by us.

This meant release from a suspense more intolerable than the most perilous action. To calmly wait where we could do nothing, while our destiny was being wrought out by forces operating in the darkness, was a terrible trial of nerve. But it was well borne. Brown, Knight, and Wilson, who were exposed to view, exhibited no more impatience than was to be expected of men in their assumed situation. Those of us in the boxcar talked in whispers only, and examined the priming of our pistols. We understood that we were waiting for a delayed train, and well knew the fearful possibilities of an obstructed track, with the speedy detection, and fight against overwhelming odds that would follow, if the train for which we waited did not arrive sooner than pursuers from Big Shanty. When we recognized the whistle of the coming train it was almost as welcome as the boom of Mitchel's cannon, which we expected to hear that evening after all our work was done. As it rumbled by us we fully expected an instant start, a swift run of a few miles, and then the hard work but pleasant excitement of bridge-burning. Alas!

Swift and frequent are the mutations of war. Success can never be assured to any enterprise in advance. The train for which we had waited with so much anxiety had no sooner stopped than we beheld on it an emblem more terrible than any comet that ever frightened a superstitious continent. Another red flag! Another train close behind! This was terrible, but what could be done?

With admirable presence of mind Andrews moderated his impatience, and asked the conductor of the newly arrived train the meaning of such an unusual obstruction of the road. His tone was commanding, and without reserve the conductor gave the full explanation. To Andrews it had a thrilling interest. The commander at Chattanooga had received information that the Yankee general Mitchel was coming by forced marches and in full strength against that town; therefore all the rolling-stock of the road had been ordered to Atlanta. This train was the first installment, but another and still longer section was behind. It was to start a few minutes after he did, and would probably not be more than ten or fifteen minutes behind.

In turn, the conductor asked Andrews who he was, and received the information that he was an agent of General Beauregard, and that he had impressed a train into military service in Atlanta, which he was running through with powder, of which Beauregard was in extreme need. Under such circumstances he greatly regretted this unfortunate detention. The conductor did not suspect the falsity of these pretenses, but told Andrews that it was very doubtful if he could get to Beauregard at Corinth by going through Chattanooga, as it was certain that Mitchel had captured Huntsville, directly on the line between them.

Andrews replied that this made no difference, as he had his orders, and should press on until they were countermanded, adding that Mitchel was probably only paying a flying visit to Huntsville, and would have to be gone soon, or find Beauregard upon him. Andrews also ordered the conductor to run far enough down the main track to allow the next train to draw in behind him, and for both trains there to wait the coming of Fuller with the regular mail. His orders were implicitly obeyed; and then to our party recommenced the awful trial of quiet waiting. One of the men outside was directed to give notice to those in the boxcar of the nature of the detention, and warn them to be ready for any emergency. Either Brown or Knight, I think, executed this commission. Leaning against our car, but without turning his eyes toward it, and speaking in a low voice, he said, "We are waiting for one of the trains the Rebels are running off from Mitchel. If we are detected before it comes, we will have to fight. Be ready." We were ready; and so intolerable is suspense that most of us would have felt as a welcome relief the command to throw open our door and spring into deadly conflict.

Slowly the leaden moments dragged themselves away. It seems scarcely creditable, but it is literally true, that for twenty-five minutes more we lay on that side track and waited—waited with minds absorbed, pulses leaping, and ears strained for the faintest sound which might give a hint as to our destiny. One precious hour had we wasted at Kingston— time enough to have burned every bridge between that place and Dalton! The whole margin of time on which we had allowed ourselves to count was two hours; now half of that was thrown away at one station, and nothing accomplished. We dared wait no longer. Andrews decided to rush ahead with the intention of meeting this extra train wherever it might be found, and forcing it to back before him to the next siding, where he could pass it. The resolution was in every way dangerous, but the danger would at least be of an active character. Just at this moment the long-expected whistle was heard, and soon the train came into plain view, bringing with it an almost interminable string of cars. The weight and length of its train had caused the long delay. Obedient to direction, it followed the first extra down the main track, and its locomotive was a long way removed from the depot when the last car cleared the upper end of the side track on which we lay. At length it had got far enough down, and it was possible for us to push on. Andrews instantly ordered the switch-tender to arrange the track so as to let us out.

But here a new difficulty presented itself. This man had been in an ill humor from the first, and was now fully convinced that something was wrong. Possibly the tone in which he was addressed irritated him still more. He therefore responded to Andrews's order by a surly refusal, and hung up the keys in the station-house. When we in the boxcar overheard his denial, we were sure that the time for fighting had come. There was no more reason for dreading the issue of a conflict at this station than at any other point, and we waited the signal with the confident expectation of victory.

But even a victory at that moment would have been most undesirable. We had no wish to shed blood unnecessarily. A telegraph office was at hand, and it was possible that before the wire could be cut a message might be flashed ahead. There were also engines in readiness for prompt pursuit, and while we might have overcome immediate opposition by the use of our firearms, our triumph would have been the signal for a close and terrible chase.

The daring coolness of Andrews removed all embarrassments. While men are hesitating and in doubt, boldness and promptness on the part of an opponent are almost sure to carry the day. Ceasing to address the switch-tender, Andrews walked hurriedly into the station, and with the truthful remark that he had no more time to waste, took down the key and began to unlock the switch. The tender cursed him terribly, and called for someone to arrest him. The crowd around also disliked the action, and began to hoot and yell; but before anyone had decided as to what ought to be done Andrews had unlocked and changed the switch, and waved his hand for the engineer to come on. It was an inexpressible relief when the cars moved forward and the sounds of strife died out. As soon as the locomotive passed to the main track, Andrews tossed the keys to the ruffled owner of them, saying, in his blandest manner, "Pardon me, sir, for being in such a hurry, but the Confederacy can't wait for every man's notions.

You'll find it is all right," and stepped on board his engine. The excitement gradually ceased, and no thought of pursuit was entertained until startling intelligence was received a few moments later from Big Shanty.

Before describing the terrible struggle above Kingston, it will be well to narrate the operations of the persons whose train had been so unceremoniously snatched from them at Big Shanty. From printed accounts published contemporaneously by several of those engaged in the pursuit, as well as from personal responses to inquiries made regarding the most material points, the writer is confident that he can tell the strange story without essential error. It is a striking commentary on the promptness of the seizure, that the bystanders generally reported that only eight men, instead of twenty, had been observed to mount the train.

William A. Fuller, conductor, Anthony Murphy, manager of the State railroad shops at Atlanta, and Jefferson Cain, engineer, stepped off their locomotive, leaving it unguarded save by the surrounding sentinels, and in perfect confidence took their seats at the breakfast-table at Big Shanty. But before they had tasted a morsel of food the quick ear of Murphy, who was seated with his back toward the window, caught the sound of escaping steam, and he exclaimed, "Fuller, who's moving your train?" Almost simultaneously the latter, who was somewhat of a ladies' man, and was bestowing polite attentions upon two or three fair passengers, saw the same movement, and sprang up, shouting, "Somebody's running off with our train!" No breakfast was eaten then. Everybody rushed through the door to the platform. The train was then fully under way, just sweeping out of sight around the first curve. With quick decision Fuller shouted to Murphy and Cain, "Come on!" and started at a full run after the flying train! This attempt to run down and catch a locomotive by a foot-race seemed so absurd that as the three, at the top of their speed, passed around the same curve, they were greeted with loud laughter and ironical cheers by the excited multitude. To all appearances it was a foolish and hopeless chase.

Yet, paradoxical as the statement may seem, this chase on foot was the wisest course possible for Fuller and his companions. What else could they do? Had they remained quietly in camp, with no show of zeal, they would have been reproached with negligence in not guarding their train more carefully, even if they were not accused with being in league with its captors. As they ran, Fuller explained the situation and his purposes to his companions. They had neither electric battery nor engine. Had they obtained horses, they would necessarily have followed the common road, instead of the railroad, and if they thought of that expedient at all, it would be as distasteful to railroad men as abandoning their ship to sailors, and they preferred leaving that course for others. It would have been wise for those who could think of nothing else to do to ride as mounted couriers to the stations ahead; but whether this was done or not I have never learned. Certainly it was not done so promptly as to influence the fortunes of the day.

But the truth is that Fuller and Murphy were at first completely deceived as to the nature of the event which had taken place. They had been warned to guard against the escape of conscript deserters from that very camp; and although they would never have suspected an attempt on the part of the conscripts to escape by capturing their engine, yet when it was seen to dash off, the thought of this warning was naturally uppermost. Even then Fuller conjectured that they would use his engine only to get a mile or two beyond the guard-line, and then abandon it. He was therefore anxious to follow closely in order to find the engine and return for his passengers at the earliest moment possible. Little did he anticipate the full magnitude of the work and the danger before him. That any Federal soldiers were within a hundred miles of Big Shanty never entered his mind or that of any other person.

For a mile or two the three footmen ran at the top of their speed, straining their eyes forward for any trace of the lost engine which they expected to see halted and abandoned at almost any point on the road. But they were soon partially undeceived as to the character of their enemies. About two miles from the place of starting they found the telegraph wire severed and a portion of it carried away. The fugitives were also reported as quietly oiling and inspecting their engine. No mere deserters would be likely to think of this. The two actions combined clearly indicated the intention of making a long run, but who the men were still remained a mystery. A few hundred yards from this place a party of workmen with a handcar was found, and these most welcome reinforcements were at once pressed into service.

Fuller's plans now became more definite and determined. He had a good handcar and abundance of willing muscle to work it. By desperate exertions, by running behind the car and pushing it up the steep grades, and then mounting and driving it furiously downhill and on the levels, it was possible to make seven or eight miles an hour; at the same time, Fuller knew that the captive engine, if held back to run on schedule time, as the reports of the workmen indicated, would make but sixteen miles per hour. Fuller bent all his thoughts and energies toward Kingston, thirty miles distant. He had been informed of the extra trains to be met at that point, and was justified in supposing that the adventurers would be greatly perplexed and hindered by them, even if they were not totally stopped. Had the seizure taken place on the preceding day, as originally planned, he might well have despaired, for then the road would have been clear. Yet he had one other resource, as will appear in due time, of which his enemies knew nothing.

Fuller did not pause to consider how he should defeat the fugitives when he had overtaken them, and he might have paid dearly for this rashness. But he could rely on help at any station, and when he had obtained the means of conveyance, as he would be sure to do at Kingston, he could easily find an overwhelming force to take with him. This Saturday was appointed as a general muster of volunteers, State militia, and conscripts, and armed soldiers were abundant in every village. But Fuller's dominant thought was that his property—the property with which he had been entrusted—was wrested from his grasp, and it was his duty to recover it, at whatever personal hazard. That any serious harm was intended to the railroad itself he probably did not yet suspect.

Talking and wearying themselves with idle conjectures, but never ceasing to work, Fuller and his party pressed swiftly on. But suddenly there was a crash, a sense of falling, and when the shock allowed them to realize what had happened, they found themselves floundering in a ditch half filled with water, and their handcar embedded in the mud beside them! They had reached the place where the first rail had been torn from the track, and had suffered accordingly. But the bank was, fortunately for them, not very high at that spot, and a few bruises were all the damage they sustained. Their handcar, which was also uninjured, was lifted on the track and driven on again. This incident increased both their caution and their respect for the men before them.

Without further mishap they reached Etowah Station, on the northern bank of the river of the same name. Here was a large bridge, which the Andrews party might have burned without loss of time had they foreseen the long detention at Kingston; but its destruction was not a part of their plan, and it was suffered to stand. The mind of Fuller grew very anxious as he approached this station. What he should find there depended, in all probability, on his power to overtake the fugitives, whose intentions seemed more formidable with each report he received of their actions. Andrews had firmly believed that no engine for pursuit could be found south of Kingston; but Fuller had a different expectation. Extensive iron-furnaces were located on the Etowah River, about five miles above the station. These works were connected with the railroad by a private track, which was the property of Major Cooper, as well as the works themselves. Murphy knew that Major Cooper had also bought an engine called the "Yonah." It had been built in the shop over which Murphy presided, and was one of the best locomotives in the State. "But where," Fuller and Murphy asked themselves, "is this engine now?" If it was in view of the adventurers as they passed, they had doubtless destroyed it, run it off the track, or carried it away with them. They could not afford to neglect such an element in the terrible game they were playing. But if it was now at the upper end of the branch at the mines, as was most probable, it would take the pursuers five miles out of their way to go for it, and even then it might not be ready to start. This diversion could not be afforded. Fuller and Murphy had come nineteen miles, and had already consumed two hours and three-quarters. The adventurers were reported as passing each station on time, and if this continued they must have reached Kingston forty-five minutes before Fuller and his companions arrived at Etowah, thirteen miles behind them. One hour and a half more to Kingston—this was the very best that could be done with the handcar. It was clear that if the "Yonah" did not come to their assistance, they were as effectually out of the race as if on the other side of the ocean. Everything now hinged on the position of that one engine.

Here we may pause to note how all coincidences, we might almost say providences, seemed to work against the bridge-burning enterprise. We were at Kingston three-quarters of an hour before our pursuers reached Etowah, thirteen miles distant. If there had been no extra trains, or if they had been sharply on time, so that we could have passed the three with a delay not exceeding fifteen or twenty minutes, which ought to have been an abundant allowance, every bridge above Kingston would have been in ashes before sundown! Or if the delay had been as great as it actually was, even then, if the locomotive "Yonah" had occupied any position excepting one, the same result would have followed. But Fuller, Murphy, and Cain, with the several armed men they had picked up at the stations passed, could not repress shouts of exultation when they saw the old "Yonah" standing on the main track, already fired up, and headed toward Kingston. It had just arrived from the mines, and in a short time would have returned again. Thus a new element of tremendous importance, which had been ignored in all our calculations, was introduced into the contest.

The pursuers seized their inestimable prize, called for all the volunteers who could snatch guns at a moment's notice, and were soon swiftly but cautiously rushing with the power of steam toward Kingston. The speed of nearly a mile a minute was in refreshing contrast to the slow and laborious progress of the handcar, and they were naturally jubilant. But what lay before them at Kingston? The frequent obstructions of the track, the continued cutting of the telegraph, and especially the cool assumption of the leader of the adventurers in calling himself a Confederate officer of high rank in charge of an impressed powder train, all conspired to deepen their conviction that some desperate scheme was on foot. But they did not pause long to listen to reports. Their eyes and their thoughts were bent toward Kingston. Had the adventurers been stopped there, or had they surprised and destroyed the trains met? The pursuers could scarcely form a conjecture as to what was before them; but the speed with which they were flying past station after station would soon end their suspense. Even the number of men on the flying train was a matter of uncertainty. At the stations passed observers reported that only four or five were seen; but the track-layers and others who had observed them at work were confident of a much larger number—twenty-five or thirty at the least.

Besides, it was by no means sure that they had not confederates in large numbers to cooperate with them at the various stations along the road. Fuller knew about how many persons had entered the train at Marietta; but it was not sure that these were all. A hundred more might be scattered along the way, at various points, ready to join in whatever strange plan was now being worked out. No conjecture of this kind that could be formed was a particle more improbable than the startling events that had already taken place. The cool courage of these pursuers, who determined to press forward and do their own duty at whatever risk, cannot be too highly rated. If they arrived at Kingston in time to unmask the pretension of the mysterious "Confederate officer," there would doubtless be a desperate fight; but the pursuers could count on assistance there, and all along the line.

Fuller reached Kingston at least an hour earlier than would have been possible with the handcar, and a single glance showed that the adventurers were gone, and his hopes of arresting them at that point were ended. They were, however, barely out of sight, and all their start had been reduced to minutes. But here again the pursuit was checked. The foresight of Andrews had blockaded the road as much as possible with the trains which had so long hindered his own movements. Two large and heavy trains stood on the main road; one of the two side tracks was occupied by the third freight, and the other by the engine of the Rome branch. There was no ready means for the passage of the "Yonah." Some precious time was employed in giving and receiving information, in telling of the seizure at Big Shanty, and hearing of the deportment of Andrews and his men at Kingston.

Then a dispute arose as to the best means of continuing the pursuit, which threatened to disunite Fuller and Murphy. The latter wished to continue the chase with the "Yonah," which was a fine engine, with large wheels; but Fuller would not wait to get the freights out of the way, and, jumping on the Rome engine, he called on all who were willing to assist him to come on. A large, enthusiastic, and well-armed company instantly volunteered; the new engine, the "Shorter," pulled out, and Murphy had only time to save himself from the disgrace of being left behind by jumping on the hindmost car as it swept past. With all the time lost in making this transfer, and in mutual explanations, the pursuers left Kingston just twenty minutes behind the Federals.

What Fuller and his friends learned at Kingston left no doubt in their minds that some deliberate and far-reaching military movement was on foot. While its precise nature was yet concealed, the probability that the road itself, and possibly Confederate towns and stores, were to be destroyed, was freely conceded. All agreed that the one thing to be done was to follow their enemies closely, and thus compel them to turn and fight or abandon their enterprise. A large force—one or two hundred well-armed men—was taken on board, and instructions left that as soon as the track could be cleared, another armed train was to follow for the purpose of rendering any needed assistance.

CHAPTER EIGHT

Spy for the Continental Army

A. A. Hoehling

In 1777, the Army of our fledgling nation needed all the help it could get. And some of that help came from spies who wore petticoats and lavish dresses—women in support of the cause of George Washington. This excerpt from A. A. Hoehling's book Women Who Spied *shows how Lydia Darragh, a Philadelphia home-maker with two sons in Washington's service, managed to get critical information to Washington's forces at critical times, resulting in success on the battlefield.*

George Washington learned the value of women spies early in America's history. In fact, although there is no evidence that he was a student of Walsingham or of others who followed him, Washington gave serious heed to the daily gleanings from a considerable number of spies, largely amateur, who worked for the Continental Army.

Not all were successful. The most tragic example was Nathan Hale, the heroic Connecticut schoolteacher. His failure as a courier that September, 1776, led to his hanging. But he taught future generations how to die.

In December of the same year, John Honeyman, a butcher who lived on the road from Trenton to Princeton, was eminently more successful. While encouraging his neighbors to think he was in the pay of the British, or even a double agent, Honeyman carried the word to Washington at Valley Forge that the Hessian garrisons in his two neighboring towns were drunk and lethargic from too much Christmas season revelry. The result was dramatic victories, first at Trenton, next at Princeton.[1]

Although General Washington did not possess the reserves to hold either prize, the success was like an injection of adrenaline to morale after the recent loss of Long Island and forts along the Hudson Palisades, the last toehold on Manhattan Island, together with the defeat at White Plains.

Then in August and October, 1777, came the brilliant victories of Bennington and Saratoga respectively, climaxing the starting months of the third year of the Revolution. At the latter, General John Burgoyne surrendered an army of nearly 6,000 men with 42 cannon and full equipment to General Horatio Gates.

However, there was no time or even full occasion for rejoicing. In between these twin triumphs, Sir William Howe marched into Philadelphia and hung out his "at home" sign. The English commander actually liked the colonists. However, Philadelphia was where all that "trouble" started, and to George III, a ruler noted for neither foresight nor common sense, the image of the Union Jack flying before Independence Hall was a warming one.

Commencing his second winter amidst the winds and snowdrifts of the Valley Forge area, General Washington maintained surprising optimism about maintaining the offensive in the face of continuing privation and dissent in the ranks.

Even as the snowflakes slanted across the dead stubble of the Pennsylvania fields, the Commander-in-Chief was asking his generals if they would recommend a winter campaign, with Philadelphia its prize.

The Marquis de Lafayette counseled what seemed obvious: give the men "a good rest in winter quarters." General Nathaniel Greene suggested any operations at this time would be "very precarious." Major General John Sullivan and others contented themselves with lengthy analyses of relative strengths of the opposing forces, in men and equipment.

Estimates of the British forces in the Philadelphia theater ranged from 6,000 all the way up to 15,000. Actually, Howe's army was not markedly larger than Washington's—then mustering approximately 11,000 effectives.

Winter in 1777, even as in 1776, did not present an auspicious setting for any offensive. Bothering Washington, nonetheless, was the suspicion that his adversary would not be wholly adverse to moving troops and mounting an attack in snow and below-freezing temperatures. Lord Howe's troops were equipped with fine rifles and artillery, warm clothing from Yorkshire's best woolen mills, and their stomachs were always filled. The British should have been able to fight at any time.

General Washington therefore had to keep abreast of Howe's intentions. As a professional engineer, the canny leader of the Patriots held no brief for guesswork. He already possessed his own intelligence service—an ancestral "G-2." It was headed by Colonel Elias Boudinot, a distinguished patriot and statesman.

The network which he spun and then endeavored, as chief spider, to dominate, was at best loose, amateurish, and operated on a catch-as-catch-can basis of expediency. It comprised farmers, merchants, itinerant artisans, country girls selling produce, almost anyone who could enter enemy-held territory unobtrusively and return with tidbits of military information.

When Philadelphia fell after the disasters of Brandywine and Germantown in September, Boudinot set up listening posts on a wide semi-circle from Red Lyon, near Chester, Pennsylvania, thirteen miles south of Philadelphia, all along the western perimeter of the occupied city to Frankford, on the northeast. Boudinot, who himself explained only that he "managed the intelligence of the Army," usually met with his agents at the Rising Sun Tavern, two miles west of Frankford and six miles north of the center of Philadelphia. In turn, the tavern rendezvous was handy to Washington's headquarters at Whitemarsh, close to Norristown and twelve miles northwest of the city. It was slightly advanced eastward from his previous Valley Forge encampment.

Boudinot entrusted the Red Lyon intelligence to Major John Clark, Jr., an imaginative young officer whose daily diary entries commenced with the preface:

"Sent in a spy today . . ."

He wanted to obtain information on arrival of reinforcements, changes of bivouacs, assemblage of wagons and other heavy equipment, even the moving of a gun emplacement. All of these chips fitted into the mosaic of the enemy's intentions, so important in the deliberations of General Washington.

During the last days of November and the first few of December, it became obvious from Major Clark's reports that the British were "in motion" within their broad Philadelphia base. This did not necessarily mean that they were on the march. But it was obvious to Clark and to his superior, Boudinot, that troops were being equipped and provisioned for something quite more than drills or even maneuvers.

What was going to happen? And when?

George Washington was sufficiently concerned to order 1,200 Rhode Island troops and 1,000 more from Virginia, Maryland, and Pennsylvania into his foremost breastworks, facing Chestnut Hill. Now he could do no more than bide his time until he obtained a better idea of the direction and strength of the possible thrust.

He could not have expected that the clinching information would emanate from a Quaker household—that of the William Darraghs on 177 South Second Street, near Spruce, in Philadelphia. Known as the "Loxley House," the comfortably appointed structure was situated across from the more sumptuous residence of Captain John Cadwalader. This farsighted patriot had used the street for drilling his "silk stocking" company of Pennsylvania militia.

General Howe himself had headquartered for a time in the Cadwalader home. Although he had requisitioned Darragh's house as a spillover for his staff, he yielded to the entreaties of both William and his slight, inconspicuous-appearing wife, Lydia. The British commander agreed to use only the parlor as a "council chamber" for staff meetings.

Lydia would never have been mistaken for a spy. She was the antithesis of Delilah, in fact or fiction. Nature had not complicated her existence with feminine beauty. However, what she lacked in ostentation or sex appeal, she amply compensated for in loyalty and quiet daring, as an opportunist and improviser.

For some weeks, Lydia had been transmitting morsels of what was going on in the occupied city to her oldest son, Lieutenant Charles Darragh, in Washington's army, via her youngest, John, who was fourteen. She reasoned that the youth was as innocent-appearing a courier as an agent could desire.

The enemy's irresolution in not commandeering the Darragh home in the first place was next compounded by his underestimation of its mistress. During the afternoon of December 2 it became apparent that an unusually important conference was to be held in the parlor. An officer notified Lydia that the General had suggested the family retire early, "as they wished to use the room that night free from interruption."

It was a singularly naive request, in that it aroused the suspicions of Mrs. Darragh. The officer might as well have told her that the British were contemplating a surprise attack on the Continental Army.

Lydia obediently went to bed. But she could not sleep. As she would recall in a letter, "a presentiment of evil" weighed upon her spirits.

Finally, she could contain her curiosity no longer. She threw back the covers, quickly slipped a dressing gown over her shoulders and tiptoed, barefooted, out of her bedroom, into the hall and down the unlighted stairway, step by step. Every squeaking of the boards, it seemed, would betray her.

However, she gained the keyhole of the parlor door a few minutes before Lord Howe's officers completed their meeting. She was in time to overhear the conference's conclusion: the British would march out of Philadelphia by night, December 4, and let loose what they hoped would be a knockout punch at General Washington's "unprepared condition." She also heard a few of the figures pertaining to the strength of the attacking forces.

She hurried upstairs, and was in bed barely in time to hear a thump-thump up the stairs, then knocks on her door. She remained silent, wondering. Then, the knocks ceased. In her feeling of guilt, Lydia did not guess the obvious—that the British officer had come only to ask her to lock up, blow out the remaining candles, and douse any coals that glowed in the grate.

She waited until his receding footsteps faded along the short corridor, then down the stairs into silence. Lydia's fears were eased. But she could not sleep.

How, she kept asking herself, could she relay to George Washington the intentions of the British? She could not conceive of a logical pretext for sending her younger son, once more, through the lines. Besides, time was short. Lydia became convinced that she and she alone must bear the responsibility of passing into American lines. Once the question was resolved, her method seemed to her obvious.

She would take a sack to the Frankford mill, for flour. Five miles northeast of the city, it lay on the route to Whitemarsh and was not too much of a walk, even for a middle-aged little lady in wintertime.

Other women, widowed or alone while their husbands fought in the army, made this trip to the mill with regularity. Like them, Lydia possessed a British pass to leave the city limits. The occupation forces had to consider food an absolute necessity.

The Quaker wife did not confide in her husband—not necessarily that she may have distrusted him, but because she was a sufficiently canny disciple of Delilah's to be aware of the perils inherent in alerting too many people to any mission. Curiously, William Darragh's only surprise and concern were in her refusal to allow her maid to accompany her. Lydia was politely adamant. Her husband remonstrated in vain.

Sack in hand, that Wednesday, December 3, in her poke bonnet and plain, ankle-length gray dress which showed that she was a Quaker, Lydia Darragh walked at a brisk clip through the frozen streets and lanes of Philadelphia.

Sentries scarcely bothered to notice, much less challenge this inconspicuous figure.

Meanwhile, Washington's patrols realized that something was up. Major Clark started a messenger toward headquarters with the intelligence that the British might be preparing an offensive. But, if so, when and where? Or was this just the incessant maneuvering and changing of regiments which were so characteristic of a large European army?

Another valuable officer, Captain Allen McLane, who was leading his one hundred hard-riding cavalrymen up and down icy, rutted paths west of the city, in the vicinity of Chestnut Hill, tried to find some hint of "motion" in that sector. It was approximately three miles in advance of the Continental Army's right wing.

McLane operated with small units in unexpected places. On a small scale, he was perhaps pioneer of the surprise and blitz technique. Once, for example, accompanied by only two or three equally daring tough officers, he smashed into a formal reception in honor of Lord Howe himself. The swashbuckling cavalrymen shot up the chandeliers, killed the Hessian guard, then remounted their horses and were away almost before the British could comprehend what had happened. Even if the military toll were not great, the party, certainly, was ruined.

Lydia arrived in the early afternoon in Frankford—a sort of no-man's-land of the Revolution[2] lightly held by the patriots. The Queen's Rangers had attempted only the month before to raid the post and take prisoners but were repulsed with losses.

She did not loiter at the mill on Frankford Creek. She asked the miller to fill her sack, promising to be back shortly.

Lydia then walked westward along Nice Town Lane toward the Rising Sun Tavern. Shortly before reaching it, Lydia was at long last challenged. It turned out, by coincidence, that her challenger was a family acquaintance, Lieutenant Colonel Thomas Craig, of the Third Pennsylvania "Mounted," popular units in the Continental Army, not quite infantry, hardly cavalry.

Craig walked beside his friend, who cautiously at first explained she was merely trying to visit her son. Then, she confided in him what she had overheard. The officer listened with interest, then suggested that she must be weary. She was.

He left her in a nearby farmhouse, asking the owners to give her supper. Then he rode off, possibly to convey Lydia Darragh's tale to headquarters. Apparently Lydia herself was not wholly certain that he would do so. And if he did, would he relay the word in time?

Still unsatisfied, Lydia hurried through her light meal and then continued by foot on the now dark, increasingly cold road toward the Rising Sun Tavern, where she had the good fortune apparently to meet Colonel Boudinot in person.

He reported in his journals,[3] "after dinner a little poor looking insignificant old woman came in and solicited leave to go into the country to buy some flour. While we were asking some questions she walked up to me and put into my hands a dirty old needlework with various small pockets in it. Surprised at this, I told her to return, she should have an answer."

The Colonel opened up the needlework to find several small pockets sewed inside. From one he removed a piece of paper rolled "into the form of a pipe shank." On the paper was fairly legible writing which revealed that Howe was coming out of the city with 5,999 men, 13 pieces of cannon, baggage wagons and 11 boats on wagon wheels (a kind of pioneering amphibious vehicle).

When Boudinot compared this "with other information" in his possession, he decided it was correct. At once he rode to Whitemarsh and conveyed to Washington personally "the naked facts without comment or opinion," as they were secreted in the needlework.

After the General had "received it with much thoughtfulness," the Colonel presented his own theory: that Howe would cross the Delaware under the pretense of marching to New York, but instead recross the river above Bristol, just north of Philadelphia, and hit the Americans from the rear, which was vulnerable.

"Deep in thought," George Washington did not utter "a single observation." Not a little frustrated at his commander's sphinx-like attitude, Boudinot repeated, "earnestly," everything he had said.

Finally, in terse words, Washington said he did not think Howe was going to cross the river, that he was carrying along the boats only as a "deception." Instead, he was certain the enemy would take a "Bye Road" and attack his army's left wing, rather than the rear.

Boudinot was to admit that he thought "the Old Fox," as Washington was often dubbed with affection, was not in this judgment so foxy. He was to confide to his diary that the General was reasoning "under a manifest mistake."

A late dispatch from Major Clark arrived about this time, giving the alarm that the British were truly "in motion," moving out of Philadelphia with "a number of flat-bottomed boats and carriages and scantlings [pieces of cut timber presumably for road surfacing or bridge building] and are busy pressing horses and wagons. No persons permitted to come out. ...."

The dashing cavalry captain, Allen McLane, sent an even more urgent warning before midnight. His scouts cantering along the Skipjack Road, near Schuylkill River, had made out shielded lanterns approaching at a distance which hinted of an army's advance units. McLane predicted without qualification that "an attempt to surprise the American camp at Whitemarsh was about to be made."

At 3: 00 A.M., Thursday, December 4, Howe's patrols opened fire on the Continental's front lines, and from a by-road as Washington had predicted. For the remainder of the early morning hours, Howe's Redcoats dug into positions along a ridge beyond Chestnut Hill, facing principally the American right, rather than the left flank as the American commander had theorized. However, what mainly mattered: the Patriots were ready. The surprise had been total failure.

"Having now so respectable a force in the field," wrote Major Benjamin Tallmadge, of Long Island, commanding the Second Regiment, Light Dragoons, "and especially the Northern Army being flushed with recent victory and hoping that the other troops would vie with them in the contest, a battle was rather desired than avoided.

"After continuing several days in his first position, by daybreak on the 7th General Howe took a new position in front of our left wing, on the flank of which I was posted with a body of horse, together with [Colonel Daniel] Morgan's[4] Light Infantry and Riflemen. We came into contact with the British Light Infantry and Dragoons in which Major [Joseph] Morris of our infantry was killed [one of twenty-seven American casualties].

"I thought a general battle inevitable, but neither general thought it prudent to descend into the plain. After continuing in this position a few days, General Howe retired to Philadelphia for winter quarters to our great surprise."

Howe subsequently contented himself with a brief explanation: ". . . the enemy's camp being as strong on their center and left as upon the right, their seeming determination to hold this position; and unwilling to expose the troops longer to the weather in this inclement season, without tents or baggage of any kind . . . I returned on the 8th."

Lydia Darragh returned to the farmhouse of her benefactor near the Rising Sun Tavern, and doubtlessly waited there until the roads cleared of military traffic. When once more in the sanctuary of 177 South Second Street, she was paid a visit by a very puzzled British officer.

"I know," he conceded, alluding to the council meeting the night of December 2, "that you were asleep for I knocked at your chamber door three times before you heard me. I am entirely at a loss to imagine who gave General Washington information of our intended attack—unless the walls of the house could speak?

"When we arrived near Whitemarsh we found all their cannon mounted and the troops prepared to receive us. And we have marched back like a parcel of fools."

General Washington, in his report to Congress, mentioned merely, "in the course of last week from a variety of intelligence I had reason to expect that General Howe was preparing to give us a general action."

The Commander-in-Chief expressed, in an order to the army, his "warmest thanks to Colonel Morgan and the officers and men of his intrepid corps for their gallant behavior in the several skirmishes with the enemy yesterday. He hopes the most spirited conduct will distinguish the whole army and gain them a just title to the praise of their country and the glory due brave men."

Another senior American officer was somewhat more succinct in summing up Morgan's role: he "messed up" the British.

Washington made no mention of Lydia Darragh. For that matter, in all of his journals, reports, and orders credit or even passing references to women are conspicuously absent. Conceivably, he shared a prevalent prejudice against the opposite sex's being identified with duties other than childbearing or housekeeping. Spying? It was scarcely feminine.

However, Tallmadge (who lived into his eighty-second year) was less reluctant to accord mention when such was indicated. Noting subsequent minor operations in Pennsylvania, Tallmadge referred to his questioning of a "country girl with eggs" coming back from the city.

And while this "young female" was volunteering information, an enemy patrol opened fire. Gallantly, Tallmadge set her up on his horse and together they galloped away, in a whirlwind of "considerable firing of pistols and not a little wheeling and charging." However, like all the iron-nerved heroines in storybooks, "she remained unmoved and never once complained of fear after she mounted my horse."

Every intent of a thoroughly dispirited Lord Howe continued to be conveyed with incredible speed to Valley Forge, to which Washington's army had now retired. The British commanding general could not outwit Boudinot's spy "management" and plucky agents such as Lydia Darragh or country girls with their baskets.

It turned out that this passive commander had asked for transfer home at the time of Burgoyne's surrender. In February, 1778, his request was granted, and the often querulous Sir Henry Clinton replaced him.

On June 18, the enemy marched out of Philadelphia, after arranging for 3,000 Tories to sail down the Delaware River aboard Royal Navy vessels, which had been under the command of Howe's brother, Admiral Richard Howe.

Not all of the Tories elected to go. Peggy Shippen, in her teens, for one, whose beauty and personal charm had earned her the title of "reigning belle" of Philadelphia society, stayed. Who could be cross with one so lovely? Certainly not the handsome and hitherto brave Major General Benedict Arnold. The Connecticut-born officer, who was a recent widower, married Peggy while he was military governor of Philadelphia—and compromised her in his plot to seize West Point, using her as a secretary in his coded correspondence with Clinton. (She followed him into what amounted to his exile in disgrace in England.)

A few Quakers had cooperated with the occupation forces. Two of them, convicted of leading British patrols against an American outpost, were hung after Philadelphia was returned to its original government.

Lydia herself went strangely unrewarded for her busy and daring mission that December night, 1777. In fact, the Friends Society subsequently decided that she and her husband, William and—certainly!—her son who had served in the army had been altogether too martial for a peace-loving religious group. So the three were expelled from membership. The young boy, John, as an adolescent, was afforded opportunity to redeem himself.

And Lydia, an obscure, imperfectly documented figure at best, faded into the peculiarly lonely oblivion of spies who have risen to unusual demands of the moment, then vanished into the wings without so much as a bow.

ENDNOTES

1. Undoubtedly there were true double agents in the Revolution. One was a somewhat shadowy figure, Ann Bates, who flitted back and forth between the lines, ultimately marrying a British officer and sailing to sanctuary in England.

2. Frankford's growing pains were not easy. Shortly after the war, a traveler wrote of "its mud and wretchedness, its barking dogs and squalling babies where society seems in a transition state from filth to cleanliness and consequently from vice to Godliness."

3. These journals, published in 1894, did not identify the Quaker woman by name, but the pages dealing with the tavern incident do, curiously, use her name in the chapter heading. This suggests that the name may have been in his original manuscript. As President of Congress after the Revolution, Boudinot signed the Treaty of Peace with England.

4. The famous Morgan had already figured prominently in the expedition against Canada, and at Saratoga would acquire new laurels in January, 1781, at the victory of Cowpens, Carolina.

Chapter Nine

The Frontier Spy

James Fenimore Cooper

James Fenimore Cooper (1789–1851) was a pioneer of American fiction who chose to focus most of his work on pioneering days. He produced so many volumes (over thirty novels alone, plus nonfiction titles) that one can practically bathe in them, if one wants to. Many do not.

Mark Twain attacked Cooper's best-known work, The Last of the Mohicans, *bitterly, creating hurt from which Cooper never quite recovered. The rap against Cooper is that his prose creeps along at a snail's pace between turgid, flowery, and awkward. Some readers and scholars find that reputation to be unfair, considering the time period in which Cooper wrote. These Cooper fans eagerly point out that much pleasure is to be found by carefully reading, or rereading, Cooper with your full attention. I certainly agree with these Cooper stalwarts, and his novels set outdoors in the wilderness mean a great deal to me. How can I ever set aside such works as the Leatherstocking series, which includes* The Last of the Mohicans?

The Spy: A Tale of the Neutral Ground, *published in 1821, was Cooper's second novel. His first,* Precaution, *published in 1820, was a clumsy Jane Austen imitation and a failure. He modeled* The Spy *as a loose imitation of Sir Walter Scott's* Waverly. *The book was a huge success, one of America's first bestsellers. The setting is the area around today's Westchester County in New York, and the time is 1778 when British and Continental forces were still locked in conflict. Cooper's titular "Spy" is Harvey Birch, working for George*

Washington and posing as a peddler, switching sides and costumes as needed to gather information.

This excerpt is from the novel's final two chapters. In one scene, the Spy (the Peddler) meets George Washington for the first time. In the next, we leap forward thirty years to find the aging Spy near the front lines in the War of 1812. Read them carefully, and you will be converted to giving Mr. James Fenimore Cooper and his works your full attention.

The commencement of the following year was passed, on the part of the Americans, in making great preparations, in conjunction with their allies, to bring the war to a close. In the South, Greene and Rawdon made a bloody campaign, that was highly honorable to the troops of the latter, but which, by terminating entirely to the advantage of the former, proved him to be the better general of the two.

New York was the point that was threatened by the allied armies; and Washington, by exciting a constant apprehension for the safety of that city, prevented such reënforcements from being sent to Cornwallis as would have enabled him to improve his success.

At length, as autumn approached, every indication was given that the final moment had arrived.

The French forces drew near to the royal lines, passing through the neutral ground, and threatened an attack in the direction of King's Bridge, while large bodies of Americans were acting in concert. By hovering around the British posts, and drawing nigh in the Jerseys, they seemed to threaten the royal forces from that quarter also. The preparations partook of the nature of both a siege and a storm. But Sir Henry Clinton, in the possession of intercepted letters from Washington, rested within his lines, and cautiously disregarded the solicitations of Cornwallis for succor.

It was at the close of a stormy day in the month of September, that a large assemblage of officers was collected near the door of a building that was situated in the heart of the Americans troops, who held the Jerseys. The age, the dress, and the dignity of deportment of most of these warriors, indicated them to be of high rank; but to one in particular was paid a deference and obedience that announced him to be of the highest. His dress was plain, but it bore the usual military distinctions of command. He was mounted on a noble animal, of a deep bay; and a group of young men, in gayer attire, evidently awaited his pleasure and did his bidding. Many a hat was lifted as its owner addressed this officer; and when he spoke, a profound attention, exceeding the respect of mere professional etiquette, was exhibited on every countenance. At length the general raised his own hat, and bowed gravely to all around him. The salute was returned, and the party dispersed, leaving the officer without a single attendant, except his body servants and one aid-de-camp. Dismounting, he stepped back a few paces, and for a moment viewed the condition of his horse with the eye of one who well understood the animal, and then, casting a brief but expressive glance at his aid, he retired into the building, followed by that gentleman.

On entering an apartment that was apparently fitted for his reception, he took a seat, and continued for a long time in a thoughtful attitude, like one in the habit of communing much with himself. During this silence, the aid-de-camp stood in expectation of his orders. At length the general raised his eyes, and spoke in those low, placid tones that seemed natural to him.

"Has the man whom I wished to see arrived, sir?"

"He waits the pleasure of your excellency."

"I will receive him here, and alone, if you please."

The aid bowed and withdrew. In a few minutes the door again opened, and a figure, gliding into the apartment, stood modestly at a distance from the general, without speaking. His entrance was unheard by the officer, who sat gazing at the fire, still absorbed in his own meditations. Several minutes passed, when he spoke to himself in an undertone,—

"Tomorrow we must raise the curtain, and expose our plans. May Heaven prosper them!"

A slight movement made by the stranger caught his ear, and he turned his head, and saw that he was not alone. He pointed silently to the fire, toward which the figure advanced, although the multitude of his garments, which seemed more calculated for disguise than comfort, rendered its warmth unnecessary. A second mild and courteous gesture motioned to a vacant chair, but the stranger refused it with a modest acknowledgment. Another pause followed, and continued for some time. At length the officer arose, and opening a desk that was laid upon the table near which he sat, took from it a small, but apparently heavy bag.

"Harvey Birch," he said, turning to the stranger, "the time has arrived when our connection must cease; henceforth and forever we must be strangers."

The peddler dropped the folds of the greatcoat that concealed his features, and gazed for a moment earnestly at the face of the speaker; then dropping his head upon his bosom, he said, meekly,—

"If it be your excellency's pleasure."

"It is necessary. Since I have filled the station which I now hold, it has become my duty to know many men, who, like yourself, have been my instruments in procuring intelligence. You have I trusted more than all; I early saw in you a regard to truth and principle, that, I am pleased to say, has never deceived me—you alone know my secret agents in the city, and on your fidelity depend, not only their fortunes, but their lives."

He paused, as if to reflect in order that full justice might be done to the peddler, and then continued,—

"I believe you are one of the very few that I have employed who have acted faithfully to our cause; and, while you have passed as a spy of the enemy, have never given intelligence that you were not permitted to divulge. To me, and to me only of all the world, you seem to have acted with a strong attachment to the liberties of America."

During this address, Harvey gradually raised his head from his bosom, until it reached the highest point of elevation; a faint tinge gathered in his cheeks, and, as the officer concluded, it was diffused over his whole countenance in a deep glow, while he stood proudly swelling with his emotions, but with eyes that sought the feet of the speaker.

"It is now my duty to pay you for these services; hitherto you have postponed receiving your reward, and the debt has become a heavy one—I wish not to undervalue your dangers; here are a hundred doubloons; remember the poverty of our country, and attribute to it the smallness of your pay."

The peddler raised his eyes to the countenance of the speaker; but, as the other held forth the money, he moved back, as if refusing the bag.

"It is not much for your services and risks, I acknowledge," continued the general, "but it is all that I have to offer; hereafter, it may be in my power to increase it."

"Does your excellency think that I have exposed my life, and blasted my character, for money?"

"If not for money, what then?"

"What has brought your excellency into the field? For what do you daily and hourly expose your precious life to battle and the halter? What is there about me to mourn, when such men as you risk their all for our country? No, no, no—not a dollar of your gold will I touch; poor America has need of it all!"

The bag dropped from the hand of the officer, and fell at the feet of the peddler, where it lay neglected during the remainder of the interview. The officer looked steadily at the face of his companion, and continued,—

"There are many motives which might govern me, that to you are unknown. Our situations are different; I am known as the leader of armies—but you must descend into the grave with the reputation of a foe to your native land. Remember that the veil which conceals your true character cannot be raised in years—perhaps never."

Birch again lowered his face, but there was no yielding of the soul in the movement.

"You will soon be old; the prime of your days is already past; what have you to subsist on?"

"These!" said the peddler, stretching forth his hands, that were already embrowned with toil.

"But those may fail you; take enough to secure a support to your age. Remember your risks and cares. I have told you that the characters of men who are much esteemed in life depend on your secrecy; what pledge can I give them of your fidelity?"

"Tell them," said Birch, advancing and unconsciously resting one foot on the bag, "tell them that I would not take the gold!"

The composed features of the officer relaxed into a smile of benevolence, and he grasped the hand of the peddler firmly.

"Now, indeed, I know you; and although the same reasons which have hitherto compelled me to expose your valuable life will still exist, and prevent my openly asserting your character, in private I can always be your friend; fail not to apply to me when in want or suffering, and so long as God giveth to me, so long will I freely share with a man who feels so nobly and acts so well. If sickness or want should ever assail you and peace once more smile upon our efforts, seek the gate of him whom you have so often met as Harper, and he will not blush to acknowledge you."

"It is little that I need in this life," said Harvey; "so long as God gives me health and honest industry, I can never want in this country; but to know that your excellency is my friend is a blessing that I prize more than all the gold of England's treasury."

The officer stood for a few moments in the attitude of intense thought. He then drew to him the desk, and wrote a few lines on a piece of paper, and gave it to the peddler.

"That Providence destines this country to some great and glorious fate I must believe, while I witness the patriotism that pervades the bosoms of her lowest citizens," he said. "It must be dreadful to a mind like yours to descend into the grave, branded as a foe to liberty; but you already know the lives that would be sacrificed, should your real character be revealed. It is impossible to do you justice now, but I fearlessly entrust you with this certificate; should we never meet again, it may be serviceable to your children."

"Children!" exclaimed the peddler, "can I give to a family the infamy of my name?"

The officer gazed at the strong emotion he exhibited with pain, and he made a slight movement towards the gold; but it was arrested by the expression of his companion's face. Harvey saw the intention, and shook his head, as he continued more mildly,—

"It is, indeed, a treasure that your excellency gives me: it is safe, too. There are men living who could say that my life was nothing to me, compared to your secrets. The paper that I told you was lost I swallowed when taken last by the Virginians. It was the only time I ever deceived your excellency, and it shall be the last; yes, this is, indeed, a treasure to me; perhaps," he continued, with a melancholy smile, "it may be known after my death who was my friend; but if it should not, there are none to grieve for me."

"Remember," said the officer, with strong emotion, "that in me you will always have a secret friend; but openly I cannot know you."

"I know it, I know it," said Birch; "I knew it when I took the service. 'Tis probably the last time that I shall ever see your excellency. May God pour down His choicest blessings on your head!" He paused, and moved towards the door. The officer followed him with eyes that expressed deep interest. Once more the peddler turned, and seemed to gaze on the placid, but commanding features of the general with regret and reverence, and, bowing low, he withdrew.

The armies of America and France were led by their illustrious commander against the enemy under Cornwallis, and terminated a campaign in triumph that had commenced in difficulties. Great Britain soon after became disgusted with the war; and the States' independence was acknowledged.

As years rolled by, it became a subject of pride among the different actors in the war, and their descendants, to boast of their efforts in the cause which had confessedly heaped so many blessings upon their country; but the name of Harvey Birch died away among the multitude of agents who were thought to have labored in secret against the rights of their countrymen. His image, however, was often present to the mind of the powerful chief, who alone knew his true character; and several times did he cause secret inquiries to be made into the other's fate, one of which only resulted in any success. By this he learned that a peddler of a different name, but similar appearance, was toiling through the new settlements that were springing up in every direction, and that he was struggling with the advance of years and apparent poverty. Death prevented further inquiries on the part of the officer, and a long period passed before he was again heard of.

It was thirty-three years after the interview which we have just related that an American army was once more arrayed against the troops of England; but the scene was transferred from Hudson's banks to those of the Niagara.

The body of Washington had long lain moldering in the tomb; but as time was fast obliterating the slight impressions of political enmity or personal envy, his name was hourly receiving new luster, and his worth and integrity each moment became more visible, not only to his countrymen, but to the world. He was already the acknowledged hero of an age of reason and truth; and many a young heart, amongst those who formed the pride of our army in 1814, was glowing with the recollection of the one great name of America, and inwardly beating with the sanguine expectation of emulating, in some degree, its renown. In no one were these virtuous hopes more vivid than in the bosom of a young officer who stood on the table rock, contemplating the great cataract, on the evening of the 25th of July of that bloody year. The person of this youth was tall and finely molded, indicating a just proportion between strength and activity; his deep black eyes were of a searching and dazzling brightness. At times, as they gazed upon the flood of waters that rushed tumultuously at his feet, there was a stern and daring look that flashed from them, which denoted the ardor of an enthusiast. But this proud expression was softened by the lines of a mouth around which there played a suppressed archness, that partook of feminine beauty. His hair shone in the setting sun like ringlets of gold, as the air from the falls gently moved the rich curls from a forehead whose whiteness showed that exposure and heat alone had given their darker hue to a face glowing with health. There was another officer standing by the side of this favored youth; and both seemed, by the interest they betrayed, to be gazing, for the first time, at the wonder of the western world. A profound silence was observed by each, until the companion of the officer that we have described suddenly started, and pointing eagerly with his sword into the abyss beneath, exclaimed,—

"See! Wharton, there is a man crossing in the very eddies of the cataract, and in a skiff no bigger than an eggshell."

"He has a knapsack—it is probably a soldier," returned the other. "Let us meet him at the ladder, Mason, and learn his tidings."

Some time was expended in reaching the spot where the adventurer was intercepted. Contrary to the expectations of the young soldiers, he proved to be a man far advanced in life, and evidently no follower of the camp. His years might be seventy, and they were indicated more by the thin hairs of silver that lay scattered over his wrinkled brow, than by any apparent failure of his system. His frame was meager and bent; but it was the attitude of habit, for his sinews were strung with the toil of half a century. His dress was mean, and manifested the economy of its owner, by the number and nature of its repairs. On his back was a scantily furnished pack, that had led to the mistake in his profession. A few words of salutation, and, on the part of the young men, of surprise, that one so aged should venture so near the whirlpools of the cataract, were exchanged; when the old man inquired, with a voice that began to manifest the tremor of age, the news from the contending armies.

"We whipped the redcoats here the other day, among the grass on the Chippewa plains," said the one who was called Mason; "since when, we have been playing hide and go seek with the ships: but we are now marching back from where we started, shaking our heads, and as surly as the devil."

"Perhaps you have a son among the soldiers," said his companion, with a milder demeanor, and an air of kindness; "if so, tell me his name and regiment, and I will take you to him."

The old man shook his head, and, passing his hand over his silver locks, with an air of meek resignation, he answered,—

"No; I am alone in the world!"

———

[Editor's note: Still in the presence of the old stranger, officer Wharton is speaking directly to Mason about his family.]

"My mother was—"

"An angel!" interrupted the old man, in a voice that startled the young soldiers by its abruptness and energy.

"Did you know her?" cried the son, with a glow of pleasure on his cheek.

The reply of the stranger was interrupted by sudden and heavy explosions of artillery, which were immediately followed by continued volleys of small arms, and in a few minutes the air was filled with the tumult of a warm and well-contested battle.

The two soldiers hastened with precipitation towards the camp, accompanied by their new acquaintance. The excitement and anxiety created by the approaching fight prevented a continuance of the con-versation, and the three held their way to the army, making occasional conjectures on the cause of the fire, and the probability of a general engagement. During their short and hurried walk, Captain Dunwoodie, however, threw several friendly glances at the old man, who moved over the ground with astonishing energy for his years, for the heart of the youth was warmed by an eulogium on a mother that he adored. In a short time they joined the regiment to which the officers belonged, when the captain, squeezing the stranger's hand, earnestly begged that he would make inquiries after him on the following morning, and that he might see him in his own tent. Here they separated.

Everything in the American camp announced an approaching strug-gle. At a distance of a few miles, the sound of cannon and musketry was heard above the roar of the cataract. The troops were soon in motion, and a movement made to support the division of the army which was already engaged. Night had set in before the reserve and irregulars reached the foot of Lundy's Lane, a road that diverged from the river and crossed a conical eminence, at no great distance from the Niagara highway. The summit of this hill was crowned with the cannon of the British, and in the flat beneath was the remnant of Scott's gallant brigade, which for a long time had held an unequal contest with distinguished bravery. A new line was interposed, and one column of the Americans directed to charge up the hill, parallel to the road. This column took the English in flank, and, bayoneting their artillerists, gained possession of the can-non. They were immediately joined by their comrades, and the enemy was swept from the hill. But large reinforcements were joining the Eng-lish general momentarily, and their troops were too brave to rest easy under the defeat. Repeated and bloody charges were made to recover the guns, but in all they were repulsed with slaughter. During the last of these struggles, the ardor of the youthful captain whom we have men-tioned urged him to lead his men some distance in advance, to scatter a daring party of the enemy. He succeeded, but in returning to the line missed his lieutenant from the station that he ought to have occupied. Soon after this repulse, which was the last, orders were given to the shat-tered troops to return to the camp. The British were nowhere to be seen, and preparations were made to take in such of the wounded as could be moved. At this moment Wharton Dunwoodie, impelled by affection for his friend, seized a lighted fusee, and taking two of his men went himself in quest of his body, where he was supposed to have fallen. Mason was found on the side of the hill, seated with great composure, but unable to walk from a fractured leg. Dunwoodie saw and flew to the side of his comrade, saying,—

"Ah! dear Tom, I knew I should find you the nearest man to the enemy."

"Softly, softly; handle me tenderly," replied the lieutenant. "No, there is a brave fellow still nearer than myself, and who he can be I know not. He rushed out of our smoke, near my platoon, to make a prisoner or some such thing, but, poor fellow, he never came back; there he lies just over the hillock. I have spoken to him several times, but I fancy he is past answering."

Dunwoodie went to the spot, and to his astonishment beheld the aged stranger.

"It is the old man who knew my mother!" cried the youth. "For her sake he shall have honorable burial; lift him, and let him be carried in; his bones shall rest on native soil."

The men approached to obey. He was lying on his back, with his face exposed to the glaring light of the fusee; his eyes were closed, as if in slumber; his lips, sunken with years, were slightly moved from their natural position, but it seemed more like a smile than a convulsion which had caused the change. A soldier's musket lay near him; his hands were pressed upon his breast, and one of them contained a substance that glittered like silver. Dunwoodie stooped, and removing the limbs, perceived the place where the bullet had found a passage to his heart. The subject of his last care was a tin box, through which the fatal lead had gone; and the dying moments of the old man must have passed in drawing it from his bosom. Dunwoodie opened it, and found a paper in which, to his astonishment, he read the following:—

Circumstances of political importance, which involve the lives and fortunes of many, have hitherto kept secret what this paper now

reveals. Harvey Birch has for years been a faithful and unrequited servant of his country. Though man does not, may God reward him for his conduct!
GEO. WASHINGTON.

It was the SPY OF THE NEUTRAL GROUND, who died as he had lived, devoted to his country, and a martyr to her liberties.

Chapter Ten

The Craft of Intelligence

Allen Dulles

The "cloak-and-dagger" figures that populate so much fiction and nonfiction about spies don't show up in accounts of the achievements of Allen Dulles as Director of the CIA under Eisenhower and Kennedy, 1953-1961. Dulles was more intellectual than the flamboyant, movie-character types, a deep thinker who put into operation a Corps of specialists, ranging from U-2 high-altitude photo-ops to listening and tracking equipment. In this excerpt from his highly praised The Craft of Intelligence, *Dulles takes on subjects that made newspaper and TV headlines when they happened. The titles of each section are editorial changes. The text is all Dulles.*

MYTH: THE CIA MAKES POLICY

I have frequently been asked what "myth" about the CIA has been the most harmful. I have hesitated in answering, I admit, because there were several to choose from, but finally chose the accusation that CIA made foreign policy, often cut across the programs laid down by the President and the Secretary of State and interfered with what ambassadors and Foreign Service officers abroad were trying to do.

This charge is untrue but extremely hard to disprove without revealing classified information. It is all the harder to disprove because to some extent it is honestly believed, and at times has even been spread, by people in government who themselves were not "in the know."

The facts are that the CIA has never carried out any action of a political nature, given any support of any nature to any persons, potentates or movements, political or otherwise, without appropriate approval at a high political level in our government outside the CIA.

In this, as well as in most such cases, there is absolutely no way to disprove such rumors. There is nothing to get your teeth into. It is only your word against the rumor market, and in this particular case high officials in the French Government did nothing to stop its spread.

A fresh and abounding group of myths about the CIA, each more fantastic than its predecessor, has been born out of the Bay of Pigs incident. A book published in May of 1964 contains a new crop of them.[1] The book is largely based on statements attributed to four brave and leading members of the Cuban brigade which went ashore at the Bay of Pigs. The responsibility for telling the story lies with Haynes Johnson, a Washington reporter. One particular bit of mythology about CIA in this book which particularly disturbed me relates to the myth I have been discussing—that CIA interferes with government policy.

In describing the last days before the invasion force pushed off for Cuba, Johnson tells us about one of the American military trainers of the brigade coopted from the American military services—an officer known to the brigade members only as "Frank." I know Frank: he is an able officer, but here he was not involved in high policy matters. His job was to see to it that the brigade got good military training. As his knowledge of Spanish was vague and as the English of the brigade members with whom he was dealing was far from perfect, there was plenty of room for misunderstanding. From what Frank has recently said, I am prone to believe that this was all a misunderstanding which the Johnson book has built up into a grave incident seemingly only to discredit the CIA.

Here is the story according to the book. Shortly before the brigade left Nicaragua for Cuba, Frank called in two of the leaders of the brigade, Pepe and Oliva (they became two of the four co-sponsors of the book). Frank told them, so they are credited with saying, that "there were forces in the Administration trying to block the invasion and Frank might be ordered to stop it." If he receives such an order, he said he would secretly inform Pepe and Oliva. Pepe remembers Frank's next words this way.

If this happens you come here and make some kind of show, as if you were putting us, the advisors, in prison, and you go ahead with the program as we have talked about it, and we will give you the whole plan, even if we are your prisoners.

This and certain related statements in the book have been widely blazoned in the American press as evidence that the CIA was preparing to thwart the orders of the President if he should have decided to call off the invasion.

This is totally false.

In the first place, Frank has denied the story.

In the second place, governing orders with respect to the brigade once it had left Puerto Cabezas would not have emanated from Nicaragua, Guatemala, or from anyone in that area. They would have come from a command post located elsewhere which had direct contact with the brigade at sea and where the authority was not in Frank's hands.

Thirdly, at the time of Frank's alleged conversation with Pepe and Oliva, I know of no forces in the administration trying to block the action. True, no decision had been reached; the entire matter was before the President for decision.

Fourth, in addition to the control of the brigade exercised through the command post as I have mentioned, the brigade at all times after it set sail for Cuba and up to the time that it entered Cuban territorial waters could have been controlled by American naval forces.

Finally, shortly after this particular incident, the President of the United States on the eve of the landing gave the order to cancel the brigade's airstrike designed to immobilize Castro's aircraft, which might, and did, attack the incoming ships. The CIA, despite its deep apprehension of the effect of this order, responded immediately and loyally to the President's decision. The brigade's airstrike was canceled as it was on the point of taking off.

MYTH: THE SOVIET SUPER SPY

Nobody minds being portrayed as invincible. I imagine the Soviets derive a good deal of satisfaction from the popular image of their intelligence officers and agents that exists in the minds of some Westerners. The value of the image is that it tends to frighten the opponent.

If I seem to have lent any support to the myth of the Soviet super spy in my earlier characterization of the Soviet intelligence officer, I would like to remind the reader that I was then writing of his training, his attitudes and his background rather than of his achievements. The examples of Soviet failures are legion. Their great networks of the past, often too large in size, eventually broke up or were exposed, both as a result of the vigorous measures of Western counterintelligence and as a result of their own internal weaknesses. Their best-trained officers make technical slips, showing that they too are fallible. Often, in situations where there is no textbook answer, no time to get instructions from headquarters and when individual decision and initiative is required, the Soviet intelligence officer fails to meet the test.

Soviet training of both intelligence officers and agents tries to drill the wayward element out of intelligence work, but it cannot be done. Harry Houghton endangered his position by spending the extra money he earned from spying on real estate ventures. He wanted to amass a fortune. Vassall spent it on fancy clothes. Each lived beyond his regular income, and this was bound, sooner or later, to attract attention. Hayhanen, the associate of Colonel Abel, one of Moscow's best spies, was an alcoholic. He was bound eventually to break up, to talk—and he did. Stashinski, the murderer, on Soviet orders, of the two Ukrainian exile leaders fell in love with a German girl and came into conflict with his KGB bosses over this relationship. It was the main cause of his defection. The Soviets seem to have taken too little note of these weaknesses.

The Soviets cannot eliminate love and sex and greed from the scene. Since they use them as weapons to ensnare people, it is strange that they fail to recognize their power to disrupt carefully planned operations.

Time and again the Soviets and satellites make serious psychological misjudgments in the people they solicit as agents. They underestimate the power of courage and honesty. Their cynical view of loyalties to other than their own kind blinds them to the dominant motives of free people.

Soviet intelligence is often overconfident, overcomplicated and overestimated. The real danger lies not in the mythical capabilities of the Soviet spy, though some are highly competent, but in the magnitude of the Soviet intelligence effort, the money it spends, the number of people it employs, the lengths to which it is willing to go to achieve its ends and the losses it is willing and able to sustain.

MYTH: AMERICANS ARE NAÏVE AND TOO NEW IN INTELLIGENCE WORK

Americans are usually proud, and rightly so, of the fact that the "conspiratorial" tendencies which seem to be natural and inbred in many other people tend to be missing from their characters and from the surroundings in which they live. The other side of the coin is that the American public, aware of this, frequently feels that both in our diplomacy and in our intelligence undertakings we are no match for the "wily foreigner." Foreigners likewise attribute to Americans a certain gullibility and naïveté. There are also other aspects of this same general notion. One is that the American official is a rather closed-minded do-gooder, a bit of a missionary, who butts into things he doesn't understand and insists on doing things his way. This is the "American" we see in Graham Greene's *The Quiet American. The Ugly American [Editor's note: 1958 novel by Eugene Burdick and William Lederer.]* gives us another angle of the same prejudice—lack of true understanding and appreciation of local peoples abroad. The number of bestsellers with this theme seems to show that it is a popular one and that we enjoy seeing our compatriots depicted as stupid people. It is little wonder then that such mischief-creating prejudices also find their way into the American and foreign criticisms of our operations abroad, including the intelligence service.

I would like to say first of all that I much prefer taking the raw material which we find in America—naïve, home-grown, even home-spun—and training such a man to be a good intelligence officer, however long the process lasts, to seeking out people who are naturally devious, conspiratorial or wily, and trying to fit them into the intelligence system. . . . [W]hen I described our norms for the potential intelligence officer . . ., I did not include such traits among them. The recruiter does not look for slippery characters. He is much more likely to shun or reject them. The American intelligence officer is trained to work in intelligence as a profession, not as a way of life. The distinction is between his occupation and his private character.

MYTH: SECRET INTELLIGENCE OPERATIONS ARE NOT IN THE AMERICAN TRADITION

There was one sensational secret operation, now in the public domain, which did worry some people in this country as being "unlawful," namely the flights of the U-2 airplane. People know a good bit about espionage as it has been carried on from time immemorial. The illegal smuggling of agents with false papers, false identities and false pretenses across the frontiers of other countries is a tactic which the Soviets have employed against us so often that we are used to it. But to send an agent over another country, out of sight and sound, more than ten miles above its soil, with a camera seemed to shock because it was so novel. Yet such are the vagaries of international law that we can do nothing when Soviet ships approach within three miles of our shores and take all the pictures they like, and we could do the same to them if we liked.

If a spy intrudes on your territory, you catch him if you can and punish him according to your laws. That applies without regard to the means of conveyance he has taken to reach his destination—railroad, automobile, balloon or aircraft or, as my forebears used to say, by shanks' mare. Espionage is not tainted with any "legality." If the territory, territorial waters or air space of another country is violated, it is an illegal act. But it is, of course, a bit difficult for a country to deny any complicity when the mode of conveyance is an aircraft of new and highly sophisticated design and performance.

As I said at the outset, some of our fellow citizens don't want anything to do with espionage of any kind. Some prefer the old-fashioned kind, popularized in the spy thrillers. Some would concede that, if you are going to do it at all, it is best to use the system that will produce the best results and is most likely to secure the information we need.

The decision to proceed with the U-2 program was based on considerations deemed in 1955 to be vital to our national security. We required the information necessary to guide our various military programs and particularly our missile program. This we could not do if we had no knowledge of the Soviet missile program. Without a better basis than we then had for gauging the nature and extent of the threat to us from surprise nuclear missile attack, our very survival might be threatened. Self-preservation is an inherent right of sovereignty. Obviously, this is not a principle to be invoked frivolously.

In retrospect, I believe that most thoughtful Americans would have expected this country to act as it did in the situation we faced in the fifties, when the missile race was on in earnest and the U-2 flights were helping to keep us informed of Soviet progress.

And while I am discussing myths and misconceptions, I might tilt at another myth connected with the U-2, namely, that Khrushchev was shocked and surprised at it all. As a matter of fact, he had known for years about the flights, though his information in the early period was not accurate in all respects. Diplomatic notes were exchanged and published well before May 1, 1960, the date of the U-2 failure, when Khrushchev's tracking techniques had become more accurate. Still, since he had been unable to do anything about the U-2, he did not wish to advertise the fact of his impotence to his own people, and he stopped sending protests.

His rage at the Paris Conference was feigned for a purpose. At the time he saw no prospect of success at the conference on the subject of Berlin. He was then in deep trouble with the Chinese Communists. Following his visit to President Eisenhower in the fall of 1959, he had been unable to placate Mao during his stop at Peking en route back from the United States. Furthermore, he was apprehensive that the Soviet people would react too favorably to President Eisenhower's planned trip to the USSR in the summer of 1960. Influenced by all these considerations, he decided to use the U-2 as a good excuse for torpedoing both the trip and the conference.

There is evidence of long debate in the Praesidium during the first two weeks of May, after the U-2 fell and before the date of the Paris Conference. The question was, I believe, whether to push the U-2 issue under the rug or use it to destroy the conference. There are also reports that Khrushchev was asked why he had not mentioned the overflight issue when he visited the President in 1959, more than six months before the U-2 came down. He is said to have remarked he didn't wish to "disturb" the spirit of Camp David.

Finally, to conclude the U-2 discussion, I should deal with one other myth, namely, that when [the pilot] Powers was downed on May 1, 1960, everybody should have kept their mouths shut and no admissions of any kind should have been made, the theory being that you don't admit espionage. It is quite true that there is an old tradition, and one which was excellent in its day and age, that you never talk about any espionage operations and that if a spy is caught, he is supposed to say nothing.

It does not always work out that way in the twentieth century. The U-2 is a case in point. It is, of course, obvious that a large number of people had to know about the building of the plane, its real purposes, its accomplishments over the five years of its useful life and also the high authority under which the project had been initiated and carried forward. In view of the unique nature of the project, its cost and complexity, this proliferation of information was inevitable. It could not be handled merely like the dispatch of a secret agent across a frontier. Of course, all these people would have known that any denial by the executive was false. Sooner or later, certainly, this would have leaked out.

But even more serious than this is the question of the responsibility of government. For the executive to have taken the position that a subordinate had exercised authority on his own to mount and carry forward such an enterprise as the U-2 operation without higher sanction would have been tantamount to admission of irresponsibility in government and that the executive was not in control of actions by subordinates which could vitally affect our national policy. This would have been an intolerable position to take. Silence on the whole affair, which I do not believe could have been maintained, would have amounted to such an admission. The fact that both in the U-2 matter and in the Bay of Pigs affair the Chief Executive assumed responsibility for what was planned as a covert operation, but had been uncovered, was, I believe, both the right decision to take and the only decision that in the circumstances could have been justified.

LITERARY MYTHS: THE SPY IN FACT AND FICTION

The spy heroes of the novelists rarely exist in real life—either on our side of the Curtain or on the other. The staff intelligence officer, at least in time of peace, is hardly ever dispatched incognito or disguised into unfriendly territory on perilous or glamorous missions. Except for the Soviet illegal who is placed abroad for long periods of time, there is no reason for an intelligence service to risk the capture and interrogation of its own officers, thereby jeopardizing its agents and possibly exposing many of its operations.

There was little resemblance between the exploits of Ian Fleming's hero, the unique James Bond, in *On Her Majesty's Secret Service*, which I read with the greatest pleasure, and the retiring and cautious behavior of the Soviet spy in the United States, Colonel Rudolf Abel. The intelligence officer, as distinct from the agent, does not usually carry weapons, concealed cameras or coded messages sewed into the lining of his pants, or, for that matter, anything that would betray him if he should be waylaid. He cannot permit himself, as do the lucky heroes of spy novels, to become entangled with luscious females who approach him in bars or step out of closets, lightly clad, in hotel rooms. Such lures might have been sent by the opposition to compromise or trap him. Sex and hardheaded intelligence operations rarely mix well.

The Soviet "new look," which uses socialite spies, like Ivanov in London and Skrypov . . . in Australia, represents an exception to this general rule. It may well be that the Soviets, having found pay dirt in the Profumo affair with its disruptive consequences, may see some advantages in using vice rings to aid blackmailing operations in later intelligence exploitation or merely to discredit persons in government positions in the Free World. This would fit in with general purposes of bringing such governments into disrepute with their own people. Certainly, from the intelligence angle, one would not expect to find items of intelligence passed via call girls to be of high reliability.

If there are dangers, tricks, plots, it is the agent who is personally involved in them, not the intelligence officer, whose duty it is to guide the agent safely. Even in the case of the agent and his own sources, the disciplines of intelligence today call for a talent for inconspicuousness that should rule out fancy living, affairs with questionable females and other such diversions. Alexander Foote, who worked for the Soviets in Switzerland, describes his first meeting during World War II with one of the most valuable agents of the Soviets. This was the man known by the code name Lucy . . .

I arrived first and awaited with some curiosity the arrival of this agent who had his lines so deep into the innermost secrets of Hitler. A quiet, nondescript little man suddenly slipped into a chair at our table and sat down. It was "Lucy" himself. Anyone less like the spy of fiction it would be hard to imagine. Consequently he was exactly what was wanted for an agent in real life. Undistinguished looking, of medium height, aged about fifty, with his mild eyes blinking behind glasses, he looked exactly like almost anyone to be found in any suburban train anywhere in the world.

Most spy romances and thrillers are written for audiences who wish to be entertained rather than educated in the business of intelligence. For the professional practitioner there is much that is exciting and engrossing in the techniques of espionage, but those untutored in the craft of intelligence would probably not find it so. And that part of actual espionage which is crucial—the successful recruitment of an important agent, the acquisition of critical information—for security reasons only finds its way into popular literature when it is seared with age.

A useful analogy is to the art of angling. In fact, I have found that good fishermen tend to make good intelligence officers. The fisherman's preparation for the catch, his consideration of the weather, the light, the currents, the depth of the water, the right bait or fly to use, the time of day to fish, the spot he chooses and the patience he shows are all a part of the art and essential to success. The moment the fish is hooked is the moment of real excitement, which even the nonfisherman can appreciate. He would not be intrigued by all the preparations, although the fisherman is, because they are vital to his craft and without them the fish is not likely to be lured and landed.

I have always been intrigued by the fact that one of the greatest author-spies in history, Daniel Defoe, never wrote a word about espionage in his major novels. In the eyes of many, Defoe is accounted one of the professionals in the early history of British intelligence. He was not only a successful operative in his own right but later became the first chief of an organized British intelligence system, a fact which was not publicly known until many years after his death. His most famous literary works, of course, are *Robinson Crusoe, Moll Flanders,* and *Journal of the Plague Year.* Try if you will to find even the slightest reference to spies or espionage in any of these books. No doubt Defoe carefully avoided writing about any actual espionage plots known to him because of political considerations and an ingrained sense of secrecy. But a man with his fertile mind could easily have invented what could have passed as a good spy story and projected it into another time and another setting. I cannot dispel the conviction altogether that he never did this because, having the inside view, he felt that for security reasons he could not give a true and full story of espionage as it was really practiced in his day, and as a novelist Defoe was above inventing something at variance with the craft.

An unusual writer on certain aspects of intelligence work is Joseph Conrad. I would venture to suggest that Conrad's Polish background is responsible for his native insights into the ways of conspiracy and the way of the spy. His own father was exiled and two of his uncles executed for their part in a plot against the Russians. The Poles have had long experience in conspiracy, as long as the Russians and, in great measure, thanks to Russian attempts to dominate them.

Being the kind of man he was, Conrad was not likely to tell a spy story for the sake of the adventure and the suspense. He was interested in the moral conflicts, in the baseness of men and their saving virtues. Conrad does not even exploit the inherent complexities of the spy stories he invents because it is not what primarily interests him.

The literature on intelligence which I find the most engrossing is of the Conrad type—stories that deal with the motivation of the spy, the informer, the traitor. Among these who have spied against their own country, there is the ideological spy, the conspiratorial spy, the venal spy and the entrapped spy. At different times in history one or the other of these motifs seems to dominate, and sometimes there is a combination of more than one motif. Klaus Fuchs was the typical ideological spy, Guy Burgess the conspiratorial type, the Swedish Colonel Stig Wennerstrom apparently was the venal spy, and William Vassall the typical case of entrapment—and finally there is the spy of fiction. And if at least we get pleasure in reading about him, let us keep him for such uses—even though he be a myth.

MISHAPS: THE STUMBLES THAT DOOM SPIES

In 1938, a Soviet intelligence officer working undercover in the United States sent a pair of pants to the cleaners. In one of the pockets, there was a batch of documents delivered by an agent employed in the Office of Naval Intelligence. It was not easy to press the pants with the documents in the pocket, so the pants presser removed them and in so doing brought to light one of the most flagrant cases of Soviet espionage in American experience up to that time. It was also one of the most flagrant instances of carelessness on the part of a trained intelligence officer on record. The officer, whose name was Gorin, was eventually returned to the Soviet Union, where he surely must have been shot for his sloppiness.

There have been some notorious cases of briefcases left behind in taxis or trains by people who should have known better. A sudden and inexplicable absent-mindedness can sometimes momentarily afflict a man who has been carefully trained in intelligence and security. But the gross mishap is usually not the fault of the intelligence officer. More often it results from the arbitrary or even the well-meaning behavior of outsiders who have no idea what the consequences of their acts may be, and from technical failures and from accidents.

The kind landlady of a rather busy roomer noticed that his spare pair of shoes was down at the heels. She took them to the cobbler's one day on her own. It was a favor. The cobbler removed the old heels and discovered that in each was a hollow compartment containing some strips of paper covered with writing. Of course he informed the police. One of my most important German sources during my days in Switzerland in World War II almost had a serious mishap because his initials were in his hat. One evening he was dining alone with me in my house in Bern. My cook detected that we were speaking German. While we were enjoying her excellent food—she was a better cook than a spy—she slipped out of the kitchen, examined the source's hat and took down his initials. The next day, she reported to her Nazi contact the fact that a man, who from his speech was obviously German, had visited me and she gave his initials.

My source was the representative in Zurich of Admiral Canaris, head of German military intelligence. He frequently visited the German Legation in Bern. When he next called there, a couple of days after our dinner, two senior members of the legation, who had already seen the cook's report, took him aside and accused him of having contact with me. He was equal to the assault. Fixing the senior of them with his eyes, he sternly remarked that he had, in fact, been dining with me, that I was one of his chief sources of intelligence about Allied affairs and that if they ever mentioned this to anyone, he would see to it that they were immediately removed from the diplomatic service. He added that his contacts with me were known only to Admiral Canaris and at the highest levels in the German government. They humbly apologized to my friend and, as far as I know, they kept their mouths shut.

Everybody learned a lesson from this—I that my cook was a spy; my German contact that he should remove his initials from his hat; and all of us that attack is the best defense and that if agent A is working with agent B, one sometimes never knows until the day of judgment who, after all, is deceiving whom. It was, of course, a close shave, and only a courageous bluff saved the day. Fortunately, in this case my contact's bona fides was quickly established. The cook's activities eventually landed her in a Swiss jail.

The little slips or oversights which can give away the whole show may sometimes be the fault of the intelligence service itself, not of the officer handling the agent, but of the technicians who produce for the agent the materials necessary to his mission—the false bottom of a suitcase that comes apart under the rough handling of a customs officer, a formula for secret writing that doesn't quite work. Forged documents are perhaps the greatest pitfall. Every intelligence service collects and studies new documents from all over the world and the modifications in old ones in order to provide agents with documents that are "authentic" in every detail and up-to-date. But occasionally there is a slip that couldn't be helped and an observant border official, who sees hundreds of passports every day, may notice that the traveler's passport has a serial number that doesn't quite jibe with the date of issue, or a visa signed by a consul who just happened to drop dead two weeks before the date he was supposed to have signed it. Even the least imaginative border control officer knows that such discrepancies can point to only one thing. No one but the agent of an intelligence service would have the facilities working for him that are needed to produce such a document, which is artistically and technically perfect except in one unfortunate detail.

Then there is fate, the unexpected intervention of impersonal forces, accidents, natural calamities, man-made obstacles that weren't there the week before, or simply the perversity of inanimate things, the malfunctioning of machinery. An agent on a mission can drop dead of a heart attack, be hit by a truck or take the plane that crashes. This may end the mission or it may do more. In March 1941, Captain Ludwig von der Osten, who had just arrived in New York to take over the direction of a network of Nazi spies in the United States, was hit by a taxi while crossing Broadway at Forty-fifth Street and fatally injured. Although a quick-thinking accomplice managed to grab his briefcase and get away, a notebook found on von der Osten's body and various papers in his hotel room pointed to the fact that he was a German masquerading as a Spaniard and undoubtedly involved in espionage. When, shortly after the accident, postal censorship at Bermuda discovered a reference to the accident in some highly suspicious correspondence that had regularly been going from the United States to Spain, the FBI was able to get on the trail of the Nazi spy ring von der Osten was to manage. In March of 1942, their work culminated in the trial and conviction of Kurt F. Ludwig and eight associates. It was Ludwig who had been with von der Osten when the taxi hit him and who had been maintaining the secret correspondence with Nazi intelligence via Spain.

One windy night during the war a parachutist was dropped into France who was supposed to make contact with the French underground. He should have landed in an open field outside the town but was blown off course and landed instead in the middle of the audience at an open-air movie. It happened to be a special showing for the SS troops stationed nearby.

There is no single field of intelligence work in which the accidental mishap is more frequent or more frustrating than in communications. One of the best illustrations of this kind of mishap can be found in a well-known literary work which couldn't have less to do with intelligence. The reader will probably recall the incident in Thomas Hardy's *Tess of the d'Urbervilles* when the important message Tess slips under Angel Clare's door slides beneath the carpet that reaches close to the sill and is never recovered by the intended recipient, with grievous consequences for all.

Messages for agents are often put into "drops" or "caches," as places of concealment are called. These may be anywhere above ground or below ground, in buildings or out of doors. The Bolsheviks, like Dr. Bancroft, Franklin's secretary, used to prefer the hollow of a tree. Today there are safer and more devious contrivances by which means papers can be protected against weather and soil for long periods of time.

In operations making use of radio communications, there can be a failure of the equipment on either the sending or receiving end. Communications making use of the mail can easily fail for at least ten good and bad reasons.

Often trains are late and a courier doesn't arrive in time to make contact with an agent who has been told not to wait longer than a certain time. To avoid this sort of accidental interruption of communications, most good operations have alternate or emergency plans which go into effect when the primary system fails, but here we begin to run into the problem of overload and overcomplexity, which is another quite distinct cause of mishaps. A person under some stress can commit just so much complex planning to memory, and will usually not have the plan written down because this is too dangerous. Or if he does have it written down, his notes may be so cryptic that he cannot decipher them when he needs to, even though when he wrote them down his shorthand seemed to be a clever and unmistakable reminder.

One of the simplest and oldest of all dodges used by intelligence in making arrangements for meetings calls for adding or subtracting days and hours from the time stipulated in a phone conversation or other message, just in case the enemy intercepts such a message. The agent has been told, let us say, to add one day and subtract two hours. Tuesday at eleven really means Wednesday at nine. When the agent was first dispatched, he knew this as well as his own name. No need to write it down in any form. Three months later, however, when he gets his first message calling him to a meeting, panic suddenly seizes him. Was it plus one day and minus two hours or was it minus one day and plus two hours? Or was it perhaps plus two days and minus one hour? Or was it ... and so on. This is, of course, a very simple instance and hardly an example of the complex arrangements often in force.

Anyone who has ever traveled under another name knows that the greatest fear is not that you will forget your new identity while signing your name in the hotel register. It is rather that after you have just signed the register, someone will walk into the lobby whom you haven't seen for twenty years, come up to you, slap you on the back and say: "Jimmy Jones, you old so-and-so, where have you been all these years?"

Any operation involving the use of a person traveling temporarily or permanently under another name always risks the one-out-of-a-thousand chance that an accidental encounter will occur with someone who knew the agent when he had another identity. Perhaps the agent can talk or joke his way out of it. The trouble is that in today's spy-conscious world the first thing most people would think of is that espionage is the real explanation. If a great deal of work has gone into building up the new identity of the agent, such an accidental encounter might just ruin everything. The Soviet illegal is usually assigned to countries where the risk of such accidental encounter is minimal if not entirely nonexistent. Yet the following instance shows how the possibility always exists and how the Soviets, as well as the rest of us, have no way really of eliminating these risks entirely.

In the Houghton-Lonsdale case, . . . the American pair called Kroger who had been operating the radio transmitter were identified after their arrest as long-term Soviet agents who had previously been active in the United States. The FBI accomplished this identification on the basis of fingerprints. Just as the identification was completed their New York office received a phone call from a gentleman who described himself as a retired football coach. The week before, *Life* magazine had shown a series of photographs of all the persons apprehended in the Lonsdale case. Thirty-five years ago, this gentleman told the FBI, he had been coaching at a large public high school in the Bronx. At that time a scrawny little fellow had tried out for the team, and he had never forgotten him. He had just seen Kroger's picture in *Life* and Kroger was that scrawny little fellow. He was absolutely certain of it. But his name wasn't Kroger, it was so-and-so. And the coach was right.

The Krogers had not tried to change their physical appearance at all. Kroger ran an open business in London of the kind that could have brought to him a variety of persons of all nationalities interested in collecting rare books. What was the chance that someone else, not necessarily the coach, who remembered him from that large public high school in the Bronx thirty or so years before would walk into his office one day in quest of a book and recognize him? Slight, but not impossible. The Soviets took the risk.

MISCHIEF-MAKING SPIES

Fabricators and swindlers have always existed in the intelligence world, but the recent growth and significance of technical and scientific discoveries, especially their military applications, has afforded new and tempting fields for the swindlers. The weakness they could exploit was the lack of detailed scientific knowledge on the part of the intelligence officer. Although every modern service will train and brief its field officers as thoroughly as possible in scientific matters of concern to it, it clearly cannot turn every intelligence officer into a full-fledged physicist or chemist. The result is that many a good field officer may go for a neat offer of information and continue working with an agent until the specialists at home have had time to analyze the data and unhappily inform him that he is in the toils of a swindler.

Immediately after World War II, the most popular swindle by all odds exploited the new and world-wide interest in atomic energy. We were swamped with what we began to call "uranium salesmen." In all the capitals of Europe, they turned up with "samples" of U-235 and U-238, in tin canisters or wrapped in cotton and stuffed into pill bottles. Sometimes they offered to sell us large quantities of the precious stuff. Sometimes they claimed their samples came from the newly opened uranium mines of Czechoslovakia, where they had excellent sources who could keep us supplied with the latest research behind the Iron Curtain. There were many variations on the theme of uranium.

The chief characteristic and the chief giveaway of the swindler, as in most swindles, is the demand for cash on the line. First comes the tempting offer accompanied by the sample, then the demand for a large sum, after which the delivery of the main goods is to follow. Since no intelligence service allows its field officers to disburse more than token sums until the headquarters has reviewed a project in all detail, it is very rare that an intelligence service actually loses any money to a swindler. All it loses is time, but this is also precious, sometimes more precious than money

After uranium, there was a vogue in infrared, then came bogus information on missiles, and no doubt at this moment the swindlers are regrouping and working up reports on the Red Chinese development of a death-ray through the use of lasers. The logic here is that the Red Chinese are behind in H-bomb research and rather than go to the expense of catching up will devote their energy to lasers.

A more laborious and less easily identifiable kind of fabrication is that produced by what we call "paper mills." They turn out reports by the yard and do not depend on hot items as the swindlers do. Often their information is plausible, well-reasoned and beautifully organized. There is only one fault with it. It doesn't come from the horse's mouth as claimed.

Shortly after World War II, a group of former military men who had escaped from one of the Balkan countries to the West promised us the plans of the latest postwar defenses on the Dalmatian coast, complete with harbor fortifications, missile ramps and the like. For this they wanted a good many thousands of dollars in gold. They agreed to show us a few samples of the papers before we paid up. These were supposed to be photocopies of official military drawings with the accompanying descriptive documents. They had allegedly procured the material from a trusted colleague, an officer who had remained behind and was now employed in the war ministry of an Iron Curtain country. In addition, there was a courier who knew the mountain passes, a brave man who had just come out with the plans and quickly returned home. He couldn't stay out in the West because his absence would be noted at home, and this was dangerous. If we wished to buy into this proposition, the courier would make a trip every month and the colleague in the war ministry would supply us with what we wanted on order.

The plans were beautiful. So were the documents. There was only one little flaw we noticed at the very first reading. Midway through one of the documents there was a statement that the new fortifications were being built by "slave" labor. Only an anti-Communist would use that term. There is, after all, no admitted slavery under Communism. Our military friends in their fervor had given themselves away. It was obvious that they themselves had drawn up the beautiful plans and documents in somebody's cellar in Munich. There was no brave courier and no friend in the war ministry, as they later admitted.

Cranks and crackpots run a close second after the fabricators as mischief-makers and time-wasters for the intelligence service. The reader would be amazed to know how many psychopaths and people with grudges and pet foibles and phobias manage to make connections with intelligence services all over the world and to tie them in knots, if only for relatively short periods of time. Again the intelligence service is vulnerable because of its standing need for information and because of the unpredictability of the quarter from which it might come.

Paranoia is by far the biggest cause of trouble. Since espionage is now in the atmosphere, it is no wonder that people with paranoid tendencies who have been disappointed in love or in business or who just don't like their neighbors will denounce their friends and foes and competitors, or even the local garbage man, as Soviet spies. During World War I, many German governesses employed by families on Long Island were denounced at one time or another and mostly for the same reason. They were seen raising and lowering their window shades at night, secretly signaling to German submarines which had surfaced offshore. Just what kind of significant information they could pass on to a submarine by lowering their shades once or twice was usually unclear, but then it is typical of paranoid delusions that there is a "bad man" close by, although it is never quite certain what he wants. Trained intelligence officers can frequently spot the crank by just this trait. There is usually very little positive substance to the crank's claim. The waiter at the "Esplanade" is spying for an Iron Curtain country. He was seen surreptitiously making notes in a corner after he had just taken overly long to serve two people who are employed in a government office. (He was probably adding up their bill.) It may later turn out that he had once accidentally spilled soup on the source, who was convinced he had done it on purpose.

Cranks and crackpots sometimes manage to wander from one intelligence service to another, and they can cause serious trouble if they are not spotted early in the game because they may have learned enough from the one experience to bring some substance to the next. A young and rather attractive girl once turned up in Switzerland with a story of her adventures behind the Iron Curtain and in West Germany and of her work in intelligence for both the Russians and one of the Allied services. Her story was long and took months to unravel. It was clear that she had been where she said she had been because she could name and describe the places and people and knew the languages of all the places. Most damning was her claim that certain Allied intelligence officers, including some Americans stationed in Germany, were working for the Soviets.

Our investigations eventually revealed that the girl had turned up as a refugee in Germany with information about the Soviets and the Poles, who had apparently employed her at one time in a purely clerical capacity. While the process of interrogation and checking was going on, she had come into contact with numerous Allied intelligence officers and had gotten to know their names. She apparently hoped for employment, but was finally turned down, since it was clear that she was a little wrong in the head. She next wandered into Switzerland, where she came to our attention. Her story by then had expanded and now included the men she had met in Germany, not in their true roles, but as actors in a great tale of espionage and duplicity. When she got through with us and went on to the next country, it is quite likely that the story got even bigger and that we who had just spoken with her also figured now as agents of the Soviets or worse. One of our people had the theory that the Russians had sent her to the West because, without any training at all, she was a perfect sabotage weapon. She could be guaranteed to waste the time of every intelligence service in Europe and prevent them from getting on with their more serious tasks.

Endnote
1. Haynes Johnson, *The Bay of Pigs* (New York: W. W. Norton & Co., Inc., 1964).

CHAPTER ELEVEN

Pinkerton's War:
The Civil War's Greatest Spy
and the Birth of the Secret Service

Jay Bonansinga

Alan Pinkerton was twenty-four when he came to America from Scotland in 1842 with his bride. He settled in the village of Dundee, Illinois, on the edge of frontier lands and continued his hard-working life as a barrel maker. Cities like Chicago, thirty-eight miles away, eventually grabbed his attention, along with police activities. He rose through the ranks to eventually become well known as a spy for the Union cause, catching the eyes of supporters of Abraham Lincoln during his Presidential bid in 1860.

When Lincoln departed Springfield, Illinois, for Washington, DC, and his inauguration in February, 1861, Pinkerton knew a dark secret. Through his associates' spying activities, and his own bold moves into the very lairs of Confederate sympathizers, he had learned of a plot to assassinate Lincoln during his train ride to Washington. The assassins—a group calling themselves the Palmetto Guards and headed by an Italian zealot named Cypriano Fernandina—planned to make their strike on Lincoln as his train stopped in Baltimore. The city was a hotbed of Southern sympathizers and anti-Lincoln sentiment.

Brought in as Lincoln's bodyguard, Pinkerton gained the President-elect's trust and put into motion the strategy that would save Abe Lincoln's life. At first, Pinkerton had been focusing on protecting bridges and other potential weak spots on the rail lines. Now he turned to putting a force of his own trusted men (and one woman) on the trains. He also rearranged and manipulated the train schedule.

This is the story of that journey, excerpted from the book Pinkerton's War: The Civil War's Greatest Spy and the Birth of the US Secret Service, *by Jay Bonansinga.*

February 11, 1861, 7:05 A.M.

A chilly drizzle strafed the frozen planks of Springfield's Western Railroad Depot. The gray morning sky hung low, as more than a thousand people thronged the platform, bumbershoots and parasols sprouting.

The man they had come to see arrived shortly after 7:00 a.m. with his oldest son by his side (the rest of his family was planning on joining him en route the next day). The tall, sinewy man carried a single trunk—which he had packed himself—tied with rope and labeled simply: "A Lincoln, White House, Washington, DC."

Before departing, the president-elect shook hands with well-wishers inside the depot house, thanking them for their thoughts. "His face was pale," wrote the *New York Herald*, "and quivered with emotion so deep as to render him almost unable to utter a single word."

Eventually words *would* come, because he was Abraham Lincoln. A few minutes before 8:00, he followed his escort—most likely his dear friend, Norman Judd, a railroad attorney and head of the Illinois Republican State Central Committee—to the private coach.

He stood on the running rail, took off his hat, turned to the crowd, and "requested silence." Then, his voice tight with emotion, he spoke these words:

My friends, no one who has never been placed in a like position can understand my feelings at this hour, nor the oppressive sadness I feel at this parting. For more than a quarter century I have lived among you, and during all that time I have received nothing but kindness at your hands. Here I have lived from youth until now, and I am an old man; here the most sacred ties of earth were assumed; here all my children were born, and here one of them lies buried. To you, dear friends, I owe all that I have, and all that I am. All the strange checkered past seems now to crowd upon my mind. Today I leave you. I go to assume a task more difficult than that which devolved upon Washington. Unless the great God who assisted him shall be with me and aid me, I must fail; but if the same Omniscient Mind and Almighty Arm that directed and protected him shall guide and support me, I shall not fail—I shall succeed. Let us all pray that the God of our fathers may not forsake us now. To Him I commend you all. Permit me to ask that with equal sincerity and faith you will invoke His wisdom and guidance for me. With these few words I must leave you, for how long I know not. Friends, one and all, I must bid you an affectionate farewell.

Pinkerton, later in his life, would go back to these words often and marvel at their eerily prophetic quality. "A strange and almost weird presentiment of grief and suffering," Pinkerton observed, "give his utterances a pathos that becomes profoundly impressive when linked with subsequent events." But on that wintry morning, no one could have imagined what those subsequent events would entail.

Abraham Lincoln, with one last deferential bow, turned and vanished inside the private coach. "Three cheers were given," reported the *Herald*, "and a few seconds afterwards the train moved slowly out of the sight of the silent gathering."

[Editor's note: As Lincoln left Springfield, heading for Washington—with stops for celebrations and layovers in Indianapolis, Philadelphia and then Harrisburg—Pinkerton was already in action. He and his agents had penetrated the inner circle of an organization determined to kill Lincoln before he became President. Pinkerton had two immediate problems: Organizing a defense of the President-Elect and convincing him that a huge change in plans was necessary.]

The conspirators had learned—most likely from members of the compromised police force—that Abraham Lincoln would have to change trains at the Calvert Street depot in Baltimore on the morning of February 23.

Upon arrival, the president-elect and his party would be loaded into carriages and taken to the Eutaw House for a brief reception. They would then proceed by horse cart to the Camden Street station, where they would board the Baltimore and Ohio train for Washington.

The most vulnerable moment in Lincoln's passage through Baltimore would occur shortly after disembarking from the incoming train. To reach his carriage, Lincoln would have to traverse a narrow vestibule between the station and its front lot.

At that point, a fake fistfight would be staged in front of the building. The few policemen at the depot would be forced to rush out to quell the row, leaving Lincoln and his party unprotected, and in the words of Pinkerton, "surrounded by a dense, excited, and hostile crowd." It would be at this vulnerable moment that the fatal shots would be fired.

A small steamer boat had been chartered and would be stationed at one of the bays or streams running into the Chesapeake. In the chaotic aftermath of the attack, the assassins would flee via steamer to Virginia and the glory of their high accomplishment.

[Editor's note: Pinkerton prevailed in a series of secret conversations with Lincoln and his close associates and aides. On the night of February 22, at a dinner in his honor at Harrisburg, Lincoln left early, feigning a headache. His movements were secret. Newspaper reporters on the scene were kept in the dark, and their telegraph wires were cut. A secret train carrying Lincoln roared toward Philadelphia where Pinkerton was waiting. He and his men would accompany Lincoln on another train to Washington, It had to pass through Baltimore, but that night the assassins would still be waiting for the scheduled train, the next day. We continue in Jay Bonansinga's words, from our excerpt from the book. This would be the most dangerous night in Abraham Lincoln's life.]

As the special train rolled out of Harrisburg—all its running lights off, its headlamp dark, its hatches and windows blacked out—a wire sparked through the lines, connecting through the American Telegraph Company office in Harrisburg, then zapping its way to Norman Judd at the Jones House.

Judd, who had remained at the hotel with Governor Curtin, assuring the dignitaries and guests that Lincoln was "resting comfortably" and that his "headache was due only to fatigue," now sprang into action. He sent a special wire to Philadelphia for one J. H. Hutchinson: It said "Plums" (Pinkerton's code name) should be advised that "Nuts" (Lincoln) had departed Harrisburg safely.

Meanwhile, back in the Harrisburg telegraph office, a young lineman named Andrew Wynne, and two other men, waited anxiously for confirmation that "Plums" had received the message.

———

The covered buggy, its windows shaded, clopped and rattled down the fire-lit streets of nighttime Philadelphia.

Seated in the coach, across from Lincoln and Lamon, Pinkerton nervously puffed his cigar. Every few moments he would turn and raise the rear shade, checking for any suspicious followers.

"It was hard to imagine anyone following them at this point in the journey," writes Richard Rowan, "yet Mr. Pinkerton, with characteristic perfection of detail, left as little to chance as humanly possible."

Pinkerton saw nothing out of the ordinary as they clattered down Market Street to 19th, then up 19th to Vine, then over to 17th Street.

As they approached the PW&B depot, Kenney instructed the driver to slow down "as if on the lookout for someone." A block from the depot, Kenney told the driver to turn down Carpenter—a narrow cross-street lined with a tall, boarded fence—which ran adjacent to the station.

Shadows engulfed the carriage as Kenney signaled for the driver to pull the reins and stop. Inside the coach's cabin, Pinkerton gave a nod and pushed open the door. In tense silence, Abraham Lincoln followed the detective and Lamon out into the cold, opaque darkness.

Pinkerton cautiously led the party around the far corner of the fence.

To avoid the prying eyes of bystanders, Pinkerton ushered the president-elect—his chiseled face obscured by his scarf, his carpetbag in tow—across the scabrous ground of the switchyard, over petrified rails and frozen, wagon-rutted earth. To a casual observer it would have been a strange sight—that long-legged man in the military coat, sidestepping icy puddles and frozen horse apples, as he followed his burly escort.

They reached the platform. They found a shed unoccupied and slipped inside it.

The time had come for Lamon, the self-styled bodyguard, to part company with his friend and former partner. In the "cold, drafty shed, with its acrid reek of smoke," Lamon reached into his pocket and pulled out a large-caliber, single-shot pocket pistol. He proffered the weapon—grip out—to his mentor.

Lincoln smiled sadly and declined the offer. Pinkerton was not amused. He clenched his fists—an involuntary tic—his way of tamping down emotion.

The detective would comment years later, "I would not for the world have it said that Mr. Lincoln had to enter the national capital armed. If fighting had to be done, it must be done by others than Mr. Lincoln."

Kate Warne was one of those "others"—now standing on the platform outside the rear sleeper car, bundled against the cold, waiting for her sick brother.

Underneath her cloak she carried her own small, single-shot pistol, along with extra charges. An African-American man named Knox stood next to her. Knox was the porter in charge of helping the "family" with their special arrangements.

In the distant cloud of steam, among the scattering of travelers, two figures emerged, slowly coming toward her. A tall, cloaked man in a muffler—hunched with apparent "infirmity"—walked gingerly along on the arm of a compact, barrel-chested man in a bowler hat.

Warne's heart most assuredly began to beat faster. This would be her greatest performance.

"Brother William!" she said, stepping forward to greet the man in the muffler, "you're indeed a sight for a loving sister's eyes!"

Lincoln gave the woman his hand, and Warne helped him up the step-rail of the rear sleeper car. George Bangs, already inside the car—also armed—greeted the twosome in the fashion of a doting older brother. The last passenger to board was the stocky, bearded man in the bowler hat.

Pinkerton paused on the foot-rail, asking Warne for the tickets.

Then he turned and called for the conductor. When Litzenberg appeared at the base of the steps, Pinkerton handed over the tickets, explaining that his sick family member was now onboard.

"The poor chap mustn't be disturbed," Pinkerton cautioned the conductor.

The conductor said he understood and waddled away, and Pinkerton vanished inside the sleeper.

Across the platform, H. F. Kenney, huddling in the shadows, proceeded with one last order of business. As Sigmund Lavine writes:

> When Kenney saw Allan enter the car, he ran up the platform as if he had just arrived and handed Conductor Litzenberg a package. Litzenberg grabbed it with one hand and signaled to the engineer with the other. Grumbling, the trainman then stowed the package in a locker under one of the seats—he was taking no chance of losing his excuse for leaving five minutes behind schedule. Moreover, he was sure the thing was valuable, otherwise, why would Mr. Felton delay the train's departure for it? Fortunately he was an honest man and made no attempt to peer inside the bundle. If he had he would have been shocked. All it contained was old newspapers!

In the moments before the train departed the station, Abraham Lincoln settled into a sleeping berth—most likely exhausted from the day's chaos and also relieved that his "performance" was complete, at least for the moment—as the three agents checked their weapons.

Although no official record exists of the specific firearms they carried, it's not implausible that Pinkerton was packing a revolver, probably a Colt model 1860, which would become the workhorse handgun for Union officers and men of Pinkerton's standing. A multiple-shot weapon, the Colt propelled its .44-caliber loads with black-powder caps.

It is likely that Warne and Bangs carried breech-loading Deringers of the single-shot variety—easily concealed in handbags and inner pockets. The .40-caliber balls were cumbersome to reload, but the pivoting barrel allowed seasoned shooters—such as Warne and Bangs—to recover quickly.

On that night, in the moments before the train rolled, cylinders spun, and breeches clicked. All was locked and loaded. It was now only a couple of minutes before 11:00.

Outside, in the darkness, the keen of the whistle pierced the cold.

The train jerked, and the last leg of Lincoln's journey to Washington—the most treacherous portion—began in a thundercloud of vapor.

Pinkerton moved through the rear hatch of the sleeper to the parapet.

His revolver, tucked and holstered inside his clerical-black coat, would have felt reassuring at this point. And so it was, there, on that windy precipice, that the husky detective lit another cigar.

As the train gathered speed, Pinkerton peered around the rear edge of the coach. Dead-ahead, in the dense, February darkness, the string of cars approached the first rail crossing along the winding, black Delaware River.

In the distance—like a twinkling star—the light of a lantern flashed. Two short blinks, then a pause, then two additional blinks. The signal told Pinkerton: "All's well! All's well!"

He puffed his stogie.

The train clattered onward, moving south, toward Wilmington.

Pinkerton had stationed his operatives at every switchyard, every crossing, and every bridge along the route. The agents used bull's-eye lanterns to send their signals. An oil-lit wick encased in a tin box, the bull's-eye utilized a refractive piece of glass behind a glowing centerpiece (hence the name). The yellow light would have flickered in the wind.

Still, as the first checkpoint passed uneventfully, Pinkerton could not relax.

A "late report" from Timothy Webster had warned Pinkerton of foul play that night among the local military regiments, ostensibly assigned to guard the railroad's property. Many of these regiments were corrupt with secessionists and were actually out to destroy tracks and bridges. Upon hearing the news, Pinkerton had immediately asked Felton to assign trustworthy workmen to go out and pretend to paint and repair all the bridges along the line that night.

These men would be secretly armed, so that they could put up a defense in case of trouble.

"The bitter cold wind stung Pinkerton's eyes," writes Lavine, "as he peered anxiously down the track, looking for the twinkling lights that blinked and vanished as quickly as a firefly's glow."

— ◦ —

Inside the swaying, thumping darkness of the sleeping car, in the warmth of a small wood-burning stove, Kate Warne marveled at the proximity of the great man. "She was thrilled," writes Warne biographer Margaret Bzovy, "that she had the opportunity to assist such a marvelous man." But according to Bzovy, Warne also wondered: "Could she actually use the gun in her pocket if she had to?"

These thoughts surely passed through Warne's mind as the president-elect, only inches away from her, made futile attempts to sleep in the cold, drafty berth.

"Lincoln was pushed up into a sleeping berth far too short for him," writes one historian, "so that his huge legs had to be doubled up."

At length, Lincoln emerged from the berth and sat with Warne and Bangs.

Huddling by the stove, the tall man chatted genially with his protectors. In a soft, low voice, Lincoln told stories of his childhood; he told jokes; he listened to Warne and Bangs tell their own stories; and before long the miles began to melt away behind them.

Meanwhile, at regular intervals, Pinkerton would appear in the rear hatchway, wind-blown and anxious, a silhouette in the moonlight, checking on his precious human cargo.

Pinkerton once again marveled at Lincoln's calm, his indomitable spirit, his good humor in the face of such a disquieting passage. "I could not then nor have I since been able to understand," Pinkerton would later observe, "how anyone, under like circumstances, could have manifested such complete mental composure and cheerful spirits."

Pinkerton, on the other hand, was not nearly as sanguine. Later in the journey, in fact, Lincoln and Pinkerton would joke about Pinkerton's almost preternatural ability to foresee dangers.

At this very moment, in fact, as Pinkerton stepped back out onto the wind-lashed perch, he felt with every fiber of his instinct that something was wrong.

The train made excellent time traversing the upper corner of Delaware and was about to cross the Maryland state line. Within minutes it would be approaching the muddy, black snake of the Susquehanna River and the treacherous territory of rebel spies and Southern sympathizers.

Pinkerton squinted against the wind to see across the dark wetlands.

As the miles clocked by, the pinpricks of firelight in the far distance, dotting a small river town, came into view: Perryman, that wasp nest of secessionism, the place where Timothy Webster had first learned of the diabolical schemes being formulated in Baltimore.

Lighting another cigar—one of the many, many Cubans he would burn down to the nub that night—Pinkerton felt certain something was amiss. He hoped his feeling of unease was merely due to his imagination, his nerves, or perhaps his lack of rest.

"He had almost no sleep for the past three nights," writes William Wise. "Maybe his gloomy feelings were the result of being so very, very weary."

The train approached Perryman. The jerk of the air brakes signaled an imminent stop.

To cross the river, the locomotive would be forced to pull onto a ferryboat—one of the first extremely dangerous and tenuous stages of the journey. Pinkerton craned his thick neck to see around the rear edge of the sleeper.

In the distant night, only blackness stared back at the burly detective.

The village of Havre de Grace—now visible on the far side of the Susquehanna—was Timothy Webster's checkpoint. Somewhere along the shadowy banks of the waterway, Webster's lantern would be the all-clear, easing Pinkerton's mind and pointing the way into Baltimore.

But no signal came: only the ominous fabric of darkness along the south bank.

FEBRUARY 23, 1861, 2:11 A.M.

Allan Pinkerton's heart raced as the train began to grind to a halt at the dock. Still no signal from the far bank. Pinkerton faced his first hard decision: He would have to hold the train, and he would have to rethink the entire route. He would also risk alarming not only his illustrious passenger but also the other travelers, potentially jeopardizing the success of the entire counterplot.

Starting toward the hatch, on his way to finding the conductor, he suddenly froze. In his peripheral vision, a faint wink of a light—just over his shoulder—flicked across the dark reaches of the Susquehanna River.

In the distance, Webster's bull's-eye twinkled faintly: One flash . . . another flash . . . pause . . . a third and fourth flash. All's well! All's well!

Meanwhile the train pulled onto the ferry.

As the boat churned and chugged noisily forward, the black surface of the water reflected the cloudless sky. Pinkerton moved his arms and legs to keep warm—and probably also to relieve the incredible tension in his bullish neck and shoulders.

The boat steamed across the river, then deposited the express on the south bank. The last leg of the journey stretched in front of the train, the beauty of the land giving lie to the menacing climate of the border state. The train clamored on.

The cathedrals of rolling hills to the west, the distant moon-gilded currents of the Chesapeake to the east, the hushed roar of Gunpowder Falls—all of it seemed to freeze and solidify in the aspic of a February chill.

They passed Havre de Grace—that hotbed of insurrection into which Webster had ridden like a vengeful ghost two weeks earlier. Pinkerton saw two flashes in the pitch . . . pause . . . then two more. They passed Magnolia—lamplight flickering in the dark. They passed over Gunpowder Bay. They passed Bowleys Quarters and Perry Hall.

Over bridges and through channels of thick forests they rumbled, as the winking of lanterns urged them toward the belly of the beast.

They crossed the outskirts of Baltimore shortly after 3:00 a.m., and soon the land flattened, and the trees cleared, and they were crossing the cinder-strewn switchyard of Calvert Station. Craning his neck, Pinkerton was relieved to see that the opulent depot—its Gothic Italian garrets rising up against the night sky, the stonework luminous in gaslight—was almost completely deserted.

"The city itself," writes Wise, "seemed to be asleep."

The train huffed into the station at exactly 3:30—precisely on time—the sparks spitting off the grinding iron wheels. The whistle shrilled. Chill winds bullwhipped across the empty platform.

Not a soul stirred.

Now Pinkerton would execute the trickiest, most dangerous maneuver of the entire journey to Washington.

———

Before slipping back into the sleeper car, Pinkerton saw, in the near distance, a railroad man in filthy dungarees amble out of the shadows. The man approached the car with an expectant expression.

Pinkerton—tense, hyperalert, ready for anything—leaned down to exchange a greeting, and the man simply whispered, "All's well."

Pinkerton gave a nod.

And now came the uncoupling.

Writes William Wise: "Their sleeping car was disconnected from the train. A team of horses came up, snorting and whinnying, and began to pull the car along the streets. Up one street and down the other, through the dangerous sleeping city."

This was the part of the journey that Pinkerton dreaded the most. He grasped the rear railing of the sleeper as the conveyance rattled along, keeping close watch on the blind alleys and dark corners of the town. Years later, in his memoir, Pinkerton would recall the ruminations crossing his mind at this point:

> The city was in profound repose as we passed through. Darkness and silence reigned over all. Perhaps at this moment, however, the reckless conspirators were astir perfecting their plans for a tragedy as infamous as any which has ever disgraced a free country—perhaps even now the holders of the red ballots were nearing themselves for their part in the dreadful work, or were tossing restlessly upon sleepless couches.

The distance between the PW&B depot and the connecting train at the Camden Street Station amounted to a few city blocks, but for Allan Pinkerton that brief horse-drawn interval would have seemed endless. His fists clenched the whole way, he prepared himself for a quick transfer.

At last, the Camden Street Station came into view in the moonlight.

Even at this hour, scattered travelers could be seen pacing across the entrance, awaiting southbound trains. Pinkerton remained on the sleeper's parapet, as the team dragged the car around the switchyard to the tracks.

Pinkerton hopped off the step-rail and turned toward the yard.

His heart practically stopped.

The track was empty. Not a single engine or car occupied the rails. No train waited to shuttle the president to his inauguration. This was not acceptable. In fact—for a man of Pinkerton's fastidious, controlling nature—this was downright catastrophic.

The detective remained stoic. He turned and climbed back up into the sleeper. He quickly told Warne and Bangs to stay alert and to stand guard while he investigated.

The burly Scot went back outside the car and found the stationmaster in his office. Careful not to appear anxious or inordinately alarmed, Pinkerton nodded a greeting and calmly asked, "Where's the train from the west?"

"Delayed," the stationmaster told him. "Maybe an hour—maybe more."

Abraham Lincoln—contorting his long limbs in the cramped berth—finally gave up trying to sleep. Or perhaps he sensed trouble.

Regardless of the reasons, as the muffled voices and footsteps of anonymous denizens rose outside the sleeper, Lincoln climbed out of the compartment and joined Warne and Bangs at the stove.

A moment later, Pinkerton returned to the sleeper car. Did Lincoln read the stiff expression on the detective's face? The man in the bowler hat explained that the Chicago train, which would convey the president to Washington, was late—already more than an hour behind schedule.

Lincoln offered a reassuring smile. "Did you anticipate this delay, too, Mr. Pinkerton?" The gentle, good-natured rib revealed something poignant developing between the two men. "If you say no, I'll be disappointed."

"Sorry to disappoint you, sir," Pinkerton retorted, "but I cannot predict the future—at least not that well."

"Are you sure, Boss?" Warne interjected. "I've been telling Mr. Lincoln about your precautions along the route, and he thinks you're capable of miracles."

"If I were capable of miracles," Pinkerton mused, "we'd already be in Washington."

The noise outside the sleeper grew. Liquor-fueled voices chortled. Scuffling footsteps approached. Perhaps the taverns had closed—or perhaps something worse was going on. Perhaps word had somehow leaked and spread of the important passenger waiting in the sleeper.

At some point—as more than one historian has suggested—Pinkerton would have likely extinguished the lights. He would have made sure that Lincoln stayed in the shadows. It would have been as dark as a tomb in that sleeper car. The minutes would have crawled.

They lowered their voices. And waited. And still the minutes dragged.

"Does this waiting make you nervous, Mr. Pinkerton?" The president-elect's Kentucky rasp broke the tense silence of the shadowy cabin. Another hour had passed. The voices outside the sleeping car had grown more feral, intoxicated, rambunctious.

Pinkerton looked down at his clenched fists. "I'm afraid that it does, Mr. Lincoln."

"In your profession," Lincoln went on, "I should think the unexpected must occur very often."

Indeed it did.

And it was about to occur again.

Inside the sleeper cabin, the sound of low, secretive voices reached a momentary lull. They had been waiting for nearly two hours now—an eternity, considering the situation—and Lincoln was temporarily out of stories. Pinkerton had just finished telling how he had become a detective, and now the muffled voices outside the car dwindled as well.

The silence ratcheted the tension with the pressure of a vise. The gloomy darkness inside the sleeper must have seemed even darker at that point. It was a sticky darkness, full of faint, unidentified noises.

Outside the shaded window closest to where Lincoln sat came the shuffling sound of drunken footsteps. The footsteps paused.

The unidentified figure—only inches away from Lincoln—began to sing.

The slurred, inarticulate, phlegmy crooning could not have sounded more sinister.

The singing seemed to go on forever. Was it a signal? Was it a taunt? Was it an overture to violence? Or was it merely the inebriated drone of a reprobate?

The song being butchered outside Lincoln's window—composed by a Northerner only two years earlier—originated in the blackface minstrel shows in New York. It was used as a "walk-around" number (in which performers preened and waved their lampblack-painted hands).

Written in high-comic style by Daniel Emmett of Bryant's Minstrels, it was sung in an exaggerated version of African-American vernacular. The song told the story of a freed black slave pining for the beautiful plantation of his youth:

> Well I wish I was in de land of cotton
> Old times dar am not forgotten
> Look away! Look away! Look away! Dixie Land.
> In Dixie Land whar I was born in,
> Early on one frosty mornin',
> Look away! Look away! Look away! Dixie Land.

For the young nation the song had been an instant success and even became a favorite of Lincoln's—it was played often during his 1860 campaign—but by 1861 the song had taken on a new context. Secessionists appropriated the sentimental tribute as an anthem of rebellion—especially the stanza that climaxes with the line, "In Dixie Land I'll take my stand / To live and die in Dixie."

The Natchez Courier would eventually crown it as "The War Song of Dixie."

But on that cold, crystalline February night, coming through the walls of a stranded sleeper car, the dissonant serenade must have put gooseflesh on the arms of the four souls waiting in the dark.

It is not unlikely that Pinkerton, Warne, and Bangs all reached for the hand-grips of their pistols.

Perhaps recognizing the volatile situation, Lincoln glanced sadly at the detective. Very softly, under his breath, the president-elect said, "No doubt there will be a great time in Dixie by and by."

Pinkerton tried to smile.

The singing continued.

"Such impressive songs," Lincoln whispered, "and sung with such moving fervor."

Warne smiled. "Oh, there are many patriots in Baltimore."

This elicited soft laughter from all the gentlemen in the sleeper.

But the laughter, alas, was short-lived.

February 23, 1861, 5:32 a.m.

Did Kate Warne jump when she finally heard the steam whistle of the connecting train shatter the predawn stillness? Perhaps she and her traveling companions all started slightly—their nerves wound as tight as armature wires.

The Chicago train rolled into the station, and the whetstone keen of iron wheels must have sent sighs of relief throughout the sleeper car. Perhaps the hammers of breech-loaded pistols were slowly, discreetly eased back into their safety positions.

Allan Pinkerton rose and exited through the rear hatch, taking his place on the parapet, as the couplers slammed and latched onto the sleeper coach.

Within minutes, the Chicago train completed its loading and transfer rituals, then slowly started out of the depot. The sleeper lurched as the engine pulled it clear.

At long last Abraham Lincoln was moving again, traveling south under the dawning light of the eastern sky.

It took only half an hour for the train to complete the last portion of its journey. Shortly after 6:00 in the morning, on February 23, 1861, the express bellowed into Washington Station in a thunderhead of vapor and noise.

When the sleeper coach finally jolted to a stop, it must have felt to Lincoln as though he had landed on a foreign shore. "Thank God this prayer meeting's over," Lincoln muttered, more to himself than anyone else.

Pinkerton exited the coach first, checking the crowded platform.

The drawn, sleepless faces of Timothy Webster and other operatives greeted "the Boss" at the foot of the step-rail. The depot swarmed with travelers arriving and departing, and Pinkerton made sure it was safe.

At last, the famous passenger appeared in the rear doorway of the sleeper with a sheepish expression. He descended the steps slowly, heavily. Writes Arthur Orrmont:

> *Surrounded by Pinkerton men, the president, exhausted from sleep-lessness and the strain of his journey, moved slowly toward the exit. A corner of his traveling shawl dragged along the ground, and Allan Pinkerton bent forward and picked it up.*

Some of the faces in the crowd turned and recognized the tall, lanky individual towering over his companions, being escorted like an anonymous king. As Lincoln approached the exit, an old friend of his, Illinois congressman Elihu Washburne, hurried up and excitedly shook the man's hand.

Accounts vary as to whether Washburne knew of the counterplot. But what is certain is this: Pinkerton worried that danger still existed, especially if the president-elect were surrounded by a crush of admirers.

"No talking here!" the detective interrupted the effusive congressman.

Washburne turned to Pinkerton and said with great indignation, "And who might *you* be, sir? Your face is unfamiliar to me."

"That's Allan Pinkerton," Lincoln told the man. "And his face won't be unfamiliar to you very long."

CHAPTER TWELVE

Beyond Repair:
The Decline and Fall of the CIA

Charles S. Faddis

Chances are, the title of Charles S. Faddis's book on one of our country's most important intelligence-gathering organizations is scary enough to get your pulse rate soaring. But hang on ... there's more! In this excerpt, Faddis takes us deep into CIA operations and reveals why it's not a pretty picture.

Imagine, if you will, a series of disasters involving naval aviation. An F-18 crashes on landing on a carrier in the Atlantic. A helicopter free-falls into the sea shortly after takeoff from a carrier in the Persian Gulf. Two jets collide during an exercise in California, killing both pilots. A fire breaks out below decks on a carrier in the Pacific, and the ship almost sinks before the flames are brought under control. A naval air-strike force going after a terrorist chemical warfare complex in the Middle East experiences unexpectedly heavy losses from air defenses and fails to destroy its target.

Now imagine what the reaction might be. The events would doubtless get a lot of attention. Press coverage would be intense. Politicians on Capitol Hill would call for inquiries. Commentators would express the usual wide variety of opinions as to the cause of the sudden spate of accidents and failures. Perhaps a commission would be appointed to look into the entire issue.

In time conclusions would be reached. It might be determined that training standards had slackened, that maintenance funds had been cut, that aging airframes had been pushed beyond their operational life cycles. Any number of corrective measures might be introduced: new training courses, inspections of all aircraft in the fleet, new flight operations procedures, and so on.

Almost certainly, however, we can say that one solution to the problems encountered would *not* be to instruct the Central Intelligence Agency to begin to build, man, equip, and operate nuclear aircraft carriers.

No matter what problems the United States Navy might be encountering in dealing with naval flight operations, no one with any common sense would think it would be a good idea to take an organization like the CIA, with no experience in flight operations at sea, and ask it to begin to take over the navy's job. We might well make the navy buckle down, tighten its standards, and clean up its act. We would certainly not ask another organization to begin to try to duplicate the incredible expertise of the US Navy in this field, compiled as it has been over many decades of operations in peace and war.

Yet remarkably, since 9/11 this is exactly the approach that we have begun to take with regard to intelligence operations. Having established that the CIA is not producing the intelligence we need, rather than concentrating on fixing it or replacing it with an organization that will get the job done, we have decided to begin to allow a host of other less capable organizations to duplicate the CIA's activities.

In any given locale abroad, therefore, at the present time, you may have half a dozen or more US intelligence and law enforcement entities all attempting to run their own strategic intelligence operations on top of, around, and through ongoing CIA intelligence activity. These organizations include not only the Defense HUMINT Service (DH), which was created to run clandestine operations against targets overseas, but also entities like the Naval Criminal Investigative Service (NCIS) and the Air Force Office of Special Investigations (AFOSI). The latter two are organizations that traditionally have run criminal investigations and focused on counterintelligence (CI). They were not built to run collection operations abroad focused on foreign targets. To the extent there is a traffic cop at all in this mess, it is the CIA chief of station, but his authority is under increasing attack, and his direction is more and more likely to be taken as advisory rather than compulsory.

I went out to be COS in a Middle Eastern nation several years ago, shortly after my predecessor and the head of the local NCIS office in that country had gotten into an epic head-butting competition. The NCIS chief had informed the COS that he was going to run collection operations of his own in the country in question. In short, he was going to have his personnel begin to recruit spies. He would keep the CIA informed, and he would coordinate to the extent he could. He was not, however, asking permission; he was moving forward no matter what the CIA thought.

My predecessor was livid. He threatened dire consequences. He fired off messages. He waited for the fire and brimstone and retribution. Nothing happened.

About that time I was processing out of headquarters and getting ready to get on a plane to head out for my new assignment. I was called into the front office of NE Division and given clear direction by my immediate superior. I was to take over as COS, I was to patch things up with NCIS, and I was to make the whole problem go away. There would be no headquarters support. No one in the CIA was really sure anymore that they had the authority to tell NCIS what to do. I was, in short, working without a net. If an op by any agency went wrong in-country on my watch, I would probably be hung, but I was not really armed with the authority to control anyone other than my own people.

As should be readily apparent by this point in the narrative, I am no apologist for the CIA. My central thesis is, after all, that the CIA needs to be replaced, as it is incapable of doing the job for which it was created. That said, whatever the level at which the CIA is performing presently in its core mission of the collection of strategic level foreign intelligence (FI), it is significantly above that of the organizations, mostly military, that are currently imposing themselves on its turf.

Part of the issue is personnel. I have known military case officers who were superb, but on average, when it comes to the running of strategic-level intelligence operations, there is no comparison between the quality of CIA case officers and those individuals who are qualified as operations officers and serving inside NCIS, AFOSI, and others. The CIA has the cream of the crop, period. This is not arrogance. Like most things it is a function of the way the system is designed. The CIA goes out and recruits case officers to perform that specific task. As I have stated earlier, the CIA does a fairly poor job of finding leaders, but it does a very good job of finding and bringing on board individuals who can recruit spies and run operations.

The military services do not recruit case officers as such. They recruit officers and enlisted personnel to perform a host of other tasks, and then they try to take some of those individuals and essentially convert them into case officers. Occasionally, they have brilliant success. More commonly, they end up with individuals who are bright, motivated, and hardworking but who simply do not have the natural skills that CIA ops officers have.

There is also, quite frankly, no comparison in experience level. The average CIA case officer is going to run more operations and make more recruitments in a single tour than his military counterpart will in his entire career. However fast the CIA is moving, and it is clearly not fast enough, it is at light speed compared to the other organizations now trying to play on the same field. The CIA case officer is also going to spend his career running agents, whereas his military counterpart is quite likely to spend at most a few years out of his entire career involved in this activity. As is true with most professions, there is only so much you can learn in training. The real education begins once you are in the field, and there is simply no substitute for repetition and exposure to actual operations.

Part of the reason is structural. DH was built to run offensive intelligence operations abroad involving the recruitment of foreign spies. That makes it an exception among the various military services I have discussed. To the extent that organizations like NCIS have been involved in intelligence operations in the past, they have been limited to the running of double agents, usually American citizens, against foreign intelligence services. This is important and difficult work, but it is an entirely different business from attempting to penetrate a terrorist organization or take apart a nuclear proliferation network. A machine built to perform CI work is not by any means automatically capable of collecting FI and running foreign assets.

That said, the biggest issue regarding military humint operations has to do with bureaucracy and command structure. Today's CIA, as risk-averse and tentative as it has become, is still an infinitely more flexible and agile organization than anything that exists within military channels. While the military is thinking about putting together a proposal for an operation to be briefed to the secretary of defense for his approval, the CIA will have already initiated and concluded the operation. Particularly in today's world, in the struggle against terror, speed is everything. If you cannot move now, there is no point in moving at all. The enemy who is currently exposed and vulnerable will no longer be so by the time you finish your PowerPoint presentations and multiple video teleconferences.

I was involved several years ago in an operation directed at the capture of an al-Qaeda operative. In brief the plan for this operation involved having assets of ours bag the target and bring him to a location where he would be handed over to us. It was unclear whether our assets could pull off the snatch, but there appeared to be nothing to lose either, so we decided to move ahead.

On board in the location in question, I had a handful of officers and a quantity of firearms. I believed I could pull off the operation, but I was also aware that, as in most such situations, there was a significant chance it might be a setup. We might show up to take possession of the target and find we were the ones being served up for an ambush.

Nearby was a major US military presence. Included in that presence were military intelligence and special operations types. I made the decision to approach them and request their assistance. They had the ability to supplement our capabilities significantly.

The first couple of conversations went well. The guys I was talking to were friends whom I knew well. We socialized regularly, and I had bought them any number of beers. We seemed well on our way to getting an op off the ground in short order.

Then I showed up for the third meeting, the one at which we were really going to hammer out details and a timetable. I walked into the office where we had met the first two times, and I was told by a clerk that the meeting had been moved into the auditorium down the hall. Confused, I walked down the hall of the military command's headquarters building and into the auditorium.

I was expecting to see the handful of individuals with whom I had met before. They were there, but so were seventy-plus other individuals. Someone was showing a PowerPoint presentation on a large screen in the front of the room. I was directed to a seat and then spent the better part of the next hour listening to individuals I did not know discuss the details of the impending operation. The meeting ended without any concrete decisions on any subject. I learned that there would be another planning session in a week, after which a briefing was planned for the general officer in charge of the area of operations.

I left the room stunned. One of my prime contacts in the military command in question pulled me aside in the hallway and told me that he had just been informed that a general officer at a location a thousand miles away was now going to assume direct tactical control of the actual rendezvous with the asset who would be bringing the captured al-Qaeda leader to us. Based on information that would be relayed to him, this general officer would then decide whether to proceed with taking custody of the prisoner and give instructions to us via radio.

I pulled the plug. I reminded my contact that this was a CIA operation and the military was supporting. I was not going to take direction from a general officer in a command center a thousand miles away about whether to trust my own asset. I was going to make the call on what to do at the rendezvous based on my knowledge of the individuals involved; my sense of the overall situation; and, ultimately, my gut. There was no way any of that was going to translate to a command post in a remote location. I walked away. That night I gave the green light for the operation to proceed, and things were put in motion.

Ultimately, the op failed, not because of anything to do with what was discussed above but simply because the assets on the ground where the target was located botched the snatch and were captured. Nothing ventured, nothing gained. We moved on to new targets and the search for new ways to get at the senior al-Qaeda individuals we were hunting.

My point herein is that the kind of procedures employed by the US military in this case are representative of the way in which that large, complex, often cumbersome organizational structure approaches operations in general. It may work well for conventional operations, although

I have my doubts in that regard as well. It is completely unsuited for intelligence operations and the kind of small-scale, fast-moving covert operations associated with them. In the world of intelligence, particularly when it comes to counterterrorism, decisions need to be made at the lowest possible level, and they need to be made now.

I have watched military case officers assigned to DH spend nine months to a year attempting to get approval to initiate human and technical operations that would have been concluded from start to finish by their CIA counterparts in less than half that time. I once saw an officer assigned to DH send off a message requesting permission to recruit a source and receive back from his headquarters an eighty-nine-page message asking for additional information on subjects so obscure and insignificant as to rival the debate over how many angels can dance on the head of a pin. Operations that would have been approved within the CIA at the level of a junior desk officer were put on hold, because it was necessary to obtain the personal signature of the Secretary of Defense in order for a DH case officer to move.

This was in most cases not a reflection on the quality of the military case officers involved. It was a product of the incredible bureaucratic inertia generated by an organizational structure that required that every decision be scrutinized by seemingly endless layers of bureaucracy and that required permission in advance for even the smallest steps. While CIA case officers were writing two-page messages detailing actions already taken, their military counterparts were drafting eighty-page submissions requesting permission to do something.

One of the horrible side effects of the refusal of senior CIA leadership to admit the full scope of the internal problems besetting that organization is that many other elements of the defense and intelligence communities have simply decided to write off the CIA and move ahead with the development of their own duplicate capabilities. Within the Department of Defense, in particular, there is a massive effort underway to stand up elements that are, on paper at least, able to perform all the tasks for which the CIA was designed. Where the director of National Intelligence stands on all this is, to me at least, unclear, but the fact remains that it is happening. If the military cannot rely upon the CIA to provide the intel they need, they will create a machine capable of getting it for them and end their reliance on the CIA entirely.

Leaving aside the horrible inefficiency of all this from a fiscal standpoint and the fact that American taxpayers are already overtaxed paying for a massive federal government, this is, from an operational perspective, an absolutely horrible idea. We will end up when this is all done with a huge, well-trained, and well-equipped military humint intelligence apparatus that will be completely incapable of moving with the speed, flexibility, and subtlety necessary to conduct intelligence operations.

I mentioned earlier the actions of Gary Schroen and those individuals who went with him into Afghanistan and constituted the first American team to enter that country in the days following September 11, 2001. That team consisted entirely of CIA officers; there were no military personnel assigned. This was not because the CIA did not want to include military personnel; it was because the Department of Defense refused to make these individuals available.

In the days leading up to the departure of Schroen's team from the United States for insertion into Afghanistan, numerous efforts were made to convince the US military to add at least a limited number of military personnel to Schroen's team. Not surprisingly, all the contacts with working-level individuals in Delta Force, Special Operations Command, and Central Command produced enthusiastic responses. There was no shortage of highly trained special operations personnel on the military side of the house who were dying for the opportunity to suit up and get into the fight. The reaction of the establishment within the Department of Defense was quite different.

No one in the military could provide a clear response as to what military forces would and would not be introduced into Afghanistan. There was an ongoing debate over what the military's mission should be. No one had decided where and when to position air assets, and as things stood there was no search-and-rescue capability to provide for the extraction of soldiers if they were wounded or became ill. The Department of Defense was reluctant to introduce personnel on the ground without having this capability. It appeared that for the time being it was just too dangerous to send US military personnel into Afghanistan.

So a small team of CIA officers, riding in an antiquated Russian helicopter acquired for the mission, made the insertion while thousands of highly trained men and women in the Special Operations community of the US military stood by and watched.

The problems with the Department of Defense did not end with the arrival of Schroen's team in-country. On October 3, 2001, he wrote the first of three field-appraisal messages from Afghanistan in an attempt to spur the US military into taking action. Bombing attacks on the Taliban had still not begun, because no infrastructure was in place to rescue downed pilots. The official word coming from headquarters was that the Department of Defense had yet to reach an agreement on what forces should be introduced and when. Meanwhile, the Afghans supporting the CIA team on the ground continued daily to demand an explanation as to when military assets would be deployed.

On October 10, 2001, Schroen received a call from CIA headquarters advising him that the logjam regarding deployment of military special operations personnel remained unbroken and suggesting that it was now his responsibility to break it. Washington, having completely dropped the ball on getting the US military into Afghanistan, was now engaging in the time-honored tradition of passing the buck. Not surprisingly, Schroen lost his cool and exploded. He was way out on a limb and desperate for support. He did not need bureaucratic games; he needed results.

Ultimately, the first US Army Special Forces A-team, ODA 555, did not arrive in Afghanistan until the evening of October 19, 2001, almost a full month behind the CIA personnel that landed with Schroen. By the time ODA 555 arrived, the CIA already had a second team on the ground, working in the area around Mazar-i-Sharif.

I am not Special Forces. I never went through the Q course at Bragg, and I have never served on an ODA. I have, however, known a lot of Special Forces operators and worked in the field with some outstanding individuals from that side of the house. I can guarantee you that the delay in getting US Army Green Berets on the ground inside Afghanistan had nothing to do with any individual's reluctance to get into the fight. In fact, I would be willing to bet that the men of ODA 555 probably had their gear packed and were ready to go to war before the sun went down on September 11, 2001.

The delay in the deployment of US military forces was caused by bureaucracy and a top-heavy command structure that required every decision to be endlessly debated, staffed, briefed, and rebriefed. It was the same reason that a simple request I made for the provision of limited military support to an asset meeting and a snatch operation turned into something resembling the planning of the D-Day invasion of Normandy.

You can't run intelligence and covert action operations this way. You will end up with a lot of shiny toys and stacks of high-speed, low-drag operators, and they will accomplish very, very little. In the world of intelligence, in many cases, less is more.

I ran into exactly the same kind of issues as Schroen when I took the first American team into northern Iraq to begin preparations for the invasion of Iraq. The plan for the invasion had already been formulated: We knew that the 10th Special Forces Group out of Fort Carson was to move into northern Iraq and pave the way for the introduction of the 4th Infantry Division. We also knew that 10th Group personnel from one of their pilot teams would be accompanying us when we entered Iraq. We had met these individuals and visited Fort Carson, and some of these personnel were, in fact, already participating in preparations for deployment.

The fact remained that when we rolled into Iraq for the first time in July of 2002 all the issues concerning 10th Group participation remained unresolved. Individuals from the military side of the house with whom we had been training and working for months stayed behind. Eight CIA officers made the initial crossing, and our Special Forces brethren did not join us until October. No one could even untangle the issues concerning use of military aircraft. We drove in, riding in commercial vehicles purchased locally for this purpose.

Maybe the best-known example of the impact of this kind of inertia and delay is what happened at Tora Bora. Reading accounts of what occurred there in the fall of 2001 makes you want to cry in frustration. To this day, individuals I know who were members of that team can hardly talk about the missed opportunities without breaking down. Plain and simple, we cornered bin Laden and his senior subordinates, and then we let them walk away.

The Jawbreaker team under Gary Berntsen's team was operating on a shoestring and a prayer in pursuing al-Qaeda into Tora Bora. They had a handful of individuals on the ground, some very questionable Afghan allies, and a transport and logistical system that depended heavily on the use of ancient discarded Soviet equipment and mules. It did not matter, because Jawbreaker had something a lot more powerful and valuable than any high technology: They had a singular focus on mission accomplishment and the willingness to do whatever it took to get the job done.

At some point in that pursuit, however, it became clear that in order to prevent the escape of the fleeing senior al-Qaeda personnel, it would be necessary to introduce American ground forces to block escape routes, close with the enemy, and finish them. Specifically, in Berntsen's mind, what was needed was at least one battalion of Rangers.

If you have never dealt with the Rangers, let me assure you as to their quality, their mettle, and their willingness to take on the seemingly impossible. These are men who will go anywhere, accomplish the mission no matter what the odds, and make whatever foe they are pitted against regret the day he confronted the United States of America. If anyone had told a Ranger battalion commander to take his men into Tora Bora, he would have responded simply by asking what time the aircraft was taking off. They would not have had any problem getting men to go in. They might have had a problem with men from other units trying to hitch a ride and get into the fight. These guys joined the US Army to destroy our enemies; a trip to the back of beyond and a chance to kill al-Qaeda would have been a dream come true.

No one gave the order. Senior officers deliberated. Briefings were conducted. Meetings were scheduled. Staff officers worked overtime to prepare PowerPoint presentations and update sitreps. Bin Laden and his key lieutenants walked out, and years later we are still trying to find many of these individuals, including bin Laden himself.

Three months after bin Laden's escape, the US military launched an operation into the same area. Using elements of the 101st Airborne and the 10th Mountain Division, they succeeded in killing hundreds of enemy fighters. The last al-Qaeda sanctuary in Afghanistan was destroyed. But not a single one of the top al-Qaeda leaders was killed or captured. It was a carefully crafted, well-executed punch, thrown three months too late.

Lest my comments be interpreted as suggesting that all the issues concerning other entities' involvement in intelligence and covert-action operations are confined to the US military, let's talk about the FBI for a while and its move into the world of human intelligence operations.

There is a fair amount of friction between the CIA and the FBI. It sort of goes with the territory. Both organizations are staffed with hard-charging, proud individuals used to getting their own way. That said, cooperation between the two is considerably better today than it has been in the past, and I have worked with a great number of FBI colleagues whom I continue to view as close personal friends as well as fellow professionals.

The two organizations are fundamentally different. They are constructed from the ground up for completely different jobs. They have different cultures, and they recruit very different types of individuals. The stereotypical CIA case officer is an individual who is at home with ambiguity and change and who expects that the plan for an op may very well have to be reformulated three times en route to an agent meeting. The stereotypical FBI agent is a guy in a dark suit and a white shirt who has the patience and attention to detail to spend years piecing together a complex criminal case out of a pile of minute facts and then ensure that it stands up to the intense standards of a criminal prosecution.

Having the CIA get into the business of criminal investigation would be a horrific idea. Leaving aside for the moment the significant constitutional-rights issues involved, the agency does not have the structure, focus, or personnel to carry out this task. It might ultimately reach the right conclusions, but it would be absolutely incapable of presenting those conclusions in an organized, evidentiary manner that would allow for prosecution and conviction.

It is an equally terrible idea to have the FBI begin to move into the realm of humint collection. In a world that requires speed and flexibility, the FBI is a stiff, slow-moving entity completely incapable of responding as required. And yet the FBI is moving into humint operations and not in a small way. It has jumped in with both feet.

Let me illustrate how ineffective this is with an example of an important terrorist case on which I was working shortly before my retirement from the CIA.

A few years ago a unit under my command developed information regarding interest on the part of a terrorist organization in the acquisition of material that would allow it to construct a weapon of mass destruction. This information was corroborated over time from multiple sources. As the picture was pieced together, it was also determined that at least some members of the organization in question had shown interest in the possibility of acquiring the necessary material from a specific location identified by us.

During operational meetings within the unit, we talked about a wide range of options to defeat this threat. It was not clear how long it might take this terrorist organization to acquire the material it was seeking, nor was it clear how quickly this group might be able to construct a weapon once it had this material in hand. Regardless, all things considered, it was clear that we were dealing with a real threat and that we needed to come up with a mechanism for taking the terrorists in question off the street.

The interest of this particular group in the acquisition of material from a specific location identified by us opened up a range of possibilities. In particular, some of the facts available suggested that it might be possible to cooperate with the FBI and to conduct a joint operation that would ultimately result in apprehension of the suspects and their successful prosecution. I, against the wise counsel of many fellow CIA officers, elected to do the corporate thing and bring the FBI into the case.

The first meeting with the FBI involved a handful of officers from their headquarters section that is charged with conducting operations against terrorist WMD programs. The second meeting, which took another two weeks to organize, involved a dozen participants from several different FBI components. There were a grand total of three CIA officers present. We were starting to feel outnumbered.

The third meeting took several more weeks to orchestrate. By this time, there were thirty-five FBI agents present. They represented a number of offices from their headquarters and three different field offices. CIA attendance remained static, with the same three officers working the op from our side. This meeting ended in a deadlock, not because of problems between the CIA and the FBI but because two of the field office representatives got into a shouting match and almost came to blows.

It had now been two months at least since we had asked the FBI to play. We were approaching the stage of the op where we had expected to be initiating operational activity on the street. In fact, we had not even yet gotten formal agreement from the FBI to participate nor could we even say with any real certainty exactly what piece of the FBI would do the op when or if it ever materialized.

Months passed. Our frustration grew. Intelligence continued to flow in showing that the threat was real and that the terrorist group's intent to acquire WMD capability remained as strong as ever. In frustration, I decided to attend the next meeting with the FBI personally in order to try to break the deadlock.

The conference room where the meeting took place was full. We had brought half a dozen CIA officers. There were close to forty FBI personnel present. During introductions, I lost track completely of who they all were or why they needed to be involved. I figured it was time to get down to brass tacks.

I told the FBI that we wanted to work with them and that we were excited about putting together an op that would result in prosecutions. I stressed, however, that the threat was growing and that we needed to move fast to head it off. I noted that we were still discussing generalities despite the fact that we would have hoped by this point to have the actual op well underway. I concluded by saying that as much as we wanted to work this target jointly, if we could not get moving soon, we might have to walk away and try to find a way to get to the target on our own.

There was a slight pause, and then one of the senior FBI agents responded by saying that if we wanted to walk away we should do so. He stated that he had no idea when they would be ready to proceed. He added that he expected that it would be many months yet and concluded his remarks by saying that actually he was not sure they were going to be able to put together an op at all and that it was possible that this target was just too difficult for them to take on. He closed by noting simply, "Maybe we can't do it."

The FBI agent who made these remarks had devoted decades of his life to the service of his country, as had many of the other FBI personnel present. They were good people who wanted to keep their fellow citizens safe and destroy the terrorist networks threatening our nation. They did not drag out the planning for this operation because they didn't care or because they were trying to make my life miserable. They did so because, working within the confines of the bureaucracy in which they served, they had no choice.

I was asking them for a quick decision and a commitment to an open-ended operation that would have to be put together as it progressed. In order to help they needed to spin up undercover operatives, commercial backstopping, and a host of technical and human capabilities, and they needed to do it now. They were incapable of doing that. I wanted someone to make a decision; there was no such someone. In their system they would be required to write a lengthy and complex operational proposal that ultimately might run to many hundreds of pages. This proposal would be scrutinized, edited, briefed, briefed again, and maybe, someday, far down the road, approved.

By that time, it would not matter what the result would be. Events would have passed us by. In all likelihood, the terrorist group in question would have succeeded in acquiring the capability it desired. If it had not, it would only be by the grace of God, not because of anything we had done.

I don't know what the resolution of this impasse was. As of the time I retired, almost a year after we began talking to the FBI, we still had not even reached the point of having an agreed-upon operational plan. I hope and pray that the CIA is not still waiting for the FBI to move. I hope somebody somewhere has moved.

Despite all the issues outlined above, the FBI is expanding daily the scope of its human intelligence operations. Once upon a time, there was a clear demarcation between the CIA and the FBI. In particular it used to be accepted as a cardinal principle that the FBI did not operate outside the United States. Those days are long gone. Not only does the FBI have an extensive collection of legal attachés around the world, they have moved heavily into running agents abroad as well. These operations may or may not be known to the CIA, and there may or may not be any coordination arranged.

To illustrate the kind of issues that arise when multiple human intelligence services are operating abroad, allow me to use a fairly benign example. Several years ago I was running operations in a country in Asia. Much of what we did was focused on the terrorist threat, and we had several productive operations that were ongoing with the local service against Internet cafés used by terrorists for communication purposes.

One day, while I was sitting in my office, a friend who worked for a local military command stopped by. He told me that he had some information for me that he thought I might find of interest. I asked him to have a seat, and then he told me a story about a conversation he had had the night before with a Special Forces sergeant he met in a bar downtown. In brief the sergeant told him that he was in-country to do some training with the local military but that while he was in-country he had also been tasked by his own chain of command to collect information on Internet cafés that might be used by terrorists for communications.

I did not hit the roof, but I was not happy. I asked my friend if he could get in touch with this sergeant. When he advised that he could, I asked him to contact the sergeant and have him come and talk to me. My friend agreed.

The next day the sergeant came to see me. He was a good man and, not surprisingly, a little chagrined that he had been called on the carpet. He explained that he had received tasking from his military command to gather information on Internet cafés in-country and that it had never occurred to him that this might cause a problem of any kind.

I told the sergeant, without going into any real detail, that there were a number of joint operations with the local liaison service that were ongoing against the cafés in question. I explained to him that these businesses were in areas where no foreigners ever went. One white face would set off alarm bells and might destroy months of work. I stressed that, in fact, in operations of this type, even the slightest misstep could mean disaster.

The sergeant understood. He promised me he would stand down, and he kept his word. As I said, he was a good man.

The fact remained that but for a lucky break and an alert friend I would never have known anything until our ops started going dead and months of backbreaking work was destroyed.

There is a lot more that could be said on this topic but very little of it in an unclassified setting. Let it suffice to say at this point that we are not just talking about involving a lot of organizations in human intelligence operations who are not very good at that kind of thing. We are talking about inviting a lot of people to play in a very tight operational space with only an extremely fuzzy understanding of who is directing traffic and who is in charge. The results are predictable: Organizations will run into each other, and the results may be catastrophic.

Back in the early 1990s, Charlie Sheen made a movie called *Beyond the Law* about a police officer in the Southwest who goes undercover to infiltrate a motorcycle gang. It's not the greatest film ever made, but it is a long way from being the worst. It is, in fact, based on the true story of an officer who actually carried out such an assignment, and it does a fairly good job of illustrating the incredible challenges such work entails.

One of the scenes in that film that is burned into my memory concerns a rally in the desert. Sheen, who by this point has been accepted into the group, is present when an FBI undercover officer, also present at the rally, is detected and confronted by members of the gang. Until this moment, Sheen is unaware that there is another undercover officer at the rally. No coordination with his office has been done by the FBI. There are two separate ops being run, and they have now crossed wires. One of them has gone south in a big way, and Sheen, still desperately exposed himself, is now faced with the prospect not only of protecting his own thin cover but of trying to think of a way to save the life of the FBI undercover as well. It's a powerful scene, and if you have ever been out on the street with a gun on your ankle and no backup, you know exactly how terrifying such a moment could be.

I'll let you watch the movie if you want to find out how this all sorts out. The point for our purposes is that this is no way to run a railroad or an operation. You can't have multiple agencies fishing in the same pond and not think you are going to have problems. Things will get screwed up. Lines will cross, and people will die.

I have a good friend in the agency who worked undercover for years inside motorcycle gangs on the East Coast. He is replete with stories about similar incidents that occurred during operations in which he was involved. One of the points he makes all the time is that your tradecraft is only as good as that of the weakest element involved in operations against a target. When he went undercover, for example, he spent the better part of a year away from his department—learning to ride, being seen, even getting the right tan lines to show he had been wearing his biker attire, not a police uniform, while riding. The bike he rode was one he built himself, and he knew it inside out.

Other organizations working the same target did not take the same care. They cut corners. They used motorcycles impounded from arrested gang members, which were often recognized by bikers at rallies the undercover officers attended. They took shortcuts in prep time and often took officers only a few months away from uniformed duty and inserted them into venues where it was highly likely they would be recognized by persons they had arrested only a short time before.

The result was not simply that the operation in question was blown or that the life of an undercover officer was endangered. The result was, as we would say in the trade, that the entire area was "heated up": It was essentially advertised to the target group that they were a focus of police interest and that undercover operatives were being utilized to penetrate them. Every other undercover attempting to work the same target would pay the price in increased scrutiny and by being put through longer and more rigorous vetting procedures.

These same principles apply to undercover work of all kinds. We cannot have a random collection of junior varsity teams trying in some haphazard fashion to crawl into the depths of al-Qaeda. We need a single, highly disciplined varsity team with laserlike focus and absolute precision.

It is strange to think that we have come to this point some sixty-plus years after the founding of the OSS, because all these issues were fully understood and appreciated then. It was, in fact, precisely because of these kinds of concerns that President Franklin Roosevelt, on the advice of Donovan and over the concerted opposition of the military services, created the Coordinator of Information, which then evolved into the OSS.

Consider, for example, the memorandum from the Secretary of War implementing Roosevelt's direction that the Coordinator of Information should be established on September 6, 1941:

Subject: Undercover Intelligence Service

The military and naval intelligence services have gone into the field of undercover intelligence to a limited extent. In the view of the appointment of the Coordinator of Information and the work which it is understood the President desires him to undertake, it is believed that the undercover intelligence of the two services should be consolidated under the Coordinator of Information. The reasons for this are that an undercover intelligence organization is much more effective if under one head than three, and that a civilian agency, such as the Coordinator of Information, has distinct advantages over any military or naval agency in the administration of such a service.

Roosevelt was not simply creating a new intelligence service; he was creating a service that would control all undercover strategic-level humint intelligence operations, and he knew exactly why he was doing it.

Kermit Roosevelt, in writing the official war history of the OSS, had this to say on the issue of whether a civilian or a military organization should run humint operations:

Secret intelligence, sabotage and subversion could not be run along standard military or bureaucratic lines. In the handling of agents the human element was primary, and it was discovered many times over that a few individuals who combined understanding of this factor with imagination in operations and objectivity in evaluating results could produce far better intelligence than could larger staffs which attempted to work on a more regular, more bureaucratic or more military basis.

Although external factors accounted for much, the notably disparate results of various competing OSS units attested the validity of the principle. Such a contrast was provided by the large but relatively unproductive SI/London staff compared with the small SI/Algiers unit which provided for Operation ANVIL, the best briefed invasion in history, as much information as the British and French services combined.

Sixty-seven years after Roosevelt and Donovan reached their conclusions about how to run effective human intelligence operations, we seem determined to relearn all the old lessons the hard way. In the midst of an open-ended worldwide conflict against a fanatical foe, as the advance of technology threatens to arm our enemies with weapons of unspeakable power, we may not have the luxury of taking our time in getting this right. The fact that we have allowed our existing strategic human intelligence organization, the CIA, to deteriorate does not mean that we were not right about the necessity to have one such single, flexible, civilian entity. We do not need a return to the chaos and confusion that characterized intelligence collection in the 1930s. We need a new OSS.

CHAPTER THIRTEEN

Memories of Sherlock Holmes:
The Final Problem

Arthur Conan Doyle

Weary of writing about Sherlock Holmes since the first novel, A Study in Scarlet, *written in 1886, Arthur Conan Doyle in 1893 published* The Final Problem, *killing Holmes and his arch-rival Professor James Moriarty on a mountain cliff and river. The story, part of the collection called* Memories of Sherlock Holmes, *caused an outcry among readers unlike any ever seen in publishing at that time. They demanded more Holmes, but Doyle had no intention of giving in. Then the publishers came to Doyle with so much money that Holmes was born again. Doyle brought him back to life in many new adventures, including the famous* Hound of the Baskervilles, *written in 1901. In his life (1859-1930) Doyle published four novels featuring Holmes and Watson, and fifty-six short stories. This excerpt from* Memories *and* The Final Problem *includes detective work of the kind Holmes is famous for, but at its core it is a spy story, immensely enjoyable despite knowing its ending. When Doyle wrote "The End" on this tale, he really thought he was putting Holmes away for good. Sherlock Holmes was much too strong for that to happen.*

It is with a heavy heart that I take up my pen to write these the last words in which I shall ever record the singular gifts by which my friend Mr. Sherlock Holmes was distinguished. In an incoherent and, as I deeply feel, an entirely inadequate fashion, I have endeavored to give some account of my strange experiences in his company from the chance which first brought us together at the period of the "Study in Scarlet," up to the time of his interference in the matter of the "Naval Treaty"—an interference which had the unquestionable effect of preventing a serious international complication. It was my intention to have stopped there, and to have said nothing of that event which has created a void in my life which the lapse of two years has done little to fill. My hand has been forced, however, by the recent letters in which Colonel James Moriarty defends the memory of his brother, and I have no choice but to lay the facts before the public exactly as they occurred. I alone know the absolute truth of the matter, and I am satisfied that the time has come when no good purpose is to be served by its suppression. As far as I know, there have been only three accounts in the public press: that in the *Journal de Geneve* on May 6th, 1891, the Reuter's dispatch in the English papers on May 7th, and finally the recent letter to which I have alluded. Of these the first and second were extremely condensed, while the last is, as I shall now show, an absolute perversion of the facts. It lies with me to tell for the first time what really took place between Professor Moriarty and Mr. Sherlock Holmes.

It may be remembered that after my marriage, and my subsequent start in private practice, the very intimate relations which had existed between Holmes and myself became to some extent modified. He still came to me from time to time when he desired a companion in his investigation, but these occasions grew more and more seldom, until I find that in the year 1890 there were only three cases of which I retain any record. During the winter of that year and the early spring of 1891, I saw in the papers that he had been engaged by the French government upon a matter of supreme importance, and I received two notes from Holmes, dated from Narbonne and from Nîmes, from which I gathered that his stay in France was likely to be a long one. It was with some surprise, therefore, that I saw him walk into my consulting-room upon the evening of April 24th. It struck me that he was looking even paler and thinner than usual.

"Yes, I have been using myself up rather too freely," he remarked, in answer to my look rather than to my words; "I have been a little pressed of late. Have you any objection to my closing your shutters?"

The only light in the room came from the lamp upon the table at which I had been reading. Holmes edged his way round the wall and flinging the shutters together, he bolted them securely.

"You are afraid of something?" I asked.

"Well, I am."

"Of what?"

"Of air-guns."

"My dear Holmes, what do you mean?"

"I think that you know me well enough, Watson, to understand that I am by no means a nervous man. At the same time, it is stupidity rather than courage to refuse to recognize danger when it is close upon you. Might I trouble you for a match?" He drew in the smoke of his cigarette as if the soothing influence was grateful to him.

"I must apologize for calling so late," said he, "and I must further beg you to be so unconventional as to allow me to leave your house presently by scrambling over your back garden wall."

"But what does it all mean?" I asked.

He held out his hand, and I saw in the light of the lamp that two of his knuckles were burst and bleeding.

"It is not an airy nothing, you see," said he, smiling. "On the contrary, it is solid enough for a man to break his hand over. Is Mrs. Watson in?"

"She is away upon a visit."

"Indeed! You are alone?"

"Quite."

"Then it makes it the easier for me to propose that you should come away with me for a week to the Continent."

"Where?"

"Oh, anywhere. It's all the same to me."

There was something very strange in all this. It was not Holmes's nature to take an aimless holiday, and something about his pale, worn face told me that his nerves were at their highest tension. He saw the question in my eyes, and, putting his finger-tips together and his elbows upon his knees, he explained the situation.

"You have probably never heard of Professor Moriarty?" said he.

"Never."

"Aye, there's the genius and the wonder of the thing!" he cried. "The man pervades London, and no one has heard of him. That's what puts him on a pinnacle in the records of crime. I tell you, Watson, in all seriousness, that if I could beat that man, if I could free society of him, I should feel that my own career had reached its summit, and I should be prepared to turn to some more placid line in life. Between ourselves, the recent cases in which I have been of assistance to the royal family of Scandinavia, and to the French republic, have left me in such a position that I could continue to live in the quiet fashion which is most congenial to me, and to concentrate my attention upon my chemical researches. But I could not rest, Watson, I could not sit quiet in my chair, if I thought that such a man as Professor Moriarty were walking the streets of London unchallenged."

"What has he done, then?"

"His career has been an extraordinary one. He is a man of good birth and excellent education, endowed by nature with a phenomenal mathematical faculty. At the age of twenty-one he wrote a treatise upon the Binomial Theorem, which has had a European vogue. On the strength of it he won the Mathematical Chair at one of our smaller universities, and had, to all appearances, a most brilliant career before him. But the man had hereditary tendencies of the most diabolical kind. A criminal strain ran in his blood, which, instead of being modified, was increased and rendered infinitely more dangerous by his extraordinary mental powers. Dark rumors gathered round him in the university town, and eventually he was compelled to resign his chair and to come down to London, where he set up as an army coach. So much is known to the world, but what I am telling you now is what I have myself discovered.

"As you are aware, Watson, there is no one who knows the higher criminal world of London so well as I do. For years past I have continually been conscious of some power behind the malefactor, some deep organizing power which forever stands in the way of the law, and throws its shield over the wrong-doer. Again and again in cases of the most varying sorts—forgery cases, robberies, murders—I have felt the presence of this force, and I have deduced its action in many of those undiscovered crimes in which I have not been personally consulted. For years I have endeavored to break through the veil which shrouded it, and at last the time came when I seized my thread and followed it, until it led me, after a thousand cunning windings, to ex-Professor Moriarty of mathematical celebrity.

"He is the Napoleon of crime, Watson. He is the organizer of half that is evil and of nearly all that is undetected in this great city. He is a genius, a philosopher, an abstract thinker. He has a brain of the first order. He sits motionless, like a spider in the center of its web, but that web has a thousand radiations, and he knows well every quiver of each of them. He does little himself. He only plans. But his agents are numerous and splendidly organized. Is there a crime to be done, a paper to be abstracted, we will say, a house to be rifled, a man to be removed—the word is passed to the Professor, the matter is organized and carried out. The agent may be caught. In that case money is found for his bail or his defense. But the central power which uses the agent is never caught—never so much as suspected. This was the organization which I deduced, Watson, and which I devoted my whole energy to exposing and breaking up.

"But the Professor was fenced round with safeguards so cunningly devised that, do what I would, it seemed impossible to get evidence which would convict in a court of law. You know my powers, my dear Watson, and yet at the end of three months I was forced to confess that I had at last met an antagonist who was my intellectual equal. My horror at his crimes was lost in my admiration at his skill. But at last he made a trip—only a little, little trip—but it was more than he could afford when I was so close upon him. I had my chance, and, starting from that point, I have woven my net round him until now it is all ready to close. In three days—that is to say, on Monday next—matters will be ripe, and the Professor, with all the principal members of his gang, will be in the hands of the police. Then will come the greatest criminal trial of the century, the clearing up of over forty mysteries, and the rope for all of them; but if we move at all prematurely, you understand, they may slip out of our hands even at the last moment.

"Now, if I could have done this without the knowledge of Professor Moriarty, all would have been well. But he was too wily for that. He saw every step which I took to draw my toils round him. Again and again he strove to break away, but I as often headed him off. I tell you, my friend, that if a detailed account of that silent contest could be written, it would take its place as the most brilliant bit of thrust-and-parry work in the history of detection. Never have I risen to such a height, and never

259

have I been so hard pressed by an opponent. He cut deep, and yet I just undercut him. This morning the last steps were taken, and three days only were wanted to complete the business. I was sitting in my room thinking the matter over, when the door opened and Professor Moriarty stood before me.

"My nerves are fairly proof, Watson, but I must confess to a start when I saw the very man who had been so much in my thoughts standing there on my threshold. His appearance was quite familiar to me. He is extremely tall and thin, his forehead domes out in a white curve, and his two eyes are deeply sunken in his head. He is clean-shaven, pale, and ascetic-looking, retaining something of the professor in his features. His shoulders are rounded from much study, and his face protrudes forward, and is forever slowly oscillating from side to side in a curiously reptilian fashion. He peered at me with great curiosity in his puckered eyes.

"'You have less frontal development than I should have expected,' said he, at last. 'It is a dangerous habit to finger loaded firearms in the pocket of one's dressing-gown.'

"The fact is that upon his entrance I had instantly recognized the extreme personal danger in which I lay. The only conceivable escape for him lay in silencing my tongue. In an instant I had slipped the revolver from the drawer into my pocket, and was covering him through the cloth. At his remark I drew the weapon out and laid it cocked upon the table. He still smiled and blinked, but there was something about his eyes which made me feel very glad that I had it there.

"'You evidently don't know me,' said he.

"'On the contrary,' I answered, 'I think it is fairly evident that I do. Pray take a chair. I can spare you five minutes if you have anything to say.'

"'All that I have to say has already crossed your mind,' said he.

"'Then possibly my answer has crossed yours,' I replied.

"'You stand fast?'

"'Absolutely.'

"He clapped his hand into his pocket, and I raised the pistol from the table. But he merely drew out a memorandum-book in which he had scribbled some dates.

"'You crossed my path on the 4th of January,' said he. 'On the 23rd you incommoded me; by the middle of February I was seriously inconvenienced by you; at the end of March I was absolutely hampered in my plans; and now, at the close of April, I find myself placed in such a position through your continual persecution that I am in positive danger of losing my liberty. The situation is becoming an impossible one.'

"'Have you any suggestion to make?' I asked.

"'You must drop it, Mr. Holmes,' said he, swaying his face about. 'You really must, you know.'

"'After Monday,' said I.

"'Tut, tut,' said he. 'I am quite sure that a man of your intelligence will see that there can be but one outcome to this affair. It is necessary that you should withdraw. You have worked things in such a fashion that we have only one resource left. It has been an intellectual treat to me to see the way in which you have grappled with this affair, and I say, unaffectedly, that it would be a grief to me to be forced to take any extreme measure. You smile, sir, but I assure you that it really would.'

"'Danger is part of my trade,' I remarked.

"'That is not danger,' said he. 'It is inevitable destruction. You stand in the way not merely of an individual, but of a mighty organization, the full extent of which you, with all your cleverness, have been unable to realize. You must stand clear, Mr. Holmes, or be trodden under foot.'

"'I am afraid,' said I, rising, 'that in the pleasure of this conversation I am neglecting business of importance which awaits me elsewhere.'

"He rose also and looked at me in silence, shaking his head sadly.

"'Well, well,' said he, at last. 'It seems a pity, but I have done what I could. I know every move of your game. You can do nothing before Monday. It has been a duel between you and me, Mr. Holmes. You hope to place me in the dock. I tell you that I will never stand in the dock. You hope to beat me. I tell you that you will never beat me. If you are clever enough to bring destruction upon me, rest assured that I shall do as much to you.'

"'You have paid me several compliments, Mr. Moriarty,' said I. 'Let me pay you one in return when I say that if I were assured of the former eventuality I would, in the interests of the public, cheerfully accept the latter.'

"'I can promise you the one, but not the other,' he snarled, and so turned his rounded back upon me, and went peering and blinking out of the room.

"That was my singular interview with Professor Moriarty. I confess that it left an unpleasant effect upon my mind. His soft, precise fashion of speech leaves a conviction of sincerity which a mere bully could not produce. Of course, you will say: 'Why not take police precautions against him?' The reason is that I am well convinced that it is from his agents the blow will fall. I have the best proofs that it would be so."

"You have already been assaulted?"

"My dear Watson, Professor Moriarty is not a man who lets the grass grow under his feet. I went out about mid-day to transact some business in Oxford Street. As I passed the corner which leads from Bentinck Street on to the Welbeck Street crossing a two-horse van furiously driven whizzed round and was on me like a flash. I sprang for the foot-path and saved myself by the fraction of a second. The van dashed round by Marylebone Lane and was gone in an instant. I kept to the pavement after that, Watson, but as I walked down Vere Street a brick came down from the roof of one of the houses, and was shattered to fragments at my feet. I called the police and had the place examined. There were slates and bricks piled up on the roof preparatory to some repairs, and they would have me believe that the wind had toppled over one of these. Of course I knew better, but I could prove nothing. I took a cab after that and reached my brother's rooms in Pall Mall, where I spent the day. Now I have come round to you, and on my way I was attacked by a rough with a bludgeon. I knocked him down, and the police have him in custody; but I can tell you with the most absolute confidence that no possible connection will ever be traced between the gentleman upon whose front teeth I have barked my knuckles and the retiring mathematical coach, who is, I dare say, working out problems upon a black-board ten miles away. You will not wonder, Watson, that my first act on entering your rooms was to close your shutters, and that I have been compelled to ask your permission to leave the house by some less conspicuous exit than the front door."

I had often admired my friend's courage, but never more than now, as he sat quietly checking off a series of incidents which must have combined to make up a day of horror.

"You will spend the night here?" I said.

"No, my friend, you might find me a dangerous guest. I have my plans laid, and all will be well. Matters have gone so far now that they can move without my help as far as the arrest goes, though my presence is necessary for a conviction. It is obvious, therefore, that I cannot do better than get away for the few days which remain before the police are at liberty to act. It would be a great pleasure to me, therefore, if you could come on to the Continent with me."

"The practice is quiet," said I, "and I have an accommodating neighbor. I should be glad to come."

"And to start to-morrow morning?"

"If necessary."

"Oh yes, it is most necessary. Then these are your instructions, and I beg, my dear Watson, that you will obey them to the letter, for you are now playing a double-handed game with me against the cleverest rogue and the most powerful syndicate of criminals in Europe. Now listen! You will dispatch whatever luggage you intend to take by a trusty messenger unaddressed to Victoria to-night. In the morning you will send for a hansom, desiring your man to take neither the first nor the second which may present itself. Into this hansom you will jump, and you will drive to the Strand end of the Lowther Arcade, handing the address to the cabman upon a slip of paper, with a request that he will not throw it away. Have your fare ready, and the instant that your cab stops, dash through the Arcade, timing yourself to reach the other side at a quarter-past nine. You will find a small brougham waiting close to the curb, driven by a fellow with a heavy black cloak tipped at the collar with red. Into this you will step, and you will reach Victoria in time for the Continental express."

"Where shall I meet you?"

"At the station. The second first-class carriage from the front will be reserved for us."

"The carriage is our rendezvous, then?"

"Yes."

It was in vain that I asked Holmes to remain for the evening. It was evident to me that he thought he might bring trouble to the roof he was under, and that that was the motive which impelled him to go. With a few hurried words as to our plans for the morrow he rose and came out with me into the garden, clambering over the wall which leads into Mortimer Street, and immediately whistling for a hansom, in which I heard him drive away.

In the morning I obeyed Holmes's injunctions to the letter. A hansom was procured with such precaution as would prevent its being one which was placed ready for us, and I drove immediately after breakfast to the Lowther Arcade, through which I hurried at the top of my speed. A brougham was waiting with a very massive driver wrapped in a dark cloak, who, the instant that I had stepped in, whipped up the horse and rattled off to Victoria Station. On my alighting there he turned the carriage, and dashed away again without so much as a look in my direction.

So far all had gone admirably. My luggage was waiting for me, and I had no difficulty in finding the carriage which Holmes had indicated, the less so as it was the only one in the train which was marked "Engaged."

My only source of anxiety now was the non-appearance of Holmes. The station clock marked only seven minutes from the time when we were due to start. In vain I searched among the groups of travelers and leave-takers for the lithe figure of my friend. There was no sign of him. I spent a few minutes in assisting a venerable Italian priest, who was endeavoring to make a porter understand, in his broken English, that his luggage was to be booked through to Paris. Then, having taken another look round, I returned to my carriage, where I found that the porter, in spite of the ticket, had given me my decrepit Italian friend as a traveling companion. It was useless for me to explain to him that his presence was an intrusion, for my Italian was even more limited than his English, so I shrugged my shoulders resignedly, and continued to look out anxiously for my friend. A chill of fear had come over me, as I thought that his absence might mean that some blow had fallen during the night. Already the doors had all been shut and the whistle blown, when—

"My dear Watson," said a voice, "you have not even condescended to say good-morning."

I turned in uncontrollable astonishment. The aged ecclesiastic had turned his face towards me. For an instant the wrinkles were smoothed away, the nose drew away from the chin, the lower lip ceased to protrude and the mouth to mumble, the dull eyes regained their fire, the drooping figure expanded. The next the whole frame collapsed again, and Holmes had gone as quickly as he had come.

"Good heavens!" I cried; "how you startled me!"

"Every precaution is still necessary," he whispered. "I have reason to think that they are hot upon our trail. Ah, there is Moriarty himself."

The train had already begun to move as Holmes spoke. Glancing back, I saw a tall man pushing his way furiously through the crowd, and waving his hand as if he desired to have the train stopped. It was too late, however, for we were rapidly gathering momentum, and an instant later had shot clear of the station.

"With all our precautions, you see that we have cut it rather fine," said Holmes, laughing. He rose, and throwing off the black cassock and hat which had formed his disguise, he packed them away in a hand-bag.

"Have you seen the morning paper, Watson?"

"No."

"You haven't seen about Baker Street, then?"

"Baker Street?"

"They set fire to our rooms last night. No great harm was done."

"Good heavens, Holmes! This is intolerable."

"They must have lost my track completely after their bludgeon-man was arrested. Otherwise they could not have imagined that I had returned to my rooms. They have evidently taken the precaution of watching you, however, and that is what has brought Moriarty to Victoria. You could not have made any slip in coming?"

"I did exactly what you advised."

"Did you find your brougham?"

"Yes, it was waiting."

"Did you recognize your coachman?"

"No."

"It was my brother Mycroft. It is an advantage to get about in such a case without taking a mercenary into your confidence. But we must plan what we are to do about Moriarty now."

"As this is an express, and as the boat runs in connection with it, I should think we have shaken him off very effectively."

"My dear Watson, you evidently did not realize my meaning when I said that this man may be taken as being quite on the same intellectual plane as myself. You do not imagine that if I were the pursuer I should allow myself to be baffled by so slight an obstacle. Why, then, should you think so meanly of him?"

"What will he do?"

"What I should do?"

"What would you do, then?"

"Engage a special."

"But it must be late."

"By no means. This train stops at Canterbury; and there is always at least a quarter of an hour's delay at the boat. He will catch us there."

"One would think that we were the criminals. Let us have him arrested on his arrival."

"It would be to ruin the work of three months. We should get the big fish, but the smaller would dart right and left out of the net. On Monday we should have them all. No, an arrest is inadmissible."

"What then?"

"We shall get out at Canterbury."

"And then?"

"Well, then we must make a cross-country journey to Newhaven, and so over to Dieppe. Moriarty will again do what I should do. He will get on to Paris, mark down our luggage, and wait for two days at the depot. In the meantime we shall treat ourselves to a couple of carpet-bags, encourage the manufactures of the countries through which we travel, and make our way at our leisure into Switzerland, via Luxembourg and Basle."

At Canterbury, therefore, we alighted, only to find that we should have to wait an hour before we could get a train to Newhaven.

I was still looking rather ruefully after the rapidly disappearing luggage-van which contained my wardrobe, when Holmes pulled my sleeve and pointed up the line.

"Already, you see," said he.

Far away, from among the Kentish woods there rose a thin spray of smoke. A minute later a carriage and engine could be seen flying along the open curve which leads to the station. We had hardly time to take our place behind a pile of luggage when it passed with a rattle and a roar, beating a blast of hot air into our faces.

"There he goes," said Holmes, as we watched the carriage swing and rock over the points. "There are limits, you see, to our friend's intelligence. It would have been a coup-de-maître had he deduced what I would deduce and acted accordingly."

"And what would he have done had he overtaken us?"

"There cannot be the least doubt that he would have made a murderous attack upon me. It is, however, a game at which two may play. The question now is whether we should take a premature lunch here, or run our chance of starving before we reach the buffet at Newhaven."

We made our way to Brussels that night and spent two days there, moving on upon the third day as far as Strasburg. On the Monday morning Holmes had telegraphed to the London police, and in the evening we found a reply waiting for us at our hotel. Holmes tore it open, and then with a bitter curse hurled it into the grate.

"I might have known it!" he groaned. "He has escaped!"

"Moriarty?"

"They have secured the whole gang with the exception of him. He has given them the slip. Of course, when I had left the country there was no one to cope with him. But I did think that I had put the game in their hands. I think that you had better return to England, Watson."

"Why?"

"Because you will find me a dangerous companion now. This man's occupation is gone. He is lost if he returns to London. If I read his character right he will devote his whole energies to revenging himself upon me. He said as much in our short interview, and I fancy that he meant it. I should certainly recommend you to return to your practice."

It was hardly an appeal to be successful with one who was an old campaigner as well as an old friend. We sat in the Strasburg salle-à-manger arguing the question for half an hour, but the same night we had resumed our journey and were well on our way to Geneva.

For a charming week we wandered up the Valley of the Rhone, and then, branching off at Leuk, we made our way over the Gemmi Pass, still deep in snow, and so, by way of Interlaken, to Meiringen. It was a lovely trip, the dainty green of the spring below, the virgin white of the winter above; but it was clear to me that never for one instant did Holmes forget the shadow which lay across him. In the homely Alpine villages or in the lonely mountain passes, I could tell by his quick glancing eyes and his sharp scrutiny of every face that passed us, that he was well convinced that, walk where we would, we could not walk ourselves clear of the danger which was dogging our footsteps.

Once, I remember, as we passed over the Gemmi, and walked along the border of the melancholy Daubensee, a large rock which had been dislodged from the ridge upon our right clattered down and roared into the lake behind us. In an instant Holmes had raced up on to the ridge, and, standing upon a lofty pinnacle, craned his neck in every direction. It was in vain that our guide assured him that a fall of stones was a common chance in the spring-time at that spot. He said nothing, but he smiled at me with the air of a man who sees the fulfillment of that which he had expected.

And yet for all his watchfulness he was never depressed. On the contrary, I can never recollect having seen him in such exuberant spirits. Again and again he recurred to the fact that if he could be assured that society was freed from Professor Moriarty he would cheerfully bring his own career to a conclusion.

"I think that I may go so far as to say, Watson, that I have not lived wholly in vain," he remarked. "If my record were closed to-night I could still survey it with equanimity. The air of London is the sweeter for my presence. In over a thousand cases I am not aware that I have ever used my powers upon the wrong side. Of late I have been tempted to look into the problems furnished by nature rather than those more superficial ones for which our artificial state of society is responsible. Your memoirs will draw to an end, Watson, upon the day that I crown my career by the capture or extinction of the most dangerous and capable criminal in Europe."

I shall be brief, and yet exact, in the little which remains for me to tell. It is not a subject on which I would willingly dwell, and yet I am conscious that a duty devolves upon me to omit no detail.

It was on the 3rd of May that we reached the little village of Meiringen, where we put up at the Englischer Hof, then kept by Peter Steiler the elder. Our landlord was an intelligent man, and spoke excellent English, having served for three years as waiter at the Grosvenor Hotel in London. At his advice, on the afternoon of the 4th we set off together, with the intention of crossing the hills and spending the night at the hamlet of Rosenlaui. We had strict injunctions, however, on no account to pass the falls of Reichenbach, which are about half-way up the hill, without making a small detour to see them.

It is indeed, a fearful place. The torrent, swollen by the melting snow, plunges into a tremendous abyss, from which the spray rolls up like the smoke from a burning house. The shaft into which the river hurls itself is an immense chasm, lined by glistening coal-black rock, and narrowing into a creaming, boiling pit of incalculable depth, which brims over and shoots the stream onward over its jagged lip. The long sweep of green water roaring forever down, and the thick flickering curtain of spray hissing forever upward, turn a man giddy with their constant whirl and clamor. We stood near the edge peering down at the gleam of the breaking water far below us against the black rocks, and listening to the half-human shout which came booming up with the spray out of the abyss.

The path has been cut half-way round the fall to afford a complete view, but it ends abruptly, and the traveler has to return as he came. We had turned to do so, when we saw a Swiss lad come running along it with a letter in his hand. It bore the mark of the hotel which we had just left, and was addressed to me by the landlord. It appeared that within a very few minutes of our leaving, an English lady had arrived who was in the last stage of consumption. She had wintered at Davos Platz, and was journeying now to join her friends at Lucerne, when a sudden hemorrhage had overtaken her. It was thought that she could hardly live a few hours, but it would be a great consolation to her to see an English doctor, and, if

I would only return, etc. The good Steiler assured me in a postscript that he would himself look upon my compliance as a very great favor, since the lady absolutely refused to see a Swiss physician, and he could not but feel that he was incurring a great responsibility.

The appeal was one which could not be ignored. It was impossible to refuse the request of a fellow-countrywoman dying in a strange land. Yet I had my scruples about leaving Holmes. It was finally agreed, however, that he should retain the young Swiss messenger with him as guide and companion while I returned to Meiringen. My friend would stay some little time at the fall, he said, and would then walk slowly over the hill to Rosenlaui, where I was to rejoin him in the evening. As I turned away I saw Holmes, with his back against a rock and his arms folded, gazing down at the rush of the waters. It was the last that I was ever destined to see of him in this world.

When I was near the bottom of the descent I looked back. It was impossible, from that position, to see the fall, but I could see the curving path which winds over the shoulder of the hill and leads to it.

Along this a man was, I remember, walking very rapidly.

I could see his black figure clearly outlined against the green behind him. I noted him, and the energy with which he walked but he passed from my mind again as I hurried on upon my errand.

It may have been a little over an hour before I reached Meiringen. Old Steiler was standing at the porch of his hotel.

"Well," said I, as I came hurrying up, "I trust that she is no worse?"

A look of surprise passed over his face, and at the first quiver of his eyebrows my heart turned to lead in my breast.

"You did not write this?" I said, pulling the letter from my pocket. "There is no sick Englishwoman in the hotel?"

"Certainly not!" he cried. "But it has the hotel mark upon it! Ha, it must have been written by that tall Englishman who came in after you had gone. He said—"

But I waited for none of the landlord's explanations. In a tingle of fear I was already running down the village street, and making for the path which I had so lately descended. It had taken me an hour to come down. For all my efforts two more had passed before I found myself at the fall of Reichenbach once more. There was Holmes's Alpine-stock still leaning against the rock by which I had left him. But there was no sign of him, and it was in vain that I shouted. My only answer was my own voice reverberating in a rolling echo from the cliffs around me.

It was the sight of that Alpine-stock which turned me cold and sick.

He had not gone to Rosenlaui, then. He had remained on that three-foot path, with sheer wall on one side and sheer drop on the other, until his enemy had overtaken him. The young Swiss had gone too. He had probably been in the pay of Moriarty, and had left the two men together. And then what had happened? Who was to tell us what had happened then?

I stood for a minute or two to collect myself, for I was dazed with the horror of the thing. Then I began to think of Holmes's own methods and to try to practice them in reading this tragedy. It was, alas, only too easy to do. During our conversation we had not gone to the end of the path, and the Alpine-stock marked the place where we had stood. The blackish soil is kept forever soft by the incessant drift of spray, and a bird would leave its tread upon it. Two lines of footmarks were clearly marked along the farther end of the path, both leading away from me. There were none returning. A few yards from the end the soil was all ploughed up into a patch of mud, and the branches and ferns which fringed the chasm were torn and bedraggled. I lay upon my face and peered over with the spray spouting up all around me. It had darkened since I left, and now I could only see here and there the glistening of moisture upon the black walls, and far away down at the end of the shaft the gleam of the broken water. I shouted; but only the same half-human cry of the fall was borne back to my ears.

But it was destined that I should after all have a last word of greeting from my friend and comrade. I have said that his Alpine-stock had been left leaning against a rock which jutted on to the path. From the top of this boulder the gleam of something bright caught my eye, and, raising my hand, I found that it came from the silver cigarette-case which he used to carry. As I took it up a small square of paper upon which it had lain fluttered down on to the ground. Unfolding it, I found that it consisted of three pages torn from his note-book and addressed to me. It was characteristic of the man that the direction was as precise, and the writing as firm and clear, as though it had been written in his study.

> *My dear Watson [it said], I write these few lines through the courtesy of Mr. Moriarty, who awaits my convenience for the final discussion of those questions which lie between us. He has been giving me a sketch of the methods by which he avoided the English police and kept himself informed of our movements. They certainly confirm the very high opinion which I had formed of his abilities. I am pleased to think that I shall be able to free society from any further effects of his presence, though I fear that it is at a cost which will give pain to my friends, and especially, my dear Watson, to you. I have already explained to you, however, that my career had in any case reached its crisis, and that no possible conclusion to it could be more congenial to me than this. Indeed, if I may make a full confession to you, I was quite convinced that the letter from Meiringen was a hoax, and I allowed you to depart on that errand under the persuasion that some development of this sort would follow. Tell Inspector Patterson that the papers which he needs to convict the gang are in pigeonhole M., done up in a blue envelope and inscribed "Moriarty." I made every disposition of my property before leaving England, and handed it to my brother Mycroft. Pray give my greetings to Mrs. Watson, and believe me to be, my dear fellow,*
> *Very sincerely yours,*
> *Sherlock Holmes*

A few words may suffice to tell the little that remains. An examination by experts leaves little doubt that a personal contest between the two men ended, as it could hardly fail to end in such a situation, in their reeling over, locked in each other's arms. Any attempt at recovering the bodies was absolutely hopeless, and there, deep down in that dreadful caldron of swirling water and seething foam, will lie for all time the most dangerous criminal and the foremost champion of the law of their generation. The Swiss youth was never found again, and there can be no doubt that he was one of the numerous agents whom Moriarty kept in his employ. As to the gang, it will be within the memory of the public how completely the evidence which Holmes had accumulated exposed their organization, and how heavily the hand of the dead man weighed upon them. Of their terrible chief few details came out during the proceedings, and if I have now been compelled to make a clear statement of his career it is due to those injudicious champions who have endeavored to clear his memory by attacks upon him whom I shall ever regard as the best and the wisest man whom I have ever known.

Chapter Fourteen

A Spy Among Friends:
Kim Philby and the Great Betrayal

Ben Macintyre

In his "Afterword" to Ben Macintyre's startling book, A Spy Among Friends, *renowned writer John le Carré describes an incident involving Philby that occurred in 1987. The Berlin Wall had come down two years before, and le Carré was attending a reception given by the Union of Soviet Writers. Le Carré says he was passed an invitation to "meet an old friend and admirer of my work." He refused. The "old friend" was Kim Philby. Le Carré says he had heard Philby was dying, and he suspected Philby was hoping to collaborate on a book with him. Le Carré had once served in Britain's MI6 Intelligence organization, Philby's home base.*

Before he had bolted to Russia in early 1963, Philby had been a high-ranking member of Britain's MI6. There he was a close friend of Nicholas Elliott, another MI6 operative who spent a great deal of time with Philby. Philby had also been posted to the US, where he became quite chummy with James Angleton, of CIA Counter-Intelligence. Information passed inadvertently by Angleton to Philby over several years resulted in the destruction of every Anglo-American spy operation that was attempted at that time.

Between his activities in MI6 and his friendships with Elliott and Angleton, Kim Philby was one of the most successful turncoat spies in history, betraying his native Britain for the KGB.

This excerpt from A Spy Among Friends *describes one among many operations Philby betrayed while posted to the US and picking up details of on-going operations from James Angleton.*

Bido Kuka crouched in the hold of the *Stormie Seas*, huddled alongside the other fighters clutching their German Schmeisser submachine guns, as the boat rose and fell queasily in the dark Adriatic swell. Kuka felt patriotic, excited, and scared. Mostly he felt seasick. A pouch filled with gold sovereigns was strapped inside his belt. Taped to the inside of his wristwatch was a single cyanide pill, for use should he fall into the hands of the Albanian secret police, the Sigurimi. In his knapsack he carried a map, medical supplies, hand grenades, enough rations to survive for a week in the mountains, Albanian currency, propaganda leaflets, and photographs of the emigre anticommunist leaders to show to the people and inspire them to rise up against the hated dictator, Enver Hoxha. Through the porthole the jagged cliffs of Karaburun rose blackly against the moonless night sky, the edge of a country Kuka had not seen for three years. The Englishmen could be heard on deck, whispering muffled orders as the boat drew inshore.

They were strange, these Englishmen, huge, sun-reddened men who spoke an incomprehensible language and laughed when there was nothing funny to laugh at. They had brought along a dog called Lean-To; one had even brought his wife. They were pretending to be on a boating holiday. The man called "Lofty" kept his binoculars trained on the cliffs. The one called "Geoffrey" rehearsed once more the procedure for operating the wireless, a bulky contraption powered by a machine that looked like a bicycle without wheels. Kuka and his eight companions smoked in nervy silence. The *Stormie Seas* edged toward the Albanian shore.

Six months earlier Bido Kuka had been recruited for Operation Valuable in a displaced-persons camp outside Rome. Kuka was a "Ballist," a member of the Balli Kombetar, the Albanian nationalist group that had fought the Nazis during the war and then the communists after it. With the communist takeover of Albania hundreds of Ballists had been arrested, tortured, and killed, and Kuka had fled with other nationalists to Italy. Since then he had spent three miserable years in Fraschetti Camp, nursing his loathing of communism, rehearsing the Balli Kombetar motto, "Albania for the Albanians, Death to the Traitors," and plotting his return. When he was approached by a fellow émigré and asked to join a new guerrilla unit for secret anticommunist operations inside Albania, he did not hesitate. As another recruit put it: "There was no question of refusing. When your life is devoted to your country you are prepared to do anything to help it."

On July 14, 1949, Kuka and a fellow Ballist named Sarni Lepenica boarded a military plane in Rome and flew to the British island of Malta in the Mediterranean. They had no travel documents. A British officer, flapping a red handkerchief by way of a recognition signal, marched them past the customs barrier and into a car. An hour later the bemused Albanians arrived at the gateway to a large castle surrounded by a moat: Fort Bingemma, a Victorian citadel on the island's southwest corner, selected by British intelligence as the ideal place from which to launch an anticommunist counterrevolution.

Over the next three months, Kuka and some thirty other Albanian recruits underwent intensive training under the watchful (if slightly mad) eye of Lieutenant Colonel David de Crespigny Smiley, an aristocratic British army officer with a legendary taste for derring-do. During the war, Smiley had fought the Italians in Abyssinia as part of the Somaliland Camel Corps, foiled a German-backed coup to unseat the King of Iraq, fought alongside Siamese guerrillas, and liberated four thousand prisoners ("all absolutely stark naked except for a ball bag") from the Japanese camp at Ubon. But it was in Albania that he earned his reputation for raw courage: in 1943 he parachuted into northern Greece and set about blowing up bridges, ambushing German troops, and training guerrillas. He emerged from the war with a deep love of Albania, a loathing for Hoxha and the communists, a Military Cross, and facial scars from a prematurely exploding briefcase. When MI6 needed someone to equip, train, and infiltrate anticommunist fighters into Albania, Smiley was the obvious choice. He was imperialist, fearless, romantic, and unwary, and in all these respects he was a neat reflection of Operation Valuable.

The training program was brief but intensive and conducted amid rigid secrecy. A series of British instructors, including an eccentric Oxford don, provided lessons in map reading, unarmed combat, machine-gun marksmanship, and operating a radio with a pedal generator. Since the instructors spoke no Albanian, and the Albanians spoke not a word of English, training was conducted in sign language. This explains why

Kuka's conception of his mission was somewhat vague: get into Albania, head for his hometown near the Greek border, sound out the possibilities for armed insurrection, then get out and report back. None of the recruits were officers, and few had any military training. Life in the camps had left some with malnutrition, and all were quite small. The British, with more than a hint of condescension, called them "the pixies."

In late September Bido Kuka and eight other recruits were taken to Otranto on the Italian coast, fifty-five miles across the Adriatic from Albania. Disguised as local fishermen, they were loaded into a fishing vessel, and at a rendezvous point twenty miles off the Albanian coast they were transferred to the *Stormie Seas*, a forty-three-ton schooner painted to resemble a pleasure boat but containing a mighty ninety-horsepower engine, concealed fuel tanks, and enough munitions to start a small war. The *Stormie Seas* was commanded by Sam Barclay and John Leatham, two intrepid former Royal Navy officers who had spent the previous year running supplies from Athens to Salonika for the forces fighting the Greek communist guerrillas. MI6 had offered them the sum of fifty pounds to transport the insurgents to the Albanian coast, which Leatham thought was more than generous: "We were looking only for free adventure and a living."

Shortly after 9:00 p.m. on October 3, two hundred yards off the Karaburun Peninsula, the heavily armed pixies clambered into two rubber boats and headed toward a cove, rowed by two stout former marines, "Lofty" Cooling and Derby Allen. The Karaburun was barely inhabited, a wild place of goat tracks and thorny scrub. Having dropped off the men and their equipment, the Englishmen rowed back to the *Stormie Seas*. Looking back at the retreating coast, they saw a light flash suddenly at the cliff top and then go out again.

The nine pixies were already heading up the cliff. The going was slow in the deep darkness. As dawn broke, they split into two parties. Bido Kuka and four others, including his friend Ramis Matuka and his cousin Ahmet, headed south toward his home region while the remaining four, led by Sarni Lepenica, headed north. As they separated, Kuka was struck by a sudden foreboding, the sensation, intense but unfocused, "that the communists were ready and waiting for them."

After a day spent hiding in a cave, Kuka and his men set off again at nightfall. In the morning they approached the village of Gjorm, a wartime center of resistance and home to many Balli Kombetar sympathizers. As they drew near, a young girl ran toward them shouting: "Brothers, you're all going to be killed!"

Breathlessly she explained that the other group had already been ambushed by government forces: three of the four had been killed, including Lepenica, and the fourth had vanished. Two days earlier no less a personage than Beqir Balluku, the Albanian army chief of staff, had arrived with hundreds of troops, and the Karaburun ridge was crawling with government forces scouring every village, track, cave, and gully for the "fascist terrorists."

Local shepherds had been instructed to report anything suspicious, on pain of death. The Albanian guerrillas thanked the girl, gratefully seized the bread and milk she offered, and ran.

At the very moment Bido Kuka was scrambling for his life through the Albanian mountains, Kim Philby was steaming toward New York aboard the RMS *Caronia*, the most luxurious ocean liner afloat. His many friends in MI5 and MI6 had given him a "memorable send-off." The *Caronia* was barely a year old, a spectacular floating hotel nicknamed the "Green Goddess" on account of her pale green livery. She was fitted with every modern luxury, including sumptuous art deco interiors, an open-air lido, and terraced decks. The only class of travel was first. Described as "a private club afloat," the liner had four hundred catering staff for seven hundred passengers. On arriving in his paneled cabin with private bathroom, Philby had found a crate of champagne awaiting him, a gift from a "disgustingly rich friend," Victor Rothschild.

Philby might have disapproved of Rothschild's riches, but he thoroughly approved of his champagne. The seven-day voyage was made all the more pleasant by the company of the cartoonist Osbert Lancaster, an affable clubland acquaintance of Philby's with a walrus mustache and a terrific thirst. Philby and Lancaster settled into the cocktail bar and started drinking their way to America. "I began to feel that I would enjoy my first transatlantic crossing," wrote Philby.

The *Caronia* docked in New York on October 7. The FBI sent out a motor launch to meet Philby; like Bido Kuka, he was whisked through customs without any of the usual formalities. That night he stayed in a high-rise hotel overlooking Central Park before catching the train to Washington, DC. Alongside the track the sumac shrubs were still in flower, but autumn was in the air and the leaves were beginning to turn. Philby's first glimpse of the American landscape took his breath away. The fall, he later wrote, is "one of the few glories of America which Americans have never exaggerated because exaggeration is impossible."

At Union Station he was met by Peter Dwyer of MI6, the outgoing station chief, and immediately plunged into a whirlwind of introductions and meetings with officials of the CIA, FBI, the State Department, and the Canadian secret service. All were delighted to shake hands with this urbane Englishman whose impressive reputation preceded him—but none more than James Jesus Angleton, his former protege, now a powerful figure in the CIA. Angleton had prepared the ground, telling his American colleagues about Philby's wartime work and how much he "admired him as a 'professional.'" The Anglo-American intelligence relationship was still close in 1949, and no two spies symbolized that intimacy more than Kim Philby and James Angleton.

Angleton remained in many ways an Englishman. "I was brought up in England in my formative years," he said many years later, "and I must confess that I learned, at least I was disciplined to learn, certain features of life, and what I regarded as duty."

Honor, loyalty, handmade suits, strong drinks, deep leather armchairs in smoky clubs: this was the England that Angleton had come to know and admire through Philby and Elliott. There was an element within American intelligence that took a more hard-eyed view of Britain's continuing claims to greatness, a younger generation unmoved by the nostalgic bonds of war, but Angleton was not of that stamp. His time in Ryder Street had left a permanent imprint on him, personally and professionally. Philby had introduced him to the arcane mysteries of the Double Cross system, the strange, endlessly reflecting conundrum of counterintelligence, and the very British idea that only a few, a select few, can be truly trusted. Philby was Angleton's souvenir of war, a time of duty, unshakable alliance, and dependability. Angleton paraded his English friend around Washington like a trophy.

While Philby was clinking glasses in Washington, on the other side of the world David Smiley waited, with mounting unease, for the Albanian guerrillas to make contact. Twice a day, morning and evening, the MI6 radio operator stationed in a large mansion on the coast of Corfu tuned in at the agreed time, but a week had passed with no word from the pixies. Finally a hasty message was picked up, sent from the caves above Gjorm where Kuka and his team were in hiding: "Things have gone wrong . . . three men killed. . . police know everything about us." The Albanians were terrified: the bulky generator gave out a high-pitched whining and when pedaled at full speed, the noise bouncing off the hills threatened to reveal them. They were running out of food and dared not descend to the village to beg or steal more. Bido Kuka persuaded the others to make a break for it and try to reach his home village of Nivica just twenty-five miles to the south. The route passed though inhospitable terrain and the government troops were doubtless still out in force, but from Nivica it was only thirty-five miles to the Greek border. A four-day trek, walking at night, skirting patrols, and hiding during daylight, brought them to the home Kuka had last seen three years earlier. He was welcomed, but cautiously. When Kuka explained that they were the vanguard of a British-backed force that would overthrow Hoxha, the villagers were skeptical: Why were they so few in number? Where were the British? Where were the guns? Kuka sensed that even here they faced mortal danger. The group declined offers to spend the night in the village. They retreated instead to the mountains and agreed to push on for the border as fast as possible in two groups: Bido Kuka, Ramis Matuka, and a third man headed south; his cousin Ahmet and the fifth man took a more direct route. Patrols were everywhere; three times Kuka's group narrowly avoided capture. They were still a dozen miles from the border, trudging through a narrow ravine, when a voice boomed out of the darkness demanding that they identify themselves or be shot down. "Who are you?" called Kuka, cocking his machine gun. "Police," came the answer. The three men opened fire. The police, dug in above them, returned fire. Ramis Matuka fell dead. Kuka and his last companion, firing wildly, fled into the woods.

Three days later, exhausted and famished, Kuka and his comrade finally reached the Greek border. They were immediately arrested, jailed by the Greek police, and interrogated. Kuka stuck to his story that he was "Enver Zenelli," the name on his forged Albanian identity card. "We said we were ordinary Albanians fleeing the country." The Greek border guards were disbelieving "and would have shot them for tuppence." After several weeks, a British officer appeared. Kuka uttered the code phrase agreed on back in Malta: "The sun has risen." Finally they were free. The survivors were flown to Athens, lodged in a safe house, and debriefed by two British intelligence officers.

By any objective estimate the first phase of Operation Valuable had been a debacle. Of the nine guerrillas who had landed in October, four were dead, one was almost certainly captured, one had vanished, the others had barely escaped with their lives, and "several Albanian civilians had also been arrested and killed," accused of aiding the guerrillas. A second landing group, arriving soon after the first, had fared little better. The Albanian forces were primed and waiting, clearly aware of the incursion, if not of its precise timing and location.

With understatement verging on fantasy, MI6 described the first phase of the operation merely as "disappointing." The loss of half the initial force was a setback but not a disaster, and the death toll was "judged by wartime standards to be acceptable." Colonel Smiley vowed to press ahead with fresh incursions, better-trained guerrillas, and greater US involvement. Albania would not be won overnight, and "it would be wrong to abandon such an important exercise," particularly now that MI6 had one of its highest fliers installed in Washington, ready and more than willing to liaise with the Americans on the next stage of Operation Valuable.

Just a few days after his arrival in Washington, Philby was appointed joint commander of the Anglo-American Special Policy Committee, responsible for running the Albanian operation with his American opposite number, James McCargar. The Americans would play an increasing role in Operation Valuable (which they code-named, perhaps more realistically, "Fiend"), not least by financing it, but Philby "was the one who made all the operational decisions."

James McCargar was a former journalist from a wealthy California family who had made a name for himself in the postwar period by arranging escape routes out of Hungary for scientists and intellectuals fleeing communism. He smuggled one Romanian woman out in the trunk of his car and then married her.

Like many American intelligence officers of the time, McCargar had an exaggerated respect for his British counterparts, and his new colleague came with glowing credentials. "Philby was a great charmer. He came to us with an enormous reputation," recalled McCargar. "One had the feeling one could have confidence in him." Philby seemed to exemplify the sort of qualities that Americans hoped to see in their British allies: cheerful, resolute, witty, and exceedingly generous with the bottle. "He had charm, warmth and an engaging, self-deprecating humor," said McCargar. "He drank a lot, but then so did we all in those days. We floated out of the war on a sea of drink without its having much effect. I considered him a friend."

Philby loved Washington, and Washington loved him. Doors were flung open, the invitations poured in, and few people needed to meet him more than once before they too considered him a friend. Aileen also seemed to find strength in Washington's welcoming atmosphere. The family moved into a large, two-story house at 4100 Nebraska Avenue, which was soon a riot of children's toys, full ashtrays, and empty bottles. In Nicholas Elliott's words, Philby was "undoubtedly devoted to his children," a trait that further endeared him to his new American friends and colleagues: here was a family man, the quintessential English gentleman, a man one could trust. Within weeks, it seems, Philby had made contact with just about everyone of note in American intelligence.

To their faces he was politeness personified; behind their backs, vituperative. There was Johnny Boyd, assistant director of the FBI ("by any objective standard, a dreadful man"); Frank Wisner, head of the Office of Policy Coordination ("balding and self-importantly running to fat"); Bill Harvey of CIA counterintelligence ("a former FBI man . . . sacked for drunkenness"); CIA chief Walter Bedell Smith ("a cold, fishy eye"); deputy CIA head and future chief Allen Dulles ("bumbling"); Bob Lamphere of the FBI ("puddingy"); and many more. The house on Nebraska

Avenue soon became a gathering place for Washington's intelligence elite. "He entertained a lot of Americans," said another CIA officer. "The wine flowed, and the whisky too." Aileen played the role of salon hostess, tottering around with trays of drinks and drinking her fair share. One guest recalled only this of Philby's parties: "They were long, and very, very wet."

Philby seemed to invite intimacy. His knowing smile, "suggestive of complicity in some private joke, conveyed an unspoken understanding of the underlying ironies of our work." He made a point of dropping in on the offices of American colleagues and counterparts in the late afternoon, knowing that his hosts would sooner or later (and usually sooner) "suggest drifting out to a friendly bar for a further round of shop talk." Trading internal information is a particular weakness of the intelligence world; spies cannot explain their work to outsiders, so they seize every opportunity to discuss it with their own kind. "Intelligence officers talk trade among themselves all the time," said one CIA officer.

"Philby was privy to a hell of a lot beyond what he should have known." The CIA and FBI were rivals, sometimes viciously so, with a peculiar social division between the two arms of American intelligence that was echoed by the competition between MI5 and MI6. Philby characterized CIA operatives as upper-class wine drinkers, while the FBI were earthier beer-drinking types. Philby was happy to drink quantities of both, with either, while trying to "please one party without offending the other." Philby's office was in the British embassy, but he was often to be found at the CIA or FBI headquarters or the Pentagon, where a room was set aside for meetings on the Albanian operation. Few subjects were out of bounds: "The sky was the limit.... He would have known as much as he wanted to find out."

James Angleton was now chief of Staff A, in command of foreign intelligence operations, and in Philby's estimation "the driving force" within the intelligence-gathering division of the CIA. A strange mystique clung to Angleton; he used the name "Lothar Metzl" and invented a cover story that he had been a Viennese café pianist before the war. Behind his house in the suburbs of North Arlington he constructed a heated greenhouse, the better to cultivate his orchids and his aura of knowing eccentricity. In the basement he polished semiprecious stones. He carried a gold fob watch; his suits and accent remained distinctly English.

Angleton tended to describe his work in fishing metaphors: "I got a few nibbles last night," he would remark obscurely after an evening trawling the files. In intelligence circles he inspired admiration, gossip, and some fear. "It was the belief within the CIA that Angleton possessed more secrets than anyone else, and grasped their meaning better than anyone else."

Harvey's, on Connecticut Avenue, was the most famous restaurant in the capital, probably the most expensive, and certainly the most exclusive. Harvey's Ladies' and Gentlemen's Oyster Saloon started serving steamed oysters, broiled lobster, and crab imperial in 1820 and had continued to do so, in colossal quantities, ever since. In 1863, notwithstanding the Civil War, Harvey's diners were getting through five hundred wagonloads of oysters a week.

Every president since Ulysses S. Grant had dined there, and the restaurant enjoyed an unrivaled reputation as the place to be seen for people of power and influence. The black waiters in pressed white uniforms were discreet, the martinis potent, the napkins stiff as cardboard, and the tables spaced far enough apart to ensure privacy for the most secret conversations. Ladies entered by a separate entrance and were not permitted in the main dining room. Most evenings, FBI director J. Edgar Hoover could be seen at his corner table, eating with Clyde Tolson, his deputy and possibly his lover. Hoover was said to be addicted to Harvey's oysters; he never paid for his meals.

Angleton and Philby began to lunch regularly at Harvey's, at first once a week, then at least every other day. They spoke on the telephone three or four times a week. Their lunches became a sort of ritual, a "habit" in Philby's words, beginning with bourbon on the rocks, proceeding through lobster and wine, and ending in brandy and cigars. Philby was impressed by both Angleton's grasp of intelligence and his appetite for food and drink. "He demonstrated regularly that overwork was not his only vice," wrote Philby; "He was one of the thinnest men I have ever met, and one of the biggest eaters. Lucky Jim!" The two men could be seen hunched in animated conversation, talking, drinking, laughing, and enjoying their shared love of secrecy. Angleton had few close friends and fewer confidants. Philby had many friends and had refined the giving and receiving of confidences to an art form. They fit one another perfectly.

"Our close association was, I am sure, inspired by genuine friendliness," wrote Philby. "But we both had ulterior motives.... By cultivating me to the full, he could better keep me under wraps. For my part, I was more than content to string him along.

"The greater the trust between us overtly, the less he would suspect covert action. Who gained most from this complex game I cannot say. But I had one big advantage. I knew what he was doing for CIA and he knew what I was doing for SIS. But the real nature of my interest was something he did not know." Beneath their friendship was an unspoken competition to see who could outthink and outdrink the other. Angleton, according to one associate, "used to pride himself that he could drink Kim under the table and still walk away with useful information. Can you imagine how much information he had to trade in those booze-ups?"

"Our discussions ranged over the whole world," Philby recalled.

They spoke of the various covert operations against the Soviet Union, the anticommunist insurgents being slipped into Albania and other countries behind the iron curtain; they discussed the intelligence operations under way in France, Italy, and Germany and resources pouring into anticommunist projects worldwide, including the recruiting of exiles for subversion behind the iron curtain. "Both CIA and SIS were up to their ears in émigré politics," wrote Philby. Angleton explained how the CIA had taken over the anti-Soviet spy network established by Reinhard Gehlen, the former chief of German intelligence on the eastern front who had offered his services to the United States after surrendering in 1945. Gehlen's spies and informants included many former Nazis, but the CIA was not choosy about its allies in the new war against Communism. By 1948 the CIA was funneling some $1.5 million (around $14.5 million today) into Gehlen's spy ring. Philby was all ears: "Many of Harvey's lobsters went to provoke Angleton into defending, with chapter and verse, the past record and current activities of the von Gehlen organization." CIA interventions in Greece and Turkey to hold back communism; covert operations in Iran, the Baltics, and Guatemala;

secret American plans in Chile, Cuba, Angola, and Indonesia; blueprints for Allied cooperation in the event of war with the USSR. All this and more was laid before Philby, between friends, as Angleton gorged and gossiped over the starched tablecloths and full glasses at Harvey's. "During those long, boozy lunches and dinners, Philby must have picked him clean," a fellow officer later wrote.

But Philby and Angleton were also professionals. After every lunch, Angleton returned to his office and dictated a long memo to his secretary, Gloria Loomis, reporting in detail his discussions with the obliging MI6 liaison chief. "Everything was written up," Loomis later insisted. Philby did likewise, dictating his own memo for MI6 to his secretary Edith Whitfield, who had accompanied him to Washington from Istanbul (much to Aileen's annoyance). Later, at home on Connecticut Avenue, Philby would write up his own notes for other eyes.

Philby liked to portray the Russian intelligence service as an organization of unparalleled efficiency. In truth, Moscow Center was frequently beset by bureaucratic bungling, inertia, and incompetence, coupled with periodic bloodletting. Before Philby's arrival, the Soviet spy outpost in Washington had been through a period of "chaotic" turbulence, with the recall of two successive residents. Initially, Philby had no direct contact with Soviet intelligence in the United States, preferring to send any information via Guy Burgess in London, as he had from Istanbul. Finally, four months after Philby's arrival, Moscow woke up to the realization that it should take better care of its veteran spy.

On March 5 a young man stepped off the ship *Batory*, newly arrived in New York harbor from Gdynia in Poland. His passport proclaimed him to be an American citizen of Polish origin named Ivan Kovalik; his real name was Valeri Mikhailovich Makayev; a thirty-two-year-old Russian intelligence officer with orders to establish himself under cover in New York and arrange a way for Philby to communicate with Moscow Center. Makayev swiftly obtained a job teaching musical composition at New York University and started an affair with a Polish dancer who owned a ballet school in Manhattan. Makayev was a good musician and one of nature's romantics, but he was a hopeless case officer. His bosses had supplied him with $25,000 for his mission, which he proceeded to spend, mostly on himself and his ballerina. Finally, Makayev got word to Philby that he had arrived. They met in New York, and Philby's newly arrived case officer handed over a new camera for photographing documents. Thereafter they would rendezvous at different points between New York and Washington, in Baltimore or Philadelphia. After nine months, Makayev had managed to set up two communication channels to Moscow, using a Finnish seaman as a courier and a postal route via an agent in London. The system was slow and cumbersome; Philby was wary of face-to-face meetings and unimpressed by his new case officer; Makayev was much more interested in ballet than in espionage. Philby was producing more valuable intelligence for Moscow than at any time in his life, yet he had never been run more incompetently.

Frank Wisner, the CIA officer in charge of insurgent operations behind the iron curtain, was baffled: every bid to undermine communism by secretly fomenting resistance within the USSR and among its satellites seemed to be going spectacularly wrong.

But Wisner, or "the Whiz," as he liked to be known, refused to be downcast, let alone change tack. Despite a disappointing start, the Albanian operation would continue: "We'll get it right next time," Wisner promised Philby.

But they did not get it right. Instead, it continued to go wrong, and not just in Albania. Funds, equipment, and arms were funneled to the anticommunist resistance in Poland, which turned out to be nothing more than a front operated by Soviet intelligence.

Anticommunist Lithuanians, Estonians, and Armenians were recruited and then dropped into their homelands by British and American planes; nationalist White Russians were sent in to continue the fight against the Bolsheviks. Almost all mysteriously disappeared. "We had agents parachuting in, floating in, walking in, boating in," said one former CIA officer. "Virtually all these operations were complete failures. . . . They were all rolled up." The CIA and MI6 kept each other informed of exactly where and when their respective teams were going in, to avoid overlap and confusion. Philby, as the liaison officer in Washington, was responsible for passing on "the timing and geographical coordinates" from one intelligence agency to another, and then another. Ukraine was considered particularly fertile ground for an insurgency, with an established resistance group active in the Carpathian Mountains. In 1949 the first British-trained team of Ukrainian insurgents was sent in with radio equipment. They were never heard from again. Two more teams followed the next year, and then three more six-man units were parachuted to drop points in Ukraine and inside the Polish border. All vanished. "I do not know what happened to the parties concerned," Philby later wrote, with ruthless irony. "But I can make an informed guess."

None of the incursions proved more catastrophic, more spectacularly valueless, than Operation Valuable. Undaunted, the British continued to train the "pixies" in Malta while the CIA established a separate training camp for Albanian insurgents, now including teams of parachutists, in a walled villa outside Heidelberg.

"We knew that they would retaliate against our families," said one recruit, "[but] we had high hopes." At the same time, MI6 prepared to drop thousands of propaganda leaflets over Albania from unmanned hot-air balloons: "The boys in London imagined a rain of pamphlets over Albanian towns with thousands of Albanians picking them out of the air, reading them and then preparing themselves for the liberation." The parachutists were flown in by Polish former RAF pilots in late 1950, crossing into Albanian airspace at a height of just two hundred feet to avoid radar.

The communist forces were ready and waiting. Two days earlier, hundreds of security police had poured into the area of the drop zone. A policeman was stationed in every village. They even knew the names of the arriving insurgents. Some of the parachutists were killed on landing, others captured. Only a few escaped. The next drop, the following July, was even more disastrous.

One group of four parachutists was mowed down immediately; another was surrounded, with two killed and two captured; the last group of four fled to a house and barricaded themselves in. The police set fire to the building and burned them all to death.

British-trained fighters continued to filter into Albania, some by boat and others on foot across the Greek border, only to be intercepted like their predecessors. Meanwhile, across Albania, the Sigurimi began rounding up relatives and friends of the insurgents. A shared surname was enough to invite suspicion. For each guerrilla as many as forty others were shot or thrown into prison.

Two captives were "tied to the back of a Jeep and dragged through the streets until their bodies were reduced to a bloody pulp." A handful of the fighters apparently escaped and sent back radio messages urging the British and Americans to send more forces.

Only much later did it emerge that the Sigurimi was running a classic double cross: the messages were sent by captives, forced to reveal their codes and transmitting with guns to their heads.

Enver Hoxha bragged: "Our famous radio game brought about the ignominious failure of the plans of the foreign enemy. . . . The bands of criminals who were dropped in by parachute or infiltrated across the border at our request came like lambs to the slaughter." Show trials were later staged with captured survivors, propaganda spectacles at which the tortured, semi-coherent defendants condemned themselves and cursed their capitalist backers before being sentenced to long prison terms from which few emerged alive.

In London and Washington, as the operation lurched from failure to calamity, morale slumped and suspicions rose. "It was obvious there was a leak somewhere," said one CIA officer. "We had several meetings, trying to figure out where the thing was going wrong. We had to ask ourselves how long we were prepared to go on dropping these young men into the bag." The British privately blamed the Americans, and vice versa. "Our security was very, very tight," insisted Colonel Smiley.

In fact, the secrecy surrounding the operation was anything but secure. Soviet intelligence had penetrated not just the Albanian émigré groups in Europe but every other community of disgruntled exiles. James Angleton learned, through his Italian contacts, that Operation Valuable had been "well and truly blown" from the start: Italian intelligence had been watching the *Stormie Seas* from the moment she set sail for Albania. Journalists had also gotten wind of the story. Once the first teams of guerrillas had been intercepted, the Albanian authorities were naturally braced for more. The operation was flawed from its inception: Hoxha was more firmly entrenched and the opposition to him much weaker than Anglo-American intelligence imagined. The planners had simply believed that

"Albania would fall from the Soviet imperial tree like a ripe plum and other fruit would soon follow." And they were simply wrong.

Operation Valuable might well have failed without Philby, but not so utterly nor so bloodily. Looking back, the planners knew whom to blame for the embarrassing and unmitigated failure.

"There is little question that Philby not only informed Moscow of overall British and American planning," wrote CIA historian Harry Rositzke, "but provided details on the individual dispatch of agent teams before they arrived in Albania." Yuri Modin, the NKVD controller in London who passed on Philby's messages to Moscow, was also explicit: "He gave us vital information about the number of men involved, the day and the time of the landing, the weapons they were bringing and their precise program of action. . . .The Soviets duly passed on Philby's information to Albanians who set up ambushes."

Philby later gloried in what he had done: "The agents we sent into Albania were armed men intent on murder, sabotage and assassination. They were quite as ready as I was to contemplate bloodshed in the service of a political ideal. They knew the risks they were running. I was serving the interests of the Soviet Union and those interests required that these men were defeated. To the extent that I helped defeat them, even if it caused their deaths, I have no regrets."

The precise death toll will never be known: somewhere between one hundred and two hundred Albanian guerrillas perished; if their families and other reprisal victims are taken into account, the figure rises into the thousands. Years later, those who had deployed the doomed Albanian insurgents came to the conclusion that, over the course of two lunch-filled years, James Angleton "gave Philby over drinks the precise coordinates for every drop zone of the CIA in Albania."

At the heart of the tragedy lay a close friendship—and a great betrayal.

Lunch at Harvey's came with a hefty bill.

Sources

"The Spy and the Traitor," by Ben Macintyre, copyright © 2018 by Ben Macintyre. Used by permission of Crown Books, an imprint of Random House, a division of Penguin Random House LLC. All rights reserved.

"The Morning They Shot the Spies," by W.C. Heinz, first published in *TRUE* magazine then collected in *When We Were One: Stories of World War II*, published in 2002 by Da Capo Press, a member of the Perseus Book Group. Reprint permission granted by Gayl B. Heinz.

"The Spy," by Michael Shaara, from *The Killer Angels*, copyright © 1974 by Michael Shaara, copyright renewed 2002 by Jeff M. Shaara and Lila E. Shaara. Used by permission of Ballantine Books, an imprint of Random House, a division of Penguin Random House LLC. All rights reserved.

"The Wolves at the Door: The True Story of America's Greatest Female Spy," by Judith L. Pearson, from *The Wolves at the Door: The True Story of America's Greatest Female Spy*, Lyons Press, 2005, 2008. Reprinted by permission.

"The Thirty-Nine Steps," by John Buchan, published by William Blackwood and Sons, Edinburgh, 1915.

"OSS," by Richard Harris Smith, from *OSS: The Secret History of America's First Central Intelligence Agency*, Lyons Press, 2005. Reprinted by permission.

"The Spies Who Stole a Train," by William Pittenger, from the book *Capturing a Locomotive*, 1881.

"Spy for the Continental Army," by A.A. Hoehling, from *Women Who Spied: True Stories of Feminine Espionage*, Madison Books, Rowman-Littlefield, 1992.

"The Frontier Spy," by James Fenimore Cooper, from *The Spy: A Tale of the Neutral Ground*, 1821.

"The Craft of Intelligence," by Allen Dulles, from *The Craft of Intelligence: America's Legendary Spy Master on the Fundamentals of Intelligence Gathering for a Free World*, Lyons Press, 2016. Reprinted by permission.

"Pinkerton's War: The Civil War's Greatest Spy and the Birth of the Secret Service," by Jay Bonansinga, from *Pinkerton's War: The Civil War's Greatest Spy and the Birth of the U.S. Secret Service*, Lyons Press, 2012. Reprinted by permission.

"Beyond Repair," by Charles S. Faddis, from *Beyond Repair: The Decline and Fall of the CIA*, Lyons Press, 2009. Reprinted by permission.

"Memories of Sherlock Holmes: The Final Problem," by Arthur Conan Doyle, from *Memories of Sherlock Holmes: The Final Problem*, 1893.

"A Spy Among Friends: Kim Philby and the Great Betrayal," by Ben Macintyre, from *A Spy Among Friends: Kim Philby and the Great Betrayal*, copyright © 2014 by Ben Macintyre. Used by permission of Crown Books, an imprint of Random House, a division of Penguin Random House LLC. All rights reserved.